Irene OLMO

I DON'T WANT TO BE A MOM

graphic mundi

Translated by Kendra Boileau

CHAPTER 1

• Child's Play •

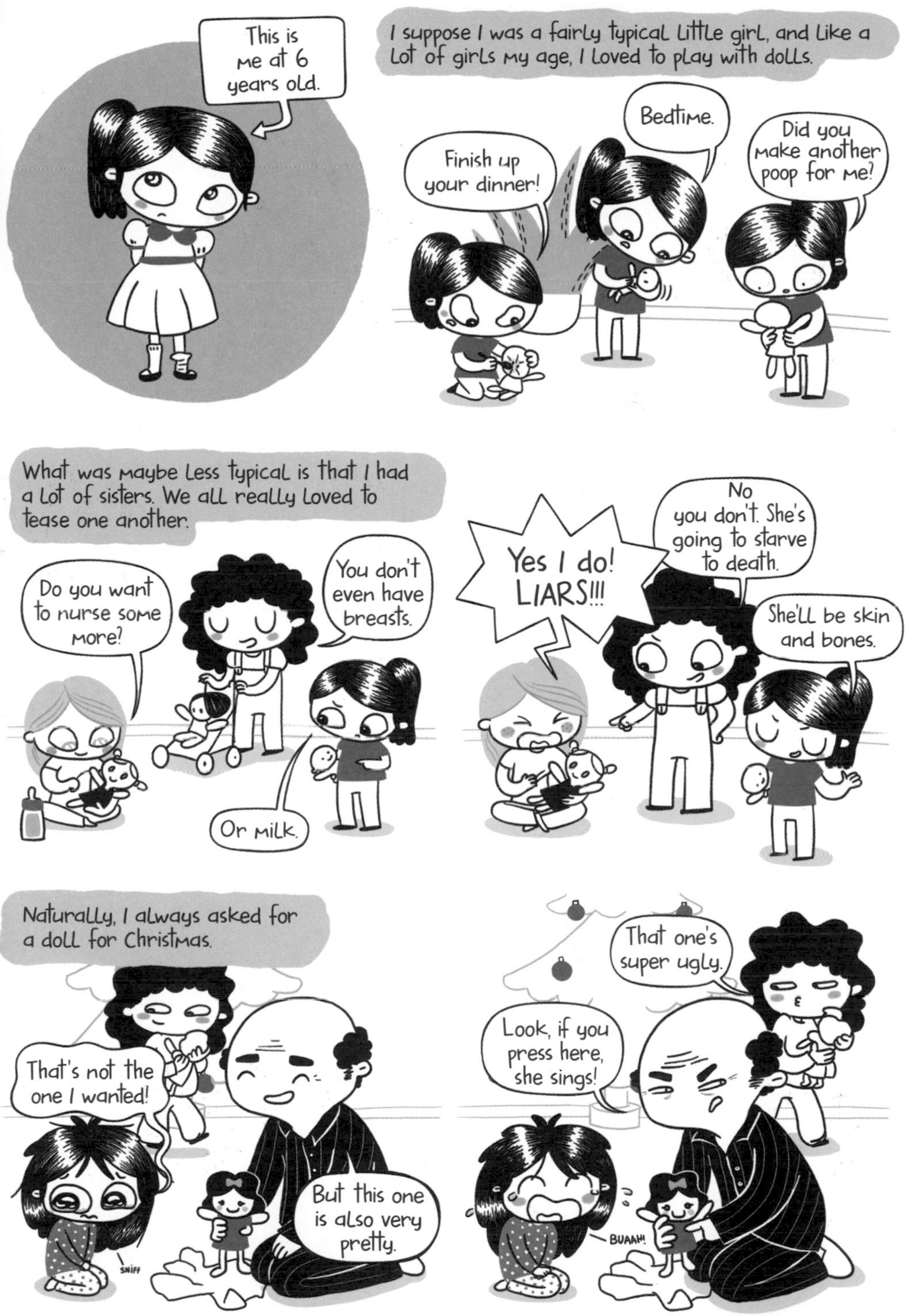
This is me at 6 years old.
I suppose I was a fairly typical little girl, and like a lot of girls my age, I loved to play with dolls.
Finish up your dinner!
Bedtime.
Did you make another poop for me?
What was maybe less typical is that I had a lot of sisters. We all really loved to tease one another.
Do you want to nurse some more?
You don't even have breasts.
Or milk.
Yes I do! LIARS!!!
No you don't. She's going to starve to death.
She'll be skin and bones.
Naturally, I always asked for a doll for Christmas.
That's not the one I wanted!
But this one is also very pretty.
SNIFF
That one's super ugly.
Look, if you press here, she sings!
BUAAH!

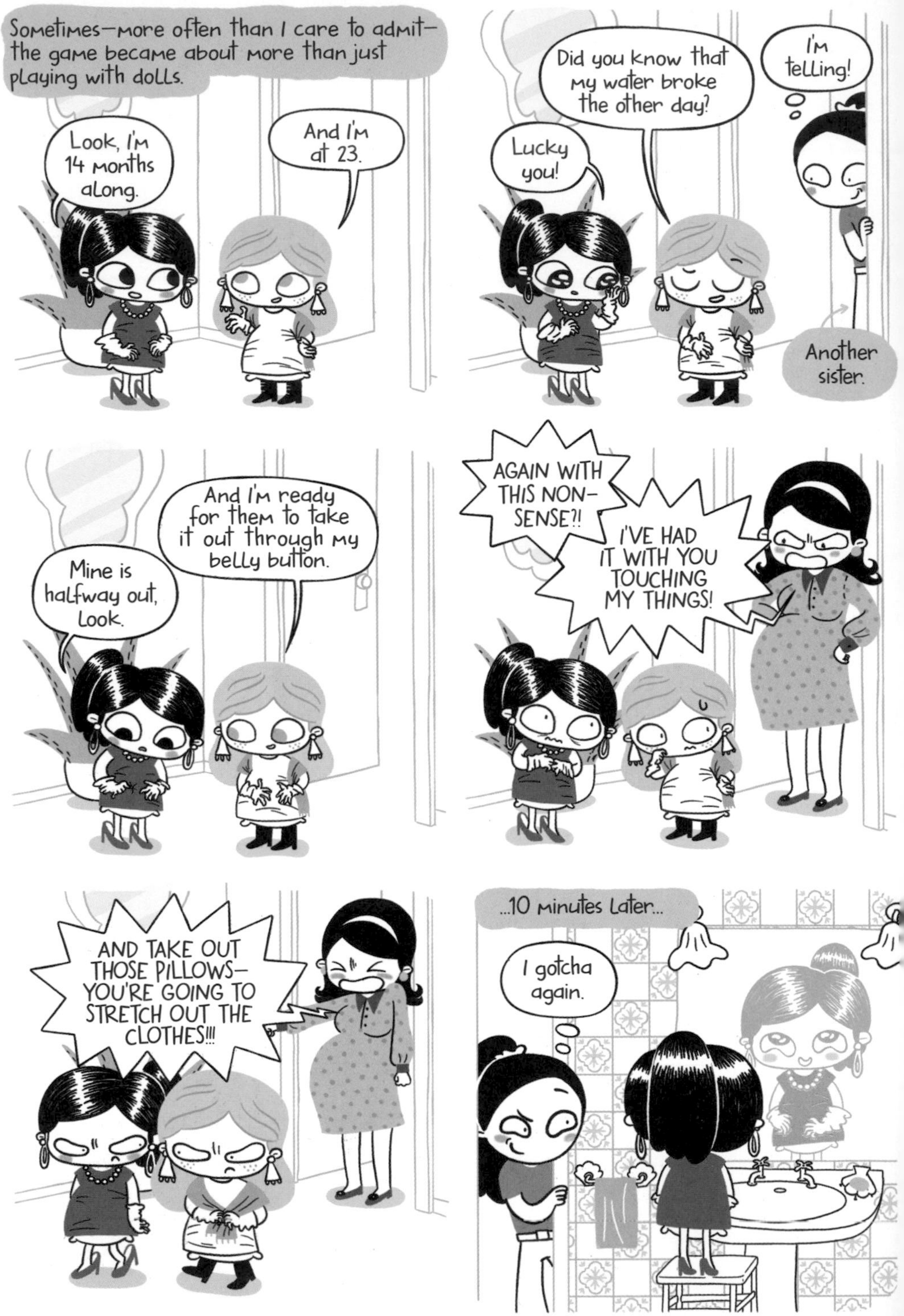
Sometimes—more often than I care to admit—the game became about more than just playing with dolls.
Look, I'm 14 months along.
And I'm at 23.
Lucky you!
Did you know that my water broke the other day?
I'm telling!
Another sister.
Mine is halfway out, look.
And I'm ready for them to take it out through my belly button.
AGAIN WITH THIS NON-SENSE?!
I'VE HAD IT WITH YOU TOUCHING MY THINGS!
AND TAKE OUT THOSE PILLOWS—YOU'RE GOING TO STRETCH OUT THE CLOTHES!!!
...10 minutes later...
I gotcha again.

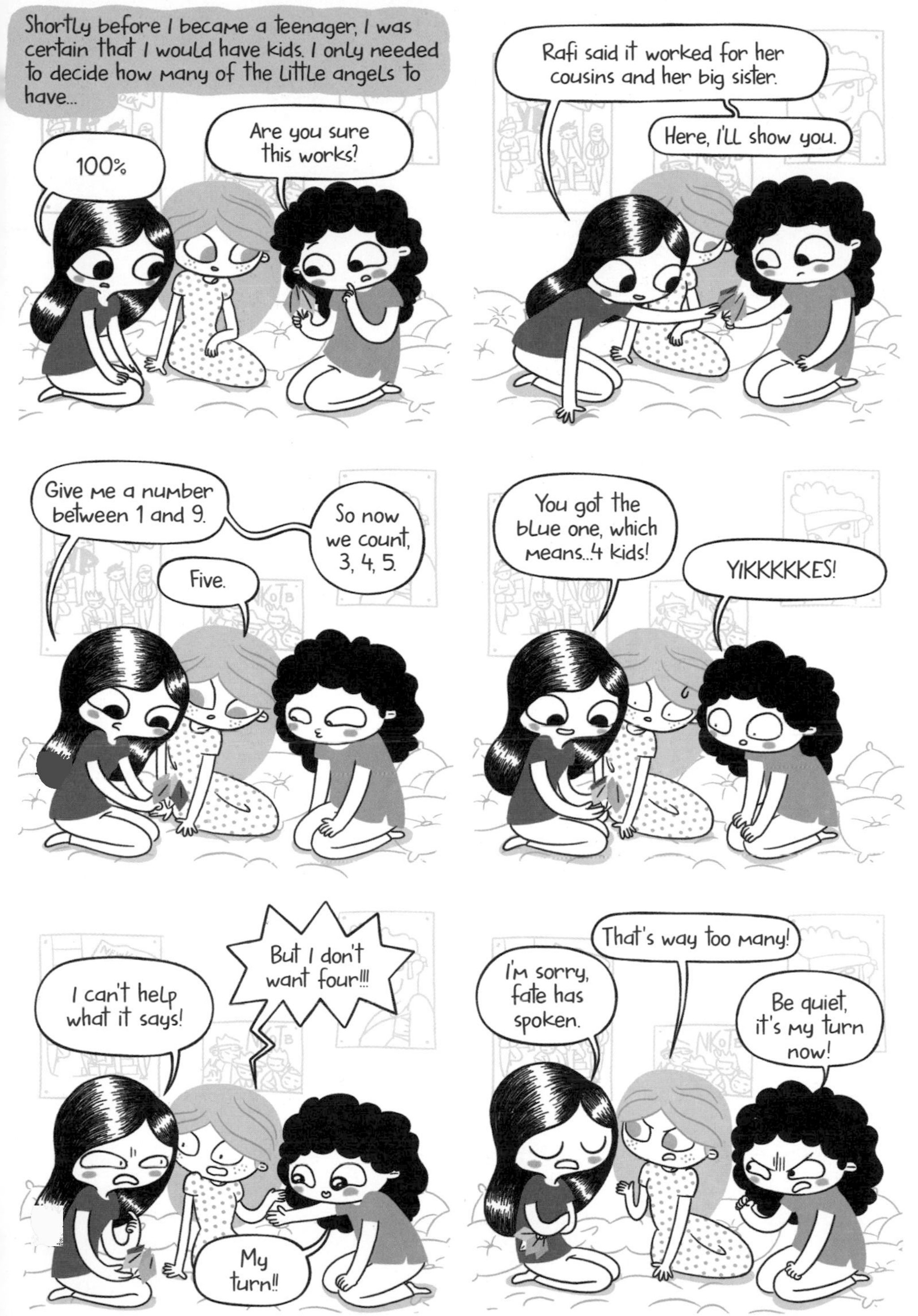
Shortly before I became a teenager, I was certain that I would have kids. I only needed to decide how many of the little angels to have...
100%
Are you sure this works?
Rafi said it worked for her cousins and her big sister.
Here, I'll show you.
Give me a number between 1 and 9.
Five.
So now we count, 3, 4, 5.
You got the blue one, which means...4 kids!
YIKKKKKES!
I can't help what it says!
But I don't want four!!!
My turn!!
I'm sorry, fate has spoken.
That's way too many!
Be quiet, it's my turn now!

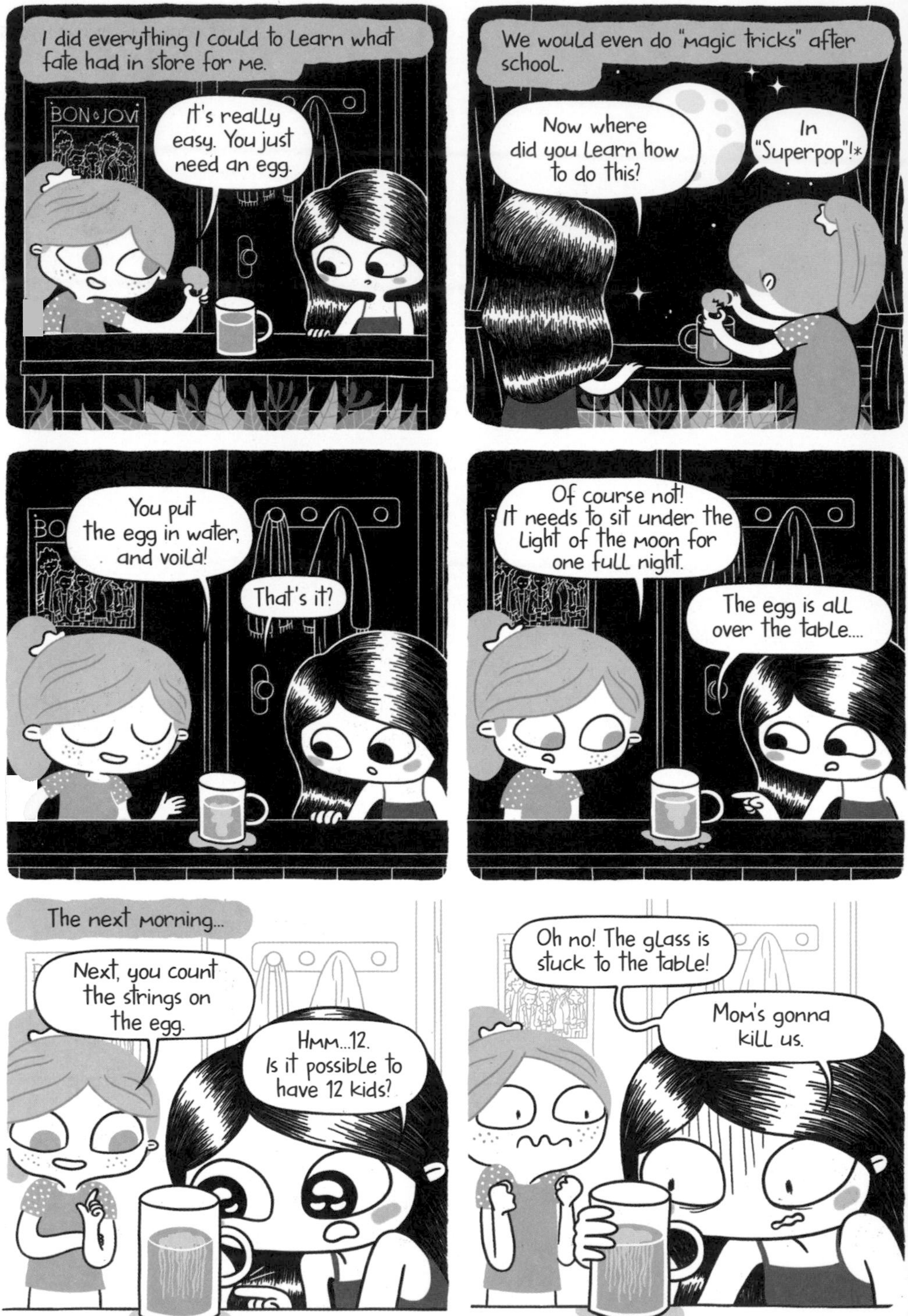
I did everything I could to learn what fate had in store for me.
BON JOVI
It's really easy. You just need an egg.
We would even do "magic tricks" after school.
Now where did you learn how to do this?
In "Superpop"!*
You put the egg in water, and voilà!
That's it?
Of course not! It needs to sit under the light of the moon for one full night.
The egg is all over the table....
The next morning...
Next, you count the strings on the egg.
Hmm...12. Is it possible to have 12 kids?
Oh no! The glass is stuck to the table!
Mom's gonna kill us.

*"Superpop" was a magazine similar to "Teen Beat" in the U.S.

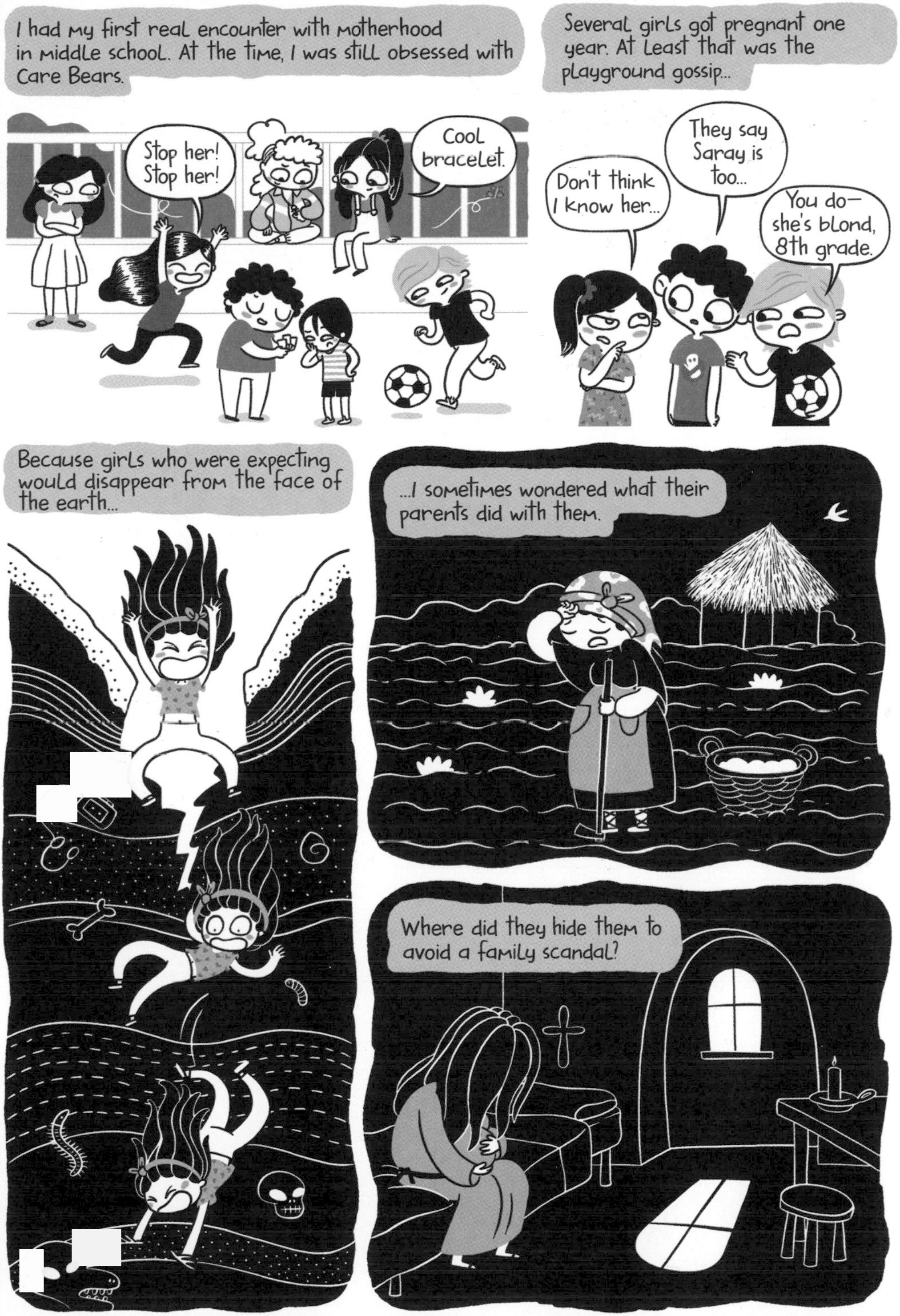
I had my first real encounter with motherhood in middle school. At the time, I was still obsessed with Care Bears.
Stop her! Stop her!
Cool bracelet.
Several girls got pregnant one year. At least that was the playground gossip...
Don't think I know her...
They say Saray is too...
You do—she's blond, 8th grade.
Because girls who were expecting would disappear from the face of the earth...
...I sometimes wondered what their parents did with them.
Where did they hide them to avoid a family scandal?

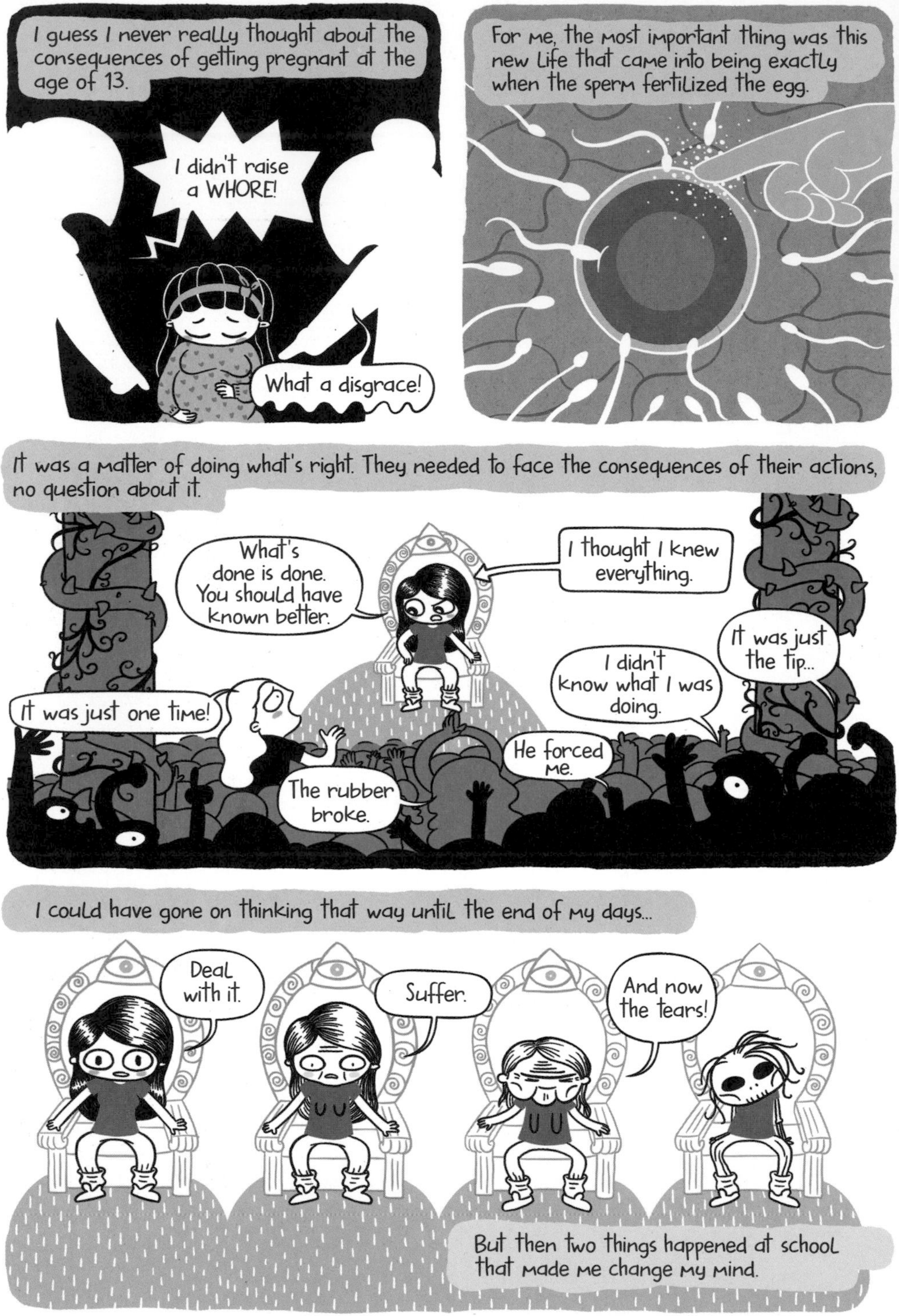
I guess I never really thought about the consequences of getting pregnant at the age of 13.
I didn't raise a WHORE!
What a disgrace!
For me, the most important thing was this new life that came into being exactly when the sperm fertilized the egg.
It was a matter of doing what's right. They needed to face the consequences of their actions, no question about it.
What's done is done. You should have known better.
I thought I knew everything.
It was just the tip...
I didn't know what I was doing.
It was just one time!
He forced me.
The rubber broke.
I could have gone on thinking that way until the end of my days...
Deal with it.
Suffer.
And now the tears!
But then two things happened at school that made me change my mind.

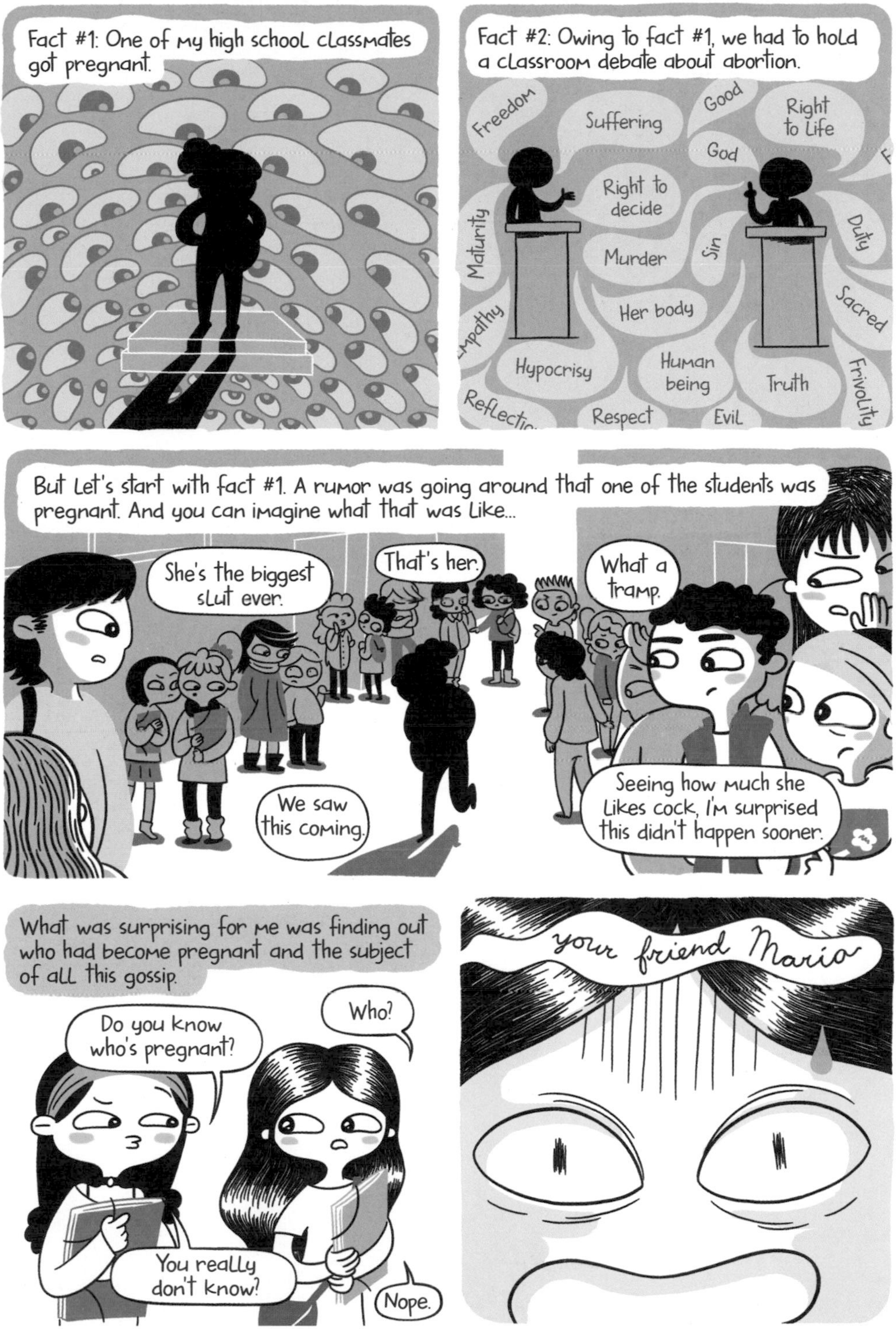

Fact #1: One of my high school classmates got pregnant.
Fact #2: Owing to fact #1, we had to hold a classroom debate about abortion.
Freedom
Suffering
Good
Right to Life
God
Right to decide
Maturity
Murder
Sin
Duty
Her body
Sacred
Hypocrisy
Human being
Truth
Frivolity
Respect
Evil
But let's start with fact #1. A rumor was going around that one of the students was pregnant. And you can imagine what that was like...
She's the biggest slut ever.
That's her.
What a tramp.
We saw this coming.
Seeing how much she likes cock, I'm surprised this didn't happen sooner.
What was surprising for me was finding out who had become pregnant and the subject of all this gossip.
Do you know who's pregnant?
Who?
You really don't know?
Nope.
your friend Maria

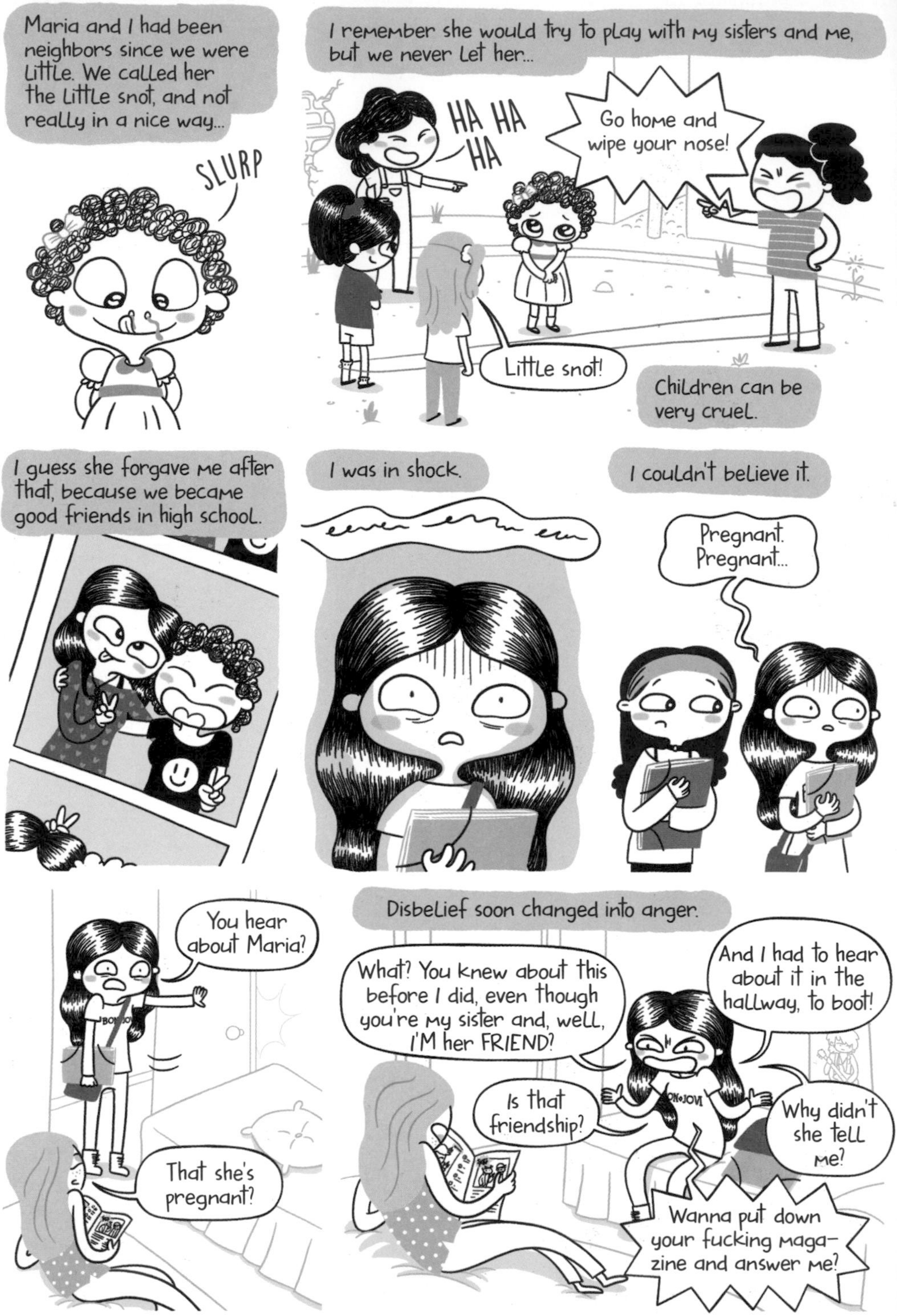

Maria and I had been neighbors since we were little. We called her the little snot, and not really in a nice way...
SLURP
I remember she would try to play with my sisters and me, but we never let her...
HA HA HA
Go home and wipe your nose!
Little snot!
Children can be very cruel.
I guess she forgave me after that, because we became good friends in high school.
I was in shock.
I couldn't believe it.
Pregnant. Pregnant...
You hear about Maria?
That she's pregnant?
Disbelief soon changed into anger.
What? You knew about this before I did, even though you're my sister and, well, I'M her FRIEND?
And I had to hear about it in the hallway, to boot!
Is that friendship?
Why didn't she tell me?
Wanna put down your fucking maga-zine and answer me?

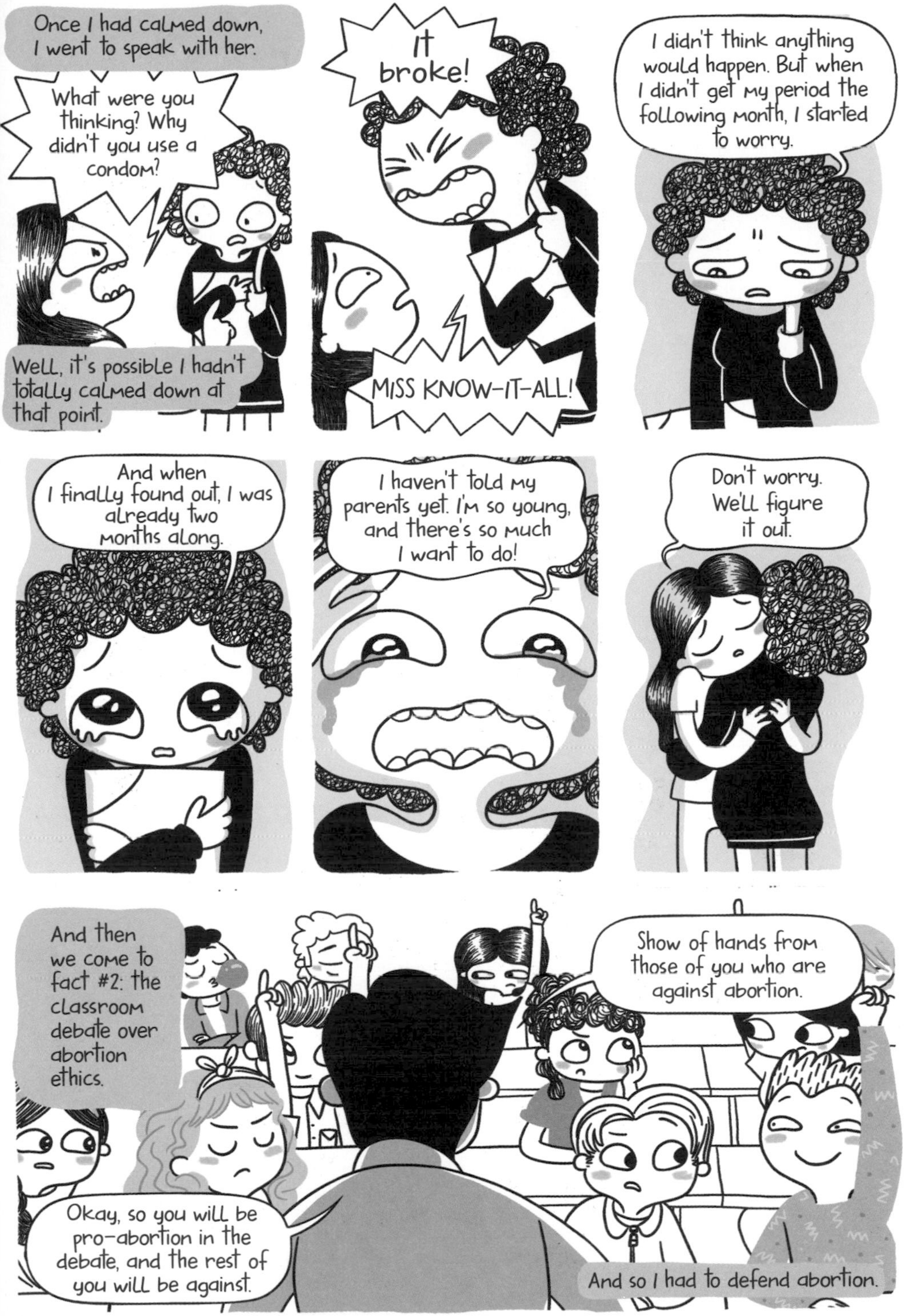
Once I had calmed down, I went to speak with her.
What were you thinking? Why didn't you use a condom?
Well, it's possible I hadn't totally calmed down at that point.
It broke!
MISS KNOW-IT-ALL!
I didn't think anything would happen. But when I didn't get my period the following month, I started to worry.
And when I finally found out, I was already two months along.
I haven't told my parents yet. I'm so young, and there's so much I want to do!
Don't worry. We'll figure it out.
And then we come to fact #2: the classroom debate over abortion ethics.
Show of hands from those of you who are against abortion.
Okay, so you will be pro-abortion in the debate, and the rest of you will be against.
And so I had to defend abortion.

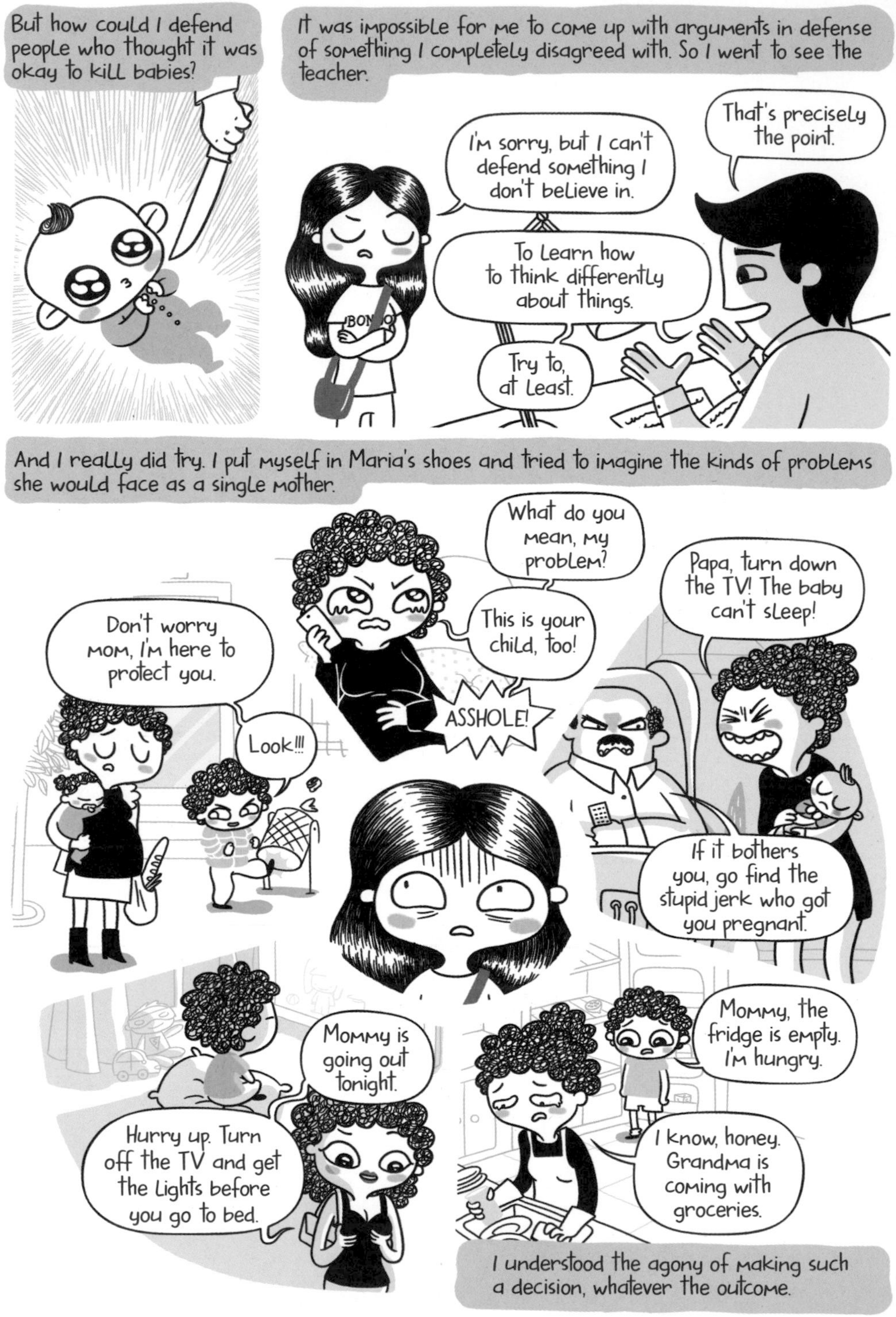
But how could I defend people who thought it was okay to kill babies?
It was impossible for me to come up with arguments in defense of something I completely disagreed with. So I went to see the teacher.
I'm sorry, but I can't defend something I don't believe in.
That's precisely the point.
To learn how to think differently about things.
Try to, at least.
And I really did try. I put myself in Maria's shoes and tried to imagine the kinds of problems she would face as a single mother.
Don't worry mom, I'm here to protect you.
Look!!!
What do you mean, my problem?
This is your child, too!
ASSHOLE!
Papa, turn down the TV! The baby can't sleep!
If it bothers you, go find the stupid jerk who got you pregnant.
Mommy is going out tonight.
Hurry up. Turn off the TV and get the lights before you go to bed.
Mommy, the fridge is empty. I'm hungry.
I know, honey. Grandma is coming with groceries.
I understood the agony of making such a decision, whatever the outcome.

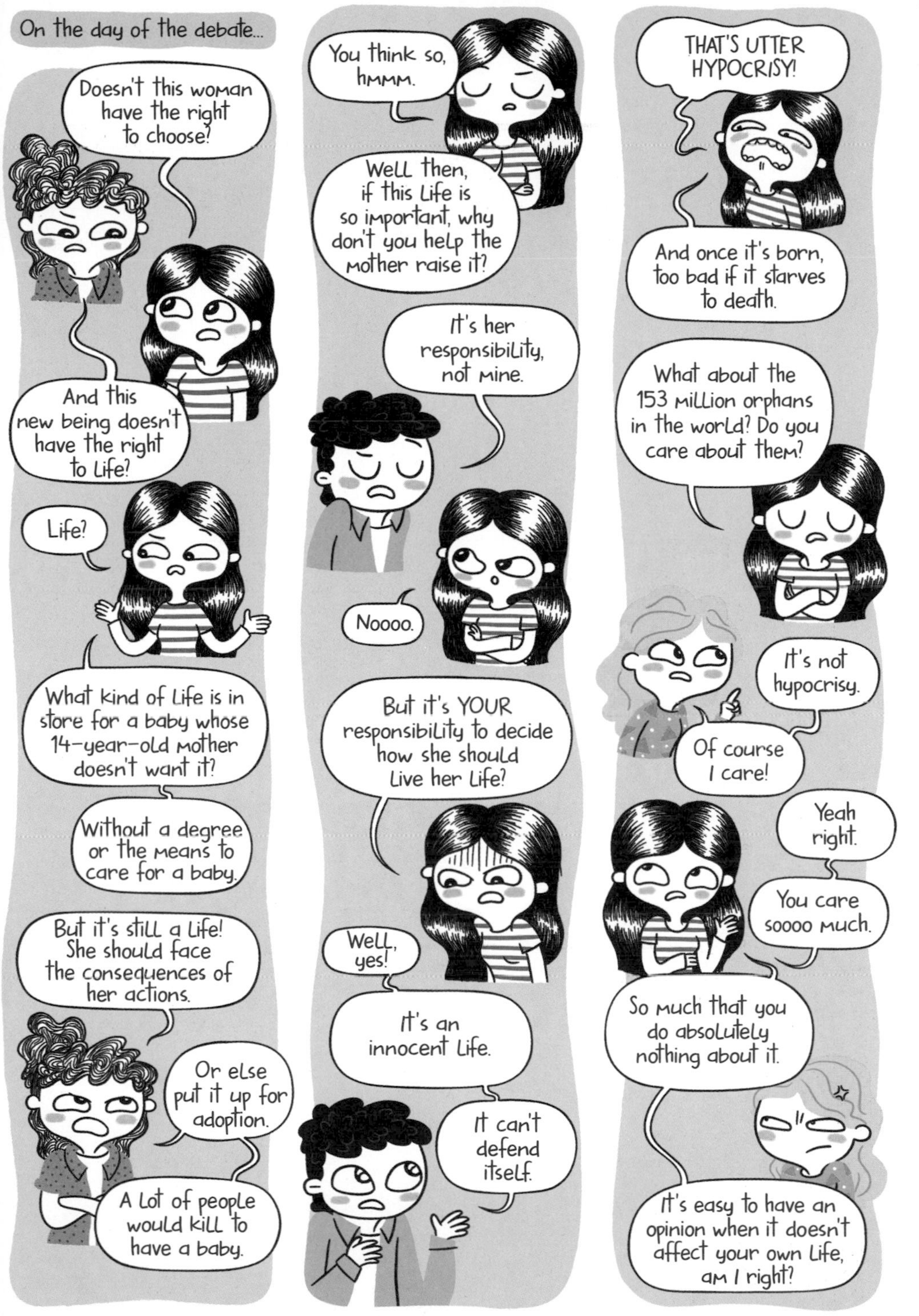
On the day of the debate...
Doesn't this woman have the right to choose?
And this new being doesn't have the right to life?
Life?
What kind of life is in store for a baby whose 14-year-old mother doesn't want it?
Without a degree or the means to care for a baby.
But it's still a life! She should face the consequences of her actions.
Or else put it up for adoption.
A lot of people would kill to have a baby.
You think so, hmmm.
Well then, if this life is so important, why don't you help the mother raise it?
It's her responsibility, not mine.
Noooo.
But it's YOUR responsibility to decide how she should live her life?
Well, yes!
It's an innocent life.
It can't defend itself.
THAT'S UTTER HYPOCRISY!
And once it's born, too bad if it starves to death.
What about the 153 million orphans in the world? Do you care about them?
It's not hypocrisy.
Of course I care!
Yeah right.
You care soooo much.
So much that you do absolutely nothing about it.
It's easy to have an opinion when it doesn't affect your own life, am I right?

This debate not only changed my mind about abortion.

It also changed how I understood the world.

I learned that reality could be very complicated.

The debate also taught me a new way of thinking. It taught me to look past the tangle of prejudices that blocked other points of view—to always question the why in everything, and to try to find my own truth.

And it prepared me for what was going to happen next.

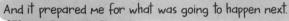

CHAPTER 2
• Strange People •

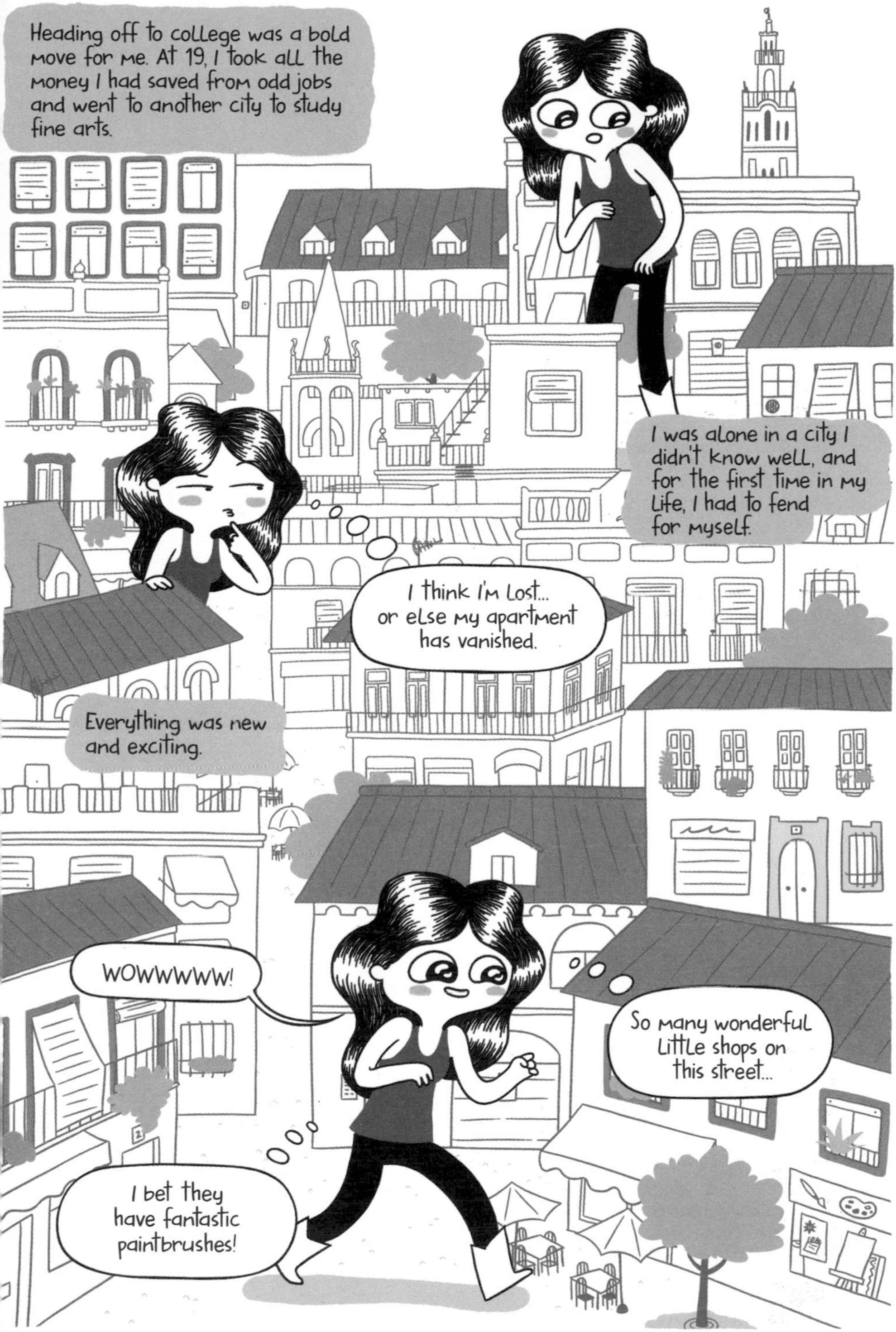
Heading off to college was a bold move for me. At 19, I took all the money I had saved from odd jobs and went to another city to study fine arts.
I was alone in a city I didn't know well, and for the first time in my life, I had to fend for myself.
I think I'm lost... or else my apartment has vanished.
Everything was new and exciting.
WOWWWWW!
So many wonderful little shops on this street...
I bet they have fantastic paintbrushes!

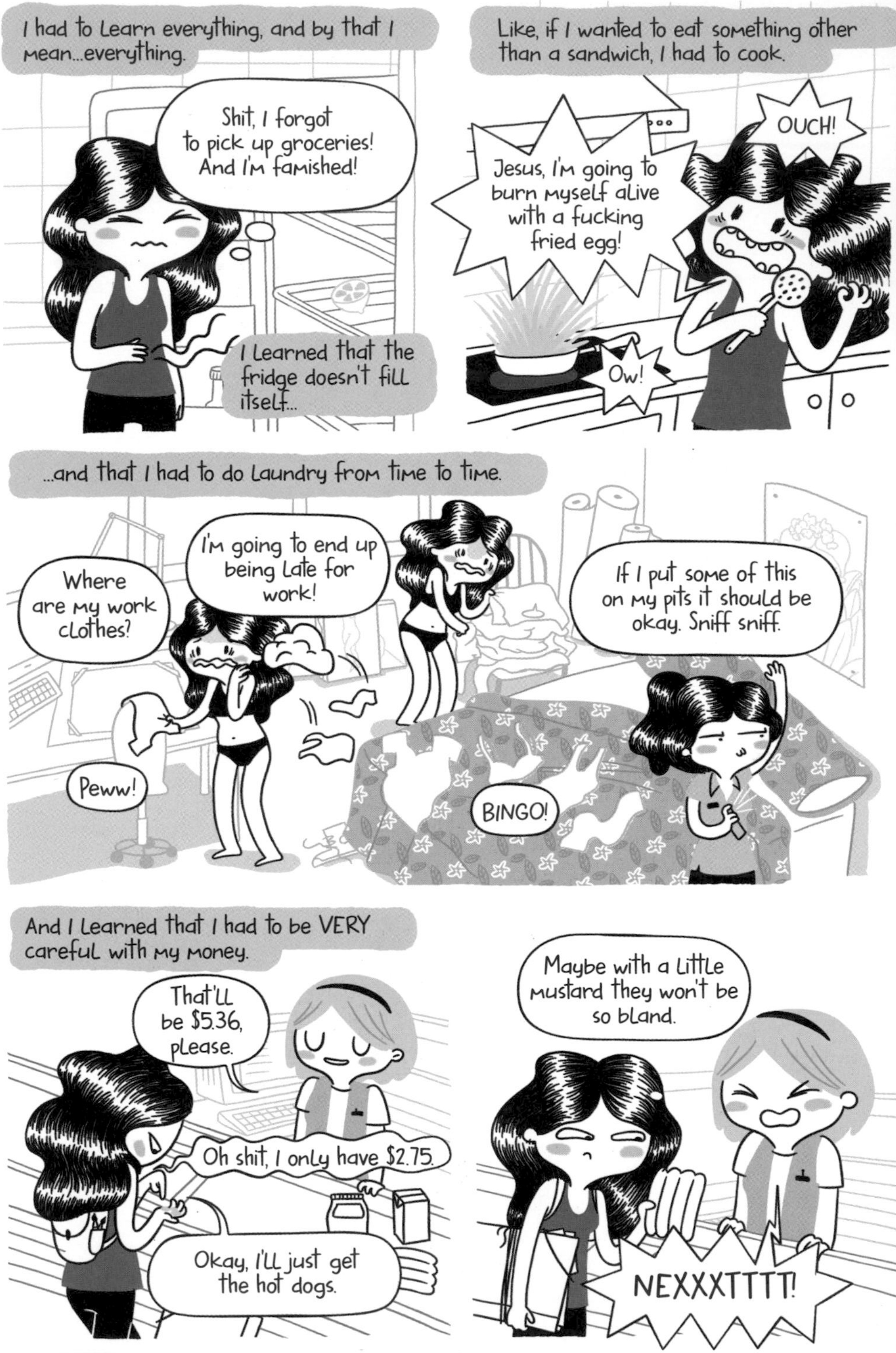
I had to learn everything, and by that I mean...everything.
Shit, I forgot to pick up groceries! And I'm famished!
I learned that the fridge doesn't fill itself...
Like, if I wanted to eat something other than a sandwich, I had to cook.
Jesus, I'm going to burn myself alive with a fucking fried egg!
OUCH!
Ow!
...and that I had to do laundry from time to time.
Where are my work clothes?
I'm going to end up being late for work!
Peww!
If I put some of this on my pits it should be okay. Sniff sniff.
BINGO!
And I learned that I had to be VERY careful with my money.
That'll be $5.36, please.
Oh shit, I only have $2.75.
Okay, I'll just get the hot dogs.
Maybe with a little mustard they won't be so bland.
NEXXXTTTT!

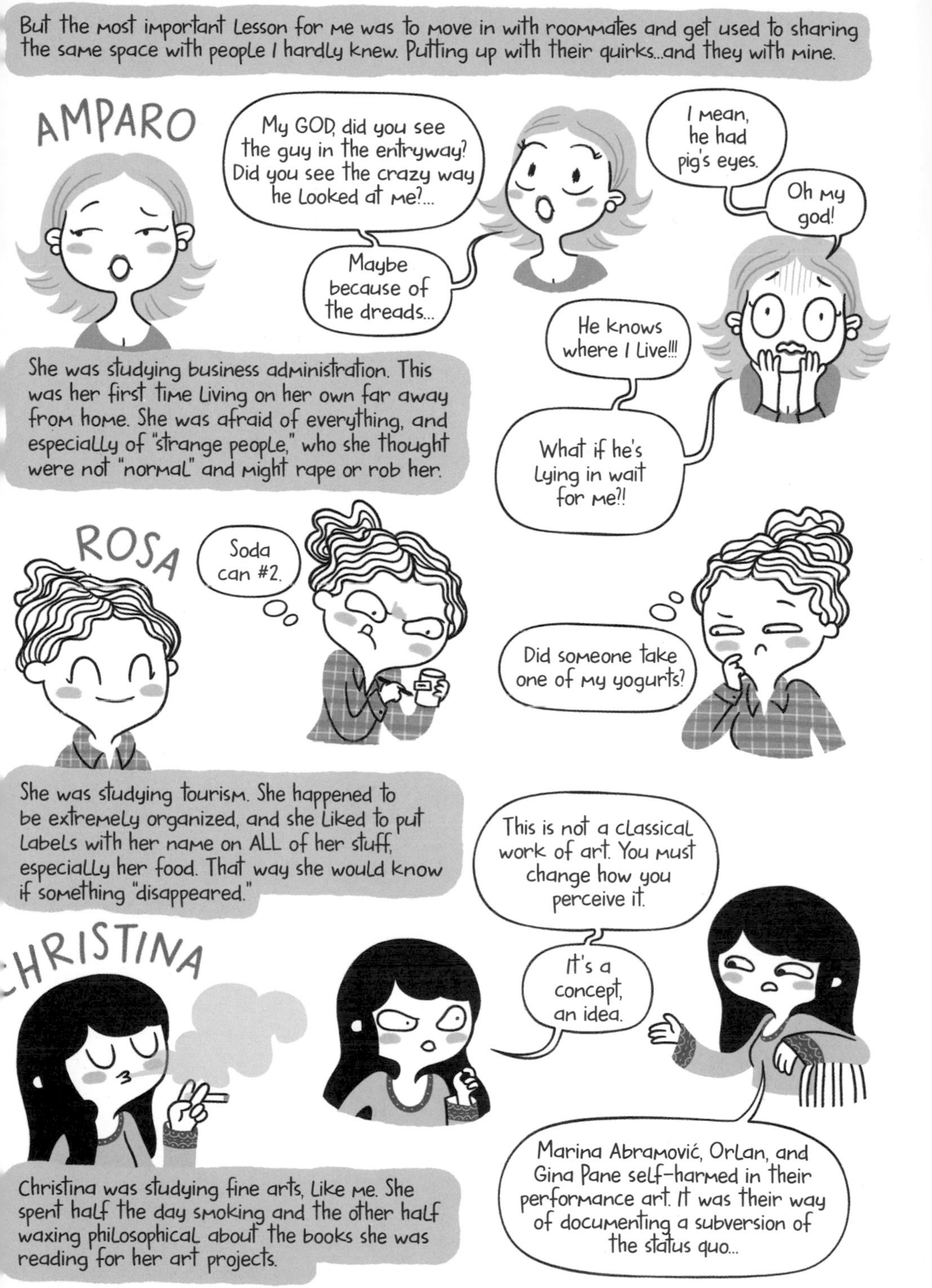
But the most important lesson for me was to move in with roommates and get used to sharing the same space with people I hardly knew. Putting up with their quirks...and they with mine.
AMPARO
My GOD, did you see the guy in the entryway? Did you see the crazy way he looked at me?...
Maybe because of the dreads...
I mean, he had pig's eyes.
Oh my god!
He knows where I live!!!
What if he's lying in wait for me?!
She was studying business administration. This was her first time living on her own far away from home. She was afraid of everything, and especially of "strange people," who she thought were not "normal" and might rape or rob her.
ROSA
Soda can #2.
Did someone take one of my yogurts?
She was studying tourism. She happened to be extremely organized, and she liked to put labels with her name on ALL of her stuff, especially her food. That way she would know if something "disappeared."
CHRISTINA
This is not a classical work of art. You must change how you perceive it.
It's a concept, an idea.
Marina Abramović, Orlan, and Gina Pane self-harmed in their performance art. It was their way of documenting a subversion of the status quo...
Christina was studying fine arts, like me. She spent half the day smoking and the other half waxing philosophical about the books she was reading for her art projects.

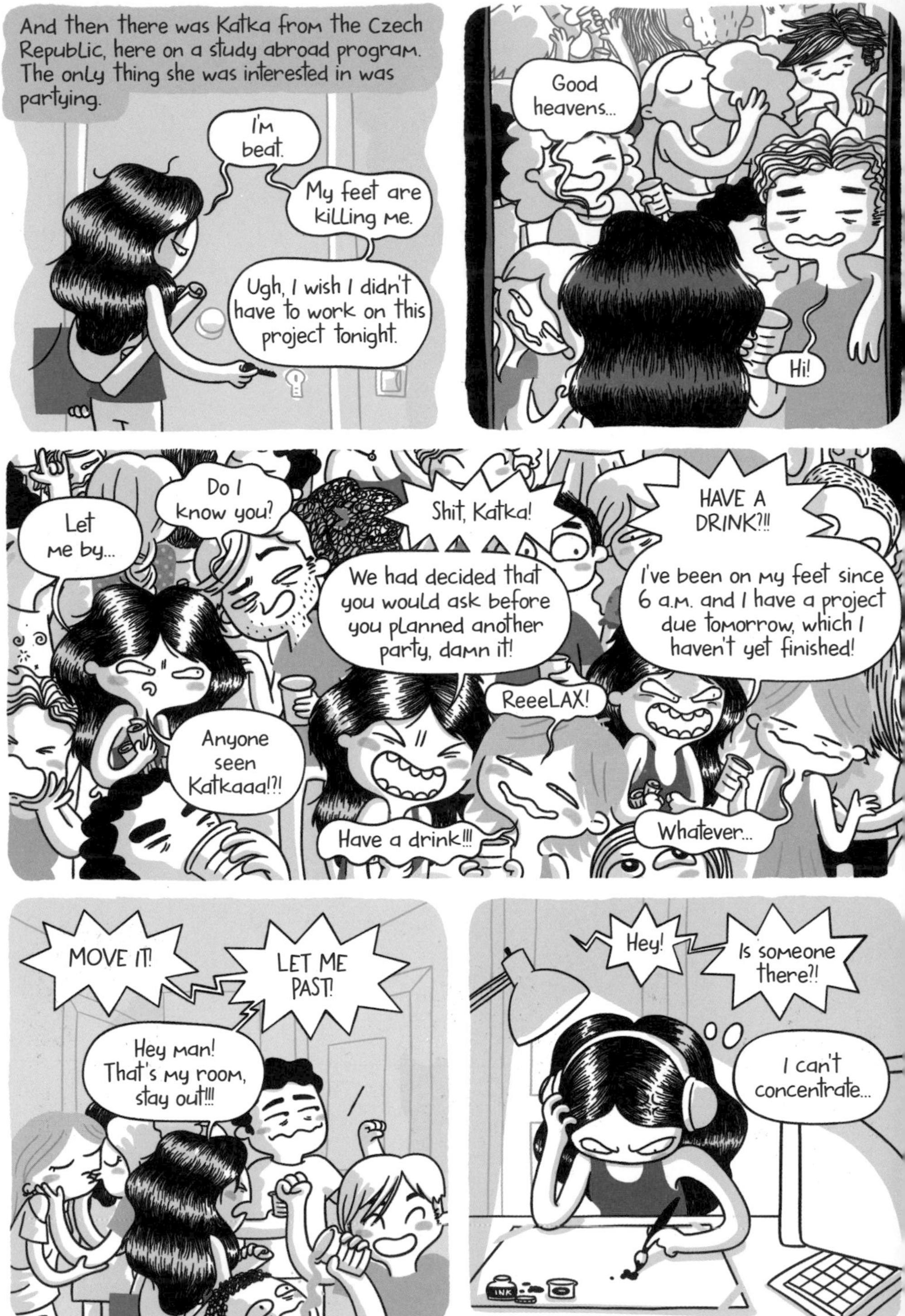
And then there was Katka from the Czech Republic, here on a study abroad program. The only thing she was interested in was partying.
I'm beat.
My feet are killing me.
Ugh, I wish I didn't have to work on this project tonight.
Good heavens...
Hi!
Let me by...
Do I know you?
Shit, Katka!
We had decided that you would ask before you planned another party, damn it!
HAVE A DRINK?!!
I've been on my feet since 6 a.m. and I have a project due tomorrow, which I haven't yet finished!
ReeeLAX!
Anyone seen Katkaaa!?!
Have a drink!!!
Whatever...
MOVE IT!
LET ME PAST!
Hey man! That's my room, stay out!!!
Hey!
Is someone there?!
I can't concentrate...
INK

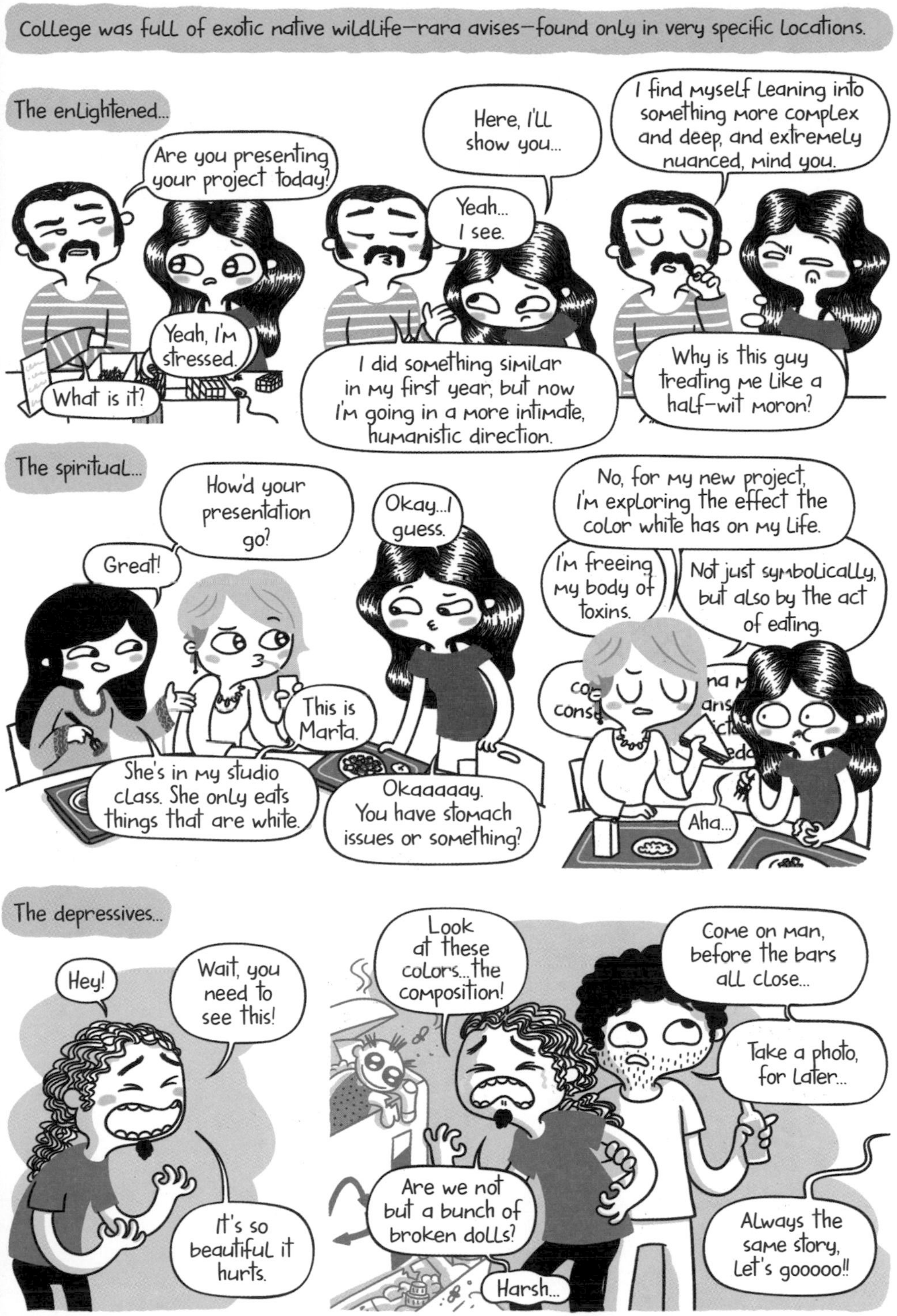
College was full of exotic native wildlife—rara avises—found only in very specific locations.
The enlightened...
Are you presenting your project today?
Yeah, I'm stressed.
What is it?
Here, I'll show you...
Yeah... I see.
I did something similar in my first year, but now I'm going in a more intimate, humanistic direction.
I find myself leaning into something more complex and deep, and extremely nuanced, mind you.
Why is this guy treating me like a half-wit moron?
The spiritual...
How'd your presentation go?
Great!
Okay...I guess.
This is Marta.
She's in my studio class. She only eats things that are white.
Okaaaaay. You have stomach issues or something?
No, for my new project, I'm exploring the effect the color white has on my life.
I'm freeing my body of toxins.
Not just symbolically, but also by the act of eating.
Aha...
The depressives...
Hey!
Wait, you need to see this!
It's so beautiful it hurts.
Look at these colors...the composition!
Come on man, before the bars all close...
Take a photo, for later...
Are we not but a bunch of broken dolls?
Harsh...
Always the same story, let's gooooo!!

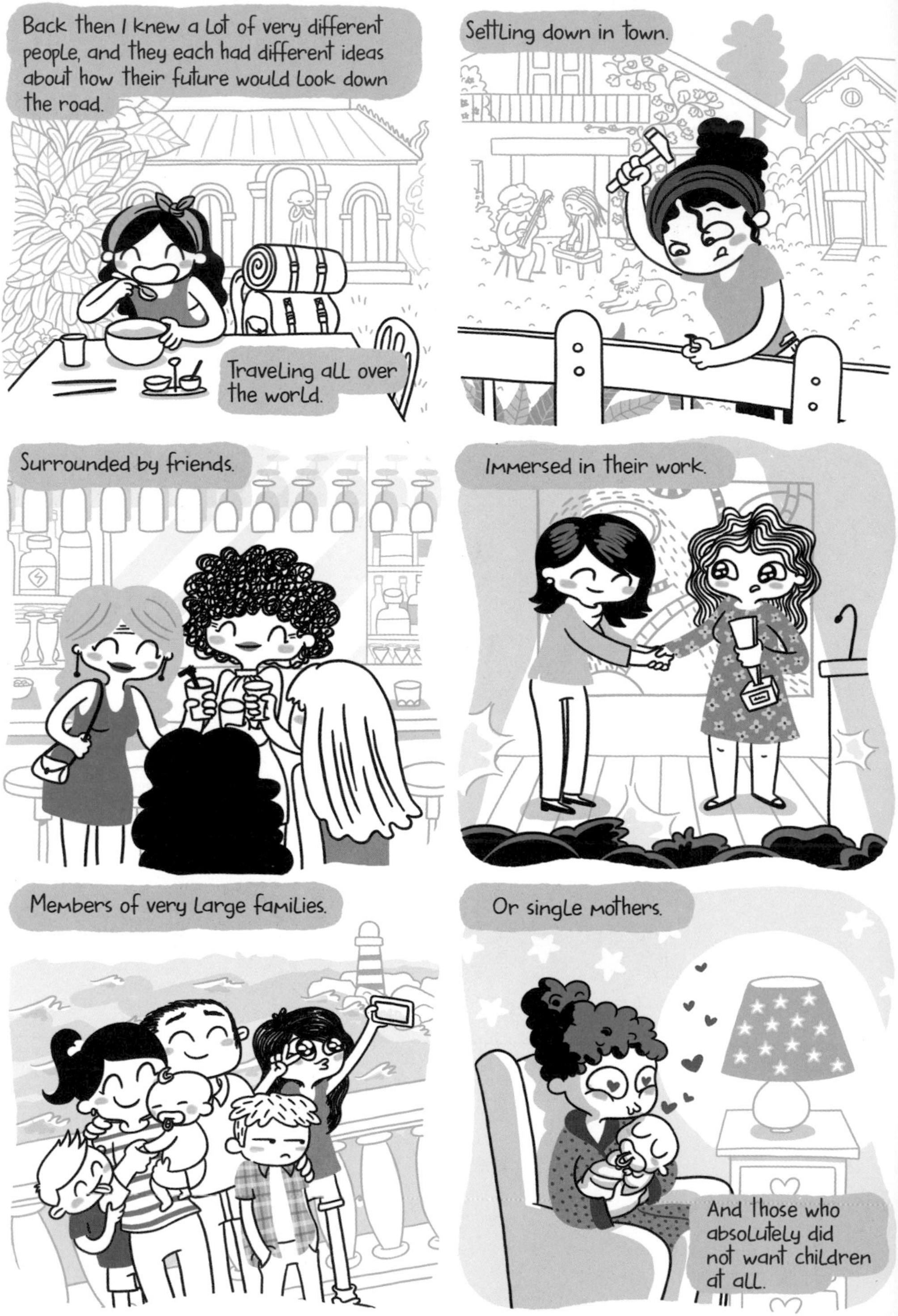
Back then I knew a lot of very different people, and they each had different ideas about how their future would look down the road.
Traveling all over the world.
Settling down in town.
Surrounded by friends.
Immersed in their work.
Members of very large families.
Or single mothers.
And those who absolutely did not want children at all.

As for me, at the time I didn't think a lot about the future, and I thought even less about being a mother and having a family. I was so completely caught up in another world.

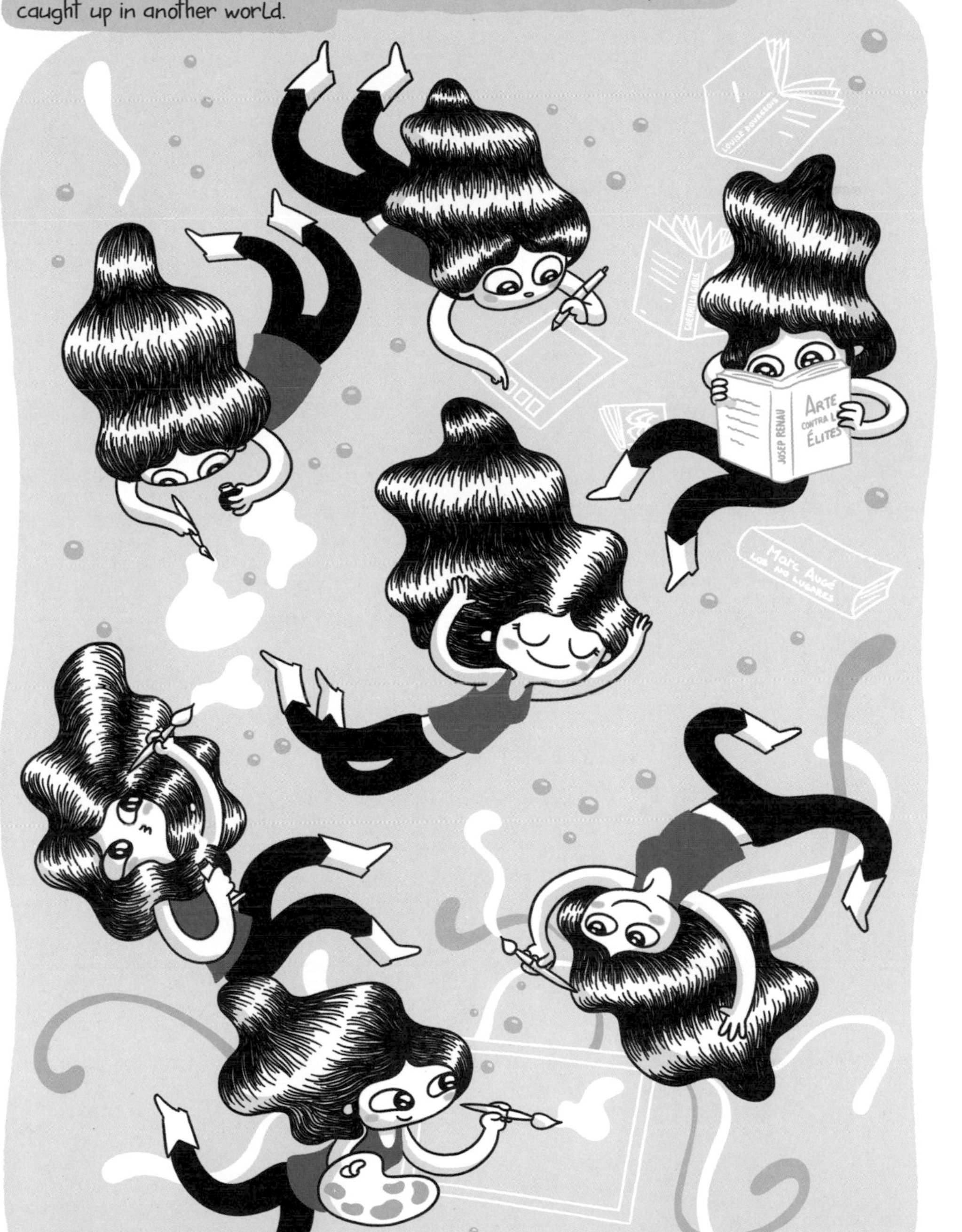
JOSEP RENAU
ARTE CONTRA L ÉLITES
Marc Augé
LOS NO LUGARES

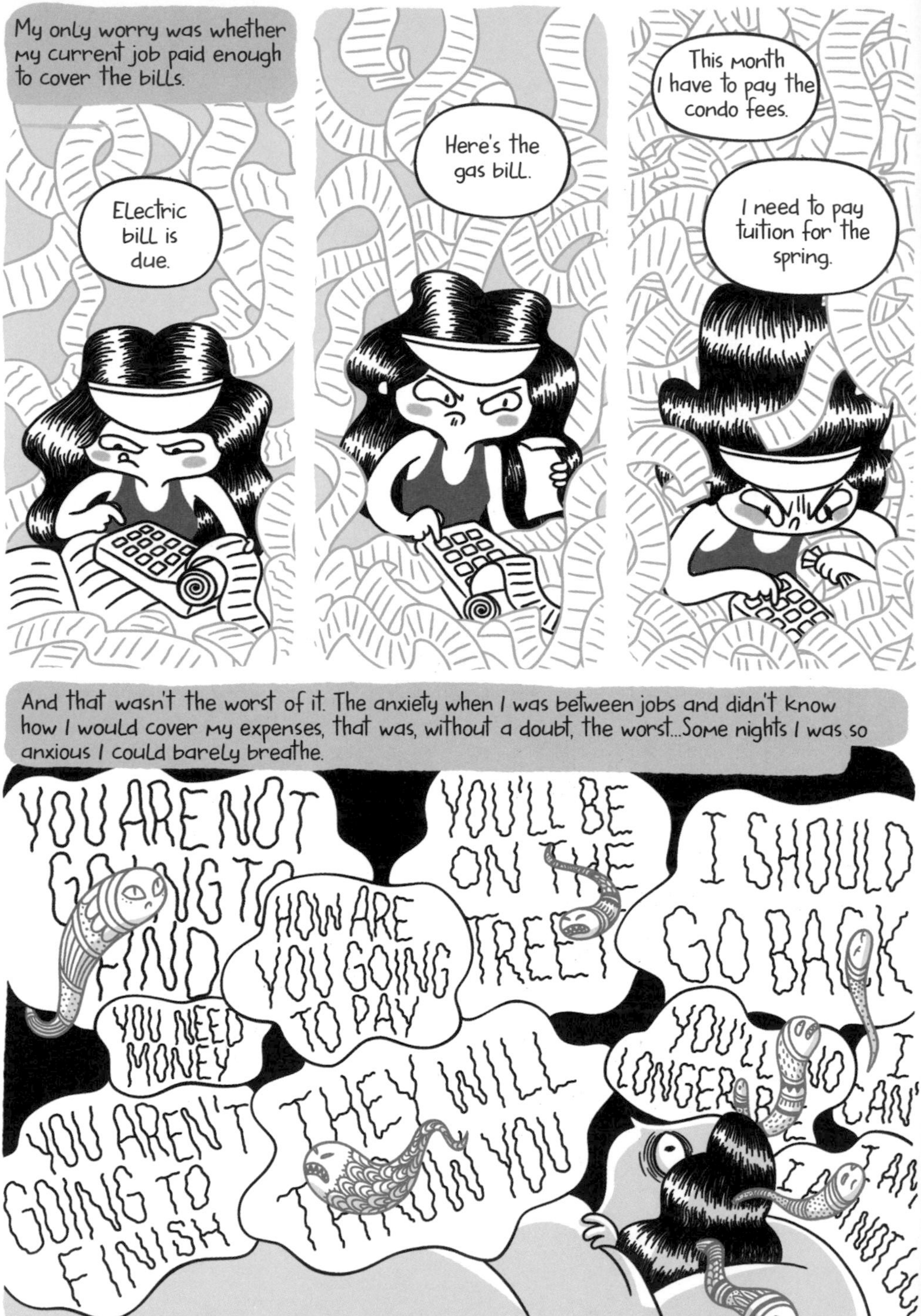
My only worry was whether my current job paid enough to cover the bills.
Electric bill is due.
Here's the gas bill.
This month I have to pay the condo fees.
I need to pay tuition for the spring.
And that wasn't the worst of it. The anxiety when I was between jobs and didn't know how I would cover my expenses, that was, without a doubt, the worst...Some nights I was so anxious I could barely breathe.
YOU ARE NOT
HOW ARE YOU GOING TO PAY
YOU NEED MONEY
I SHOULD GO BACK
YOU AREN'T GOING TO FINISH

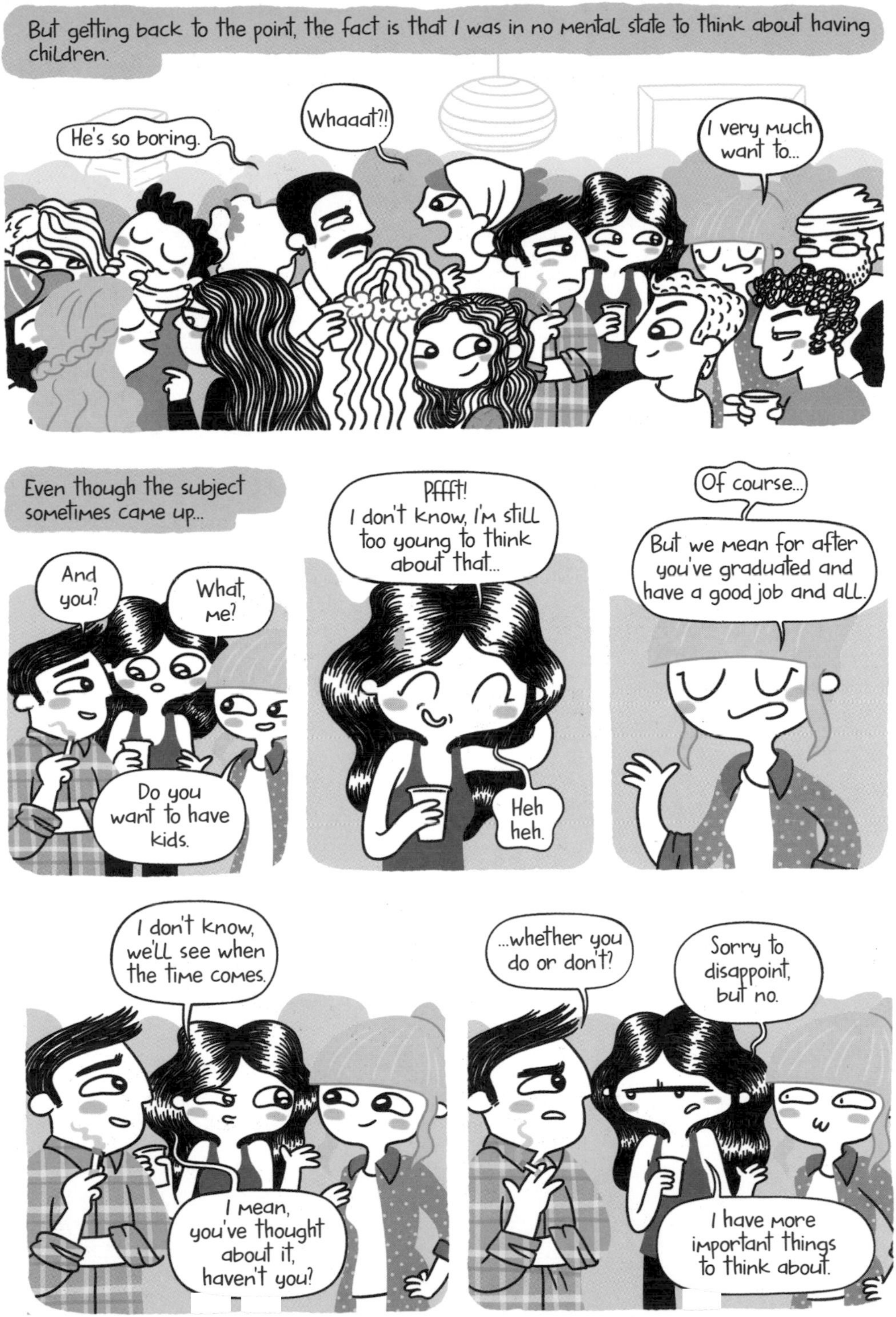
But getting back to the point, the fact is that I was in no mental state to think about having children.
He's so boring.
Whaaat?!
I very much want to...
Even though the subject sometimes came up...
And you?
What, me?
Do you want to have kids.
Pffft!
I don't know, I'm still too young to think about that...
Heh heh.
Of course...
But we mean for after you've graduated and have a good job and all.
I don't know, we'll see when the time comes.
I mean, you've thought about it, haven't you?
...whether you do or don't?
Sorry to disappoint, but no.
I have more important things to think about.

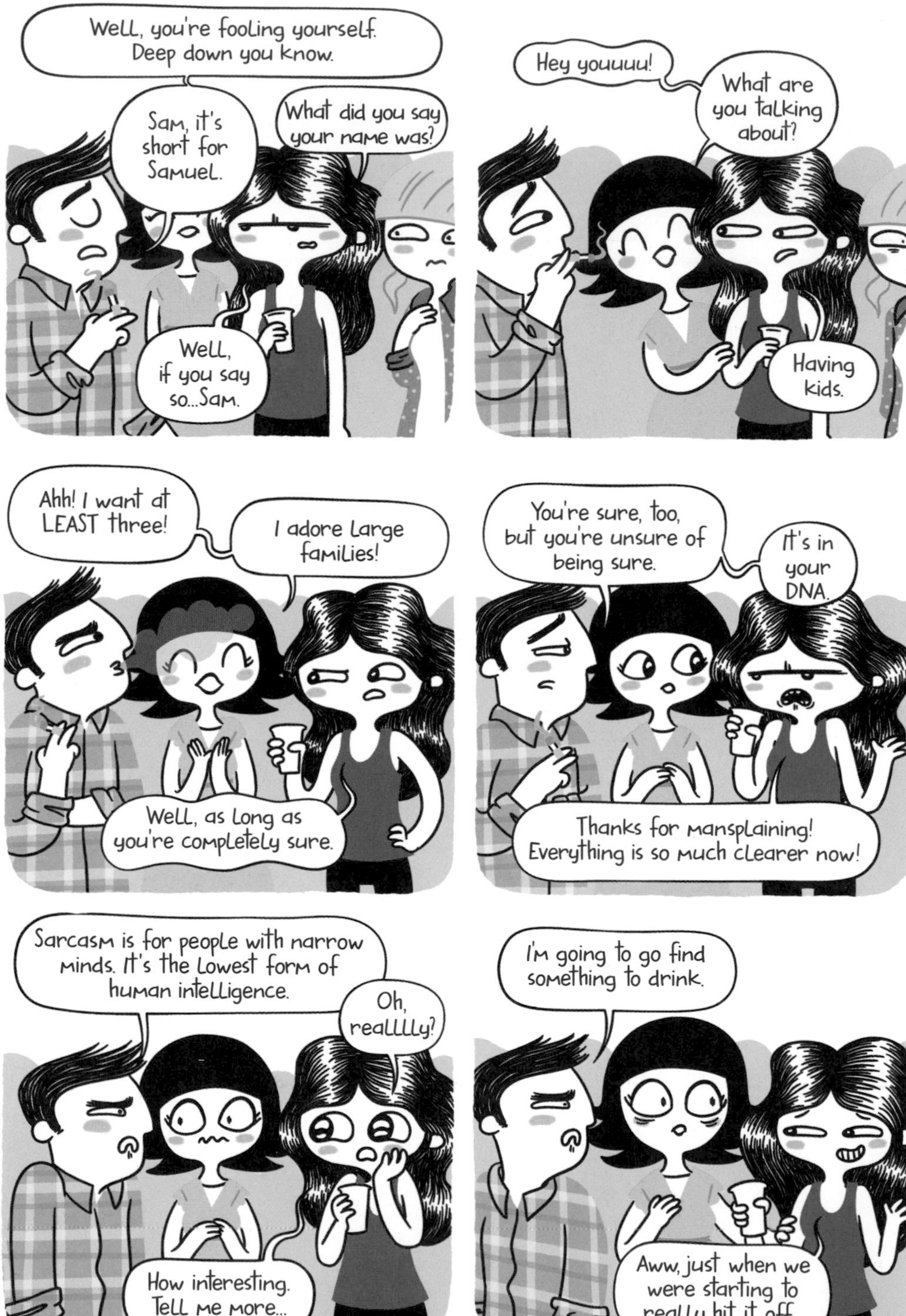
Well, you're fooling yourself. Deep down you know.
Sam, it's short for Samuel.
What did you say your name was?
Well, if you say so...Sam.
Hey youuuu!
What are you talking about?
Having kids.
Ahh! I want at LEAST three!
I adore large families!
Well, as long as you're completely sure.
You're sure, too, but you're unsure of being sure.
It's in your DNA.
Thanks for mansplaining! Everything is so much clearer now!
Sarcasm is for people with narrow minds. It's the lowest form of human intelligence.
Oh, realllly?
How interesting. Tell me more...
I'm going to go find something to drink.
Aww, just when we were starting to really hit it off...

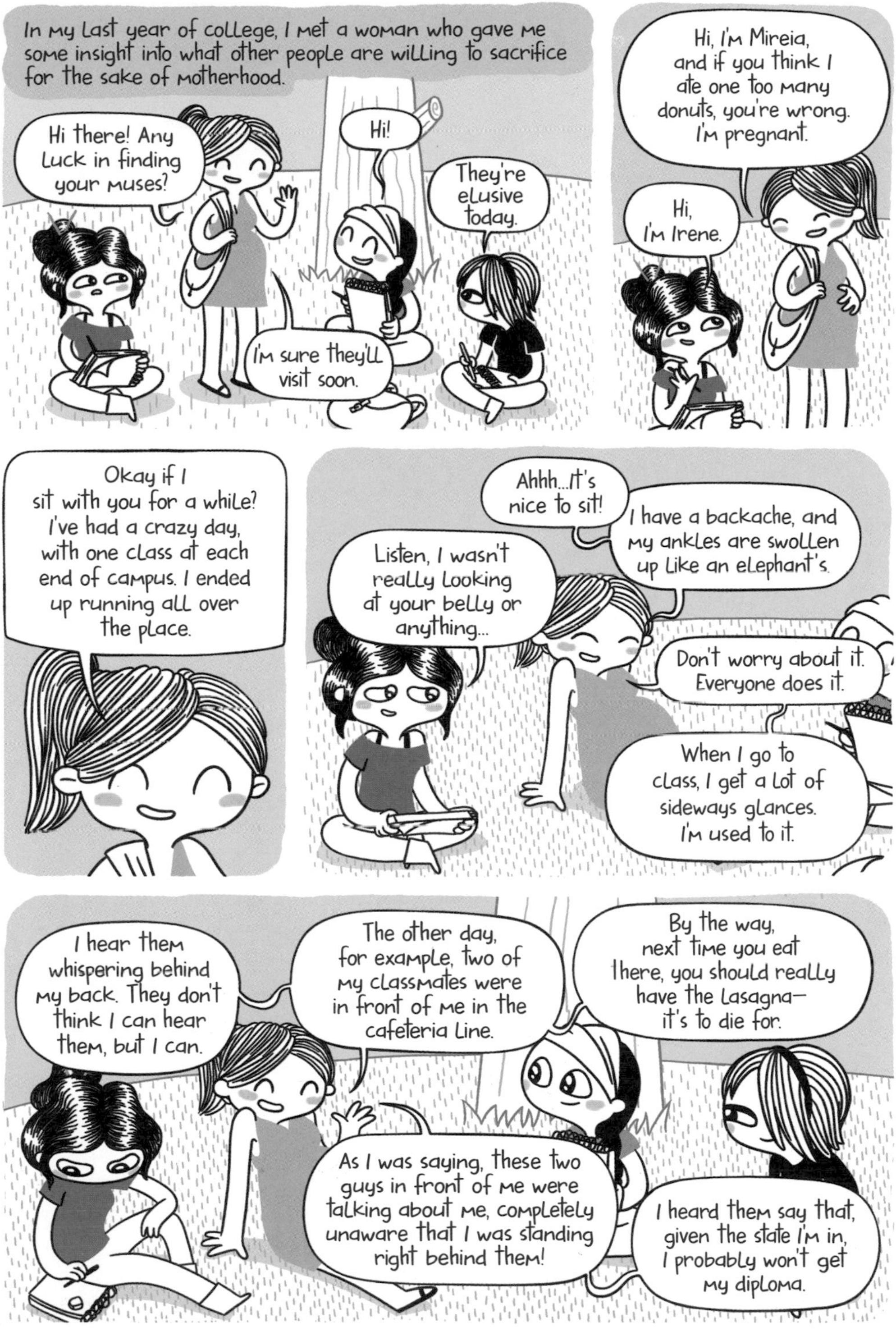
In my last year of college, I met a woman who gave me some insight into what other people are willing to sacrifice for the sake of motherhood.
Hi there! Any luck in finding your muses?
Hi!
They're elusive today.
I'm sure they'll visit soon.
Hi, I'm Mireia, and if you think I ate one too many donuts, you're wrong. I'm pregnant.
Hi, I'm Irene.
Okay if I sit with you for a while? I've had a crazy day, with one class at each end of campus. I ended up running all over the place.
Ahhh...It's nice to sit!
I have a backache, and my ankles are swollen up like an elephant's.
Listen, I wasn't really looking at your belly or anything...
Don't worry about it. Everyone does it.
When I go to class, I get a lot of sideways glances. I'm used to it.
I hear them whispering behind my back. They don't think I can hear them, but I can.
The other day, for example, two of my classmates were in front of me in the cafeteria line.
By the way, next time you eat there, you should really have the lasagna— it's to die for.
As I was saying, these two guys in front of me were talking about me, completely unaware that I was standing right behind them!
I heard them say that, given the state I'm in, I probably won't get my diploma.

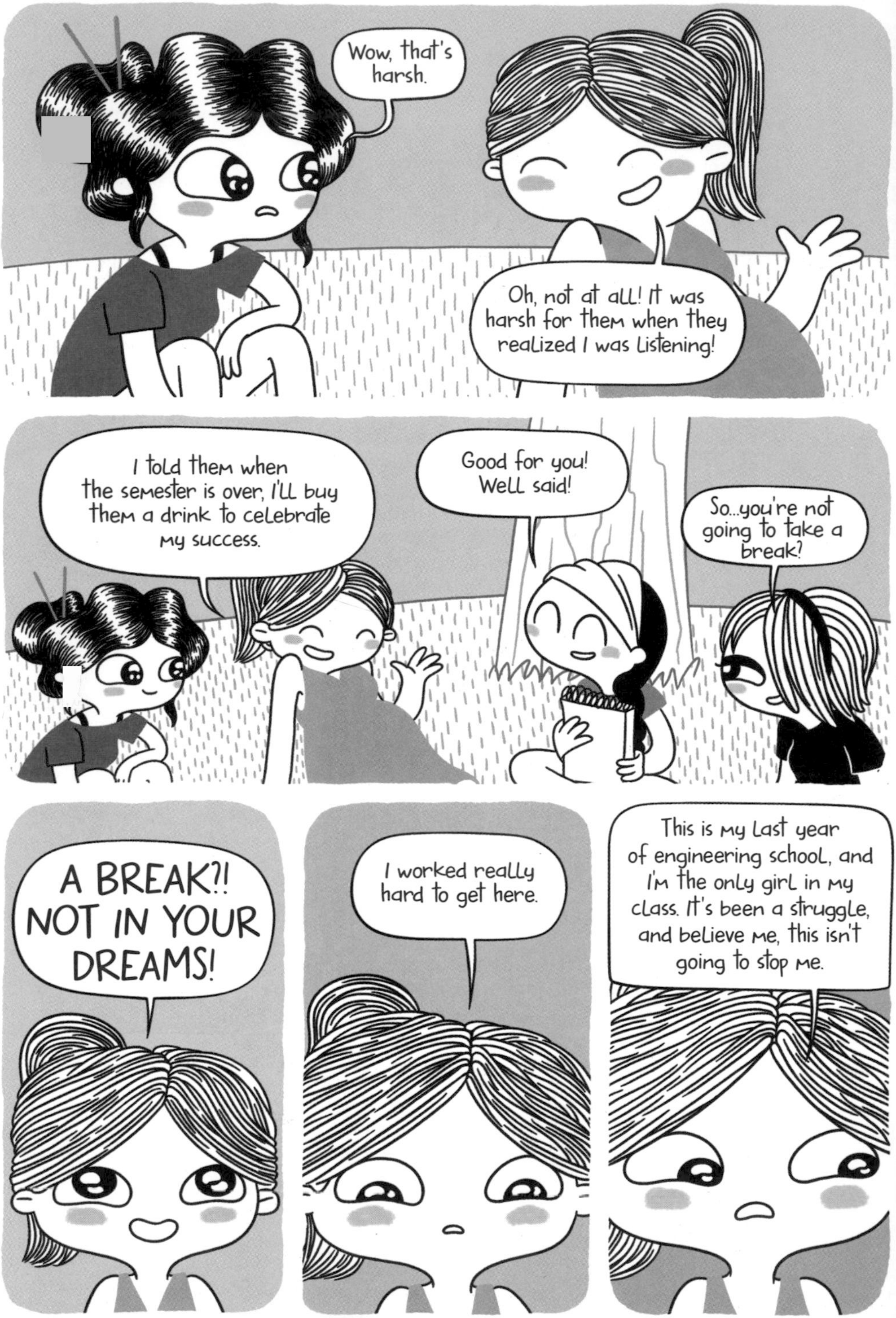
Wow, that's harsh.
Oh, not at all! It was harsh for them when they realized I was listening!
I told them when the semester is over, I'll buy them a drink to celebrate my success.
Good for you! Well said!
So...you're not going to take a break?
A BREAK?! NOT IN YOUR DREAMS!
I worked really hard to get here.
This is my last year of engineering school, and I'm the only girl in my class. It's been a struggle, and believe me, this isn't going to stop me.

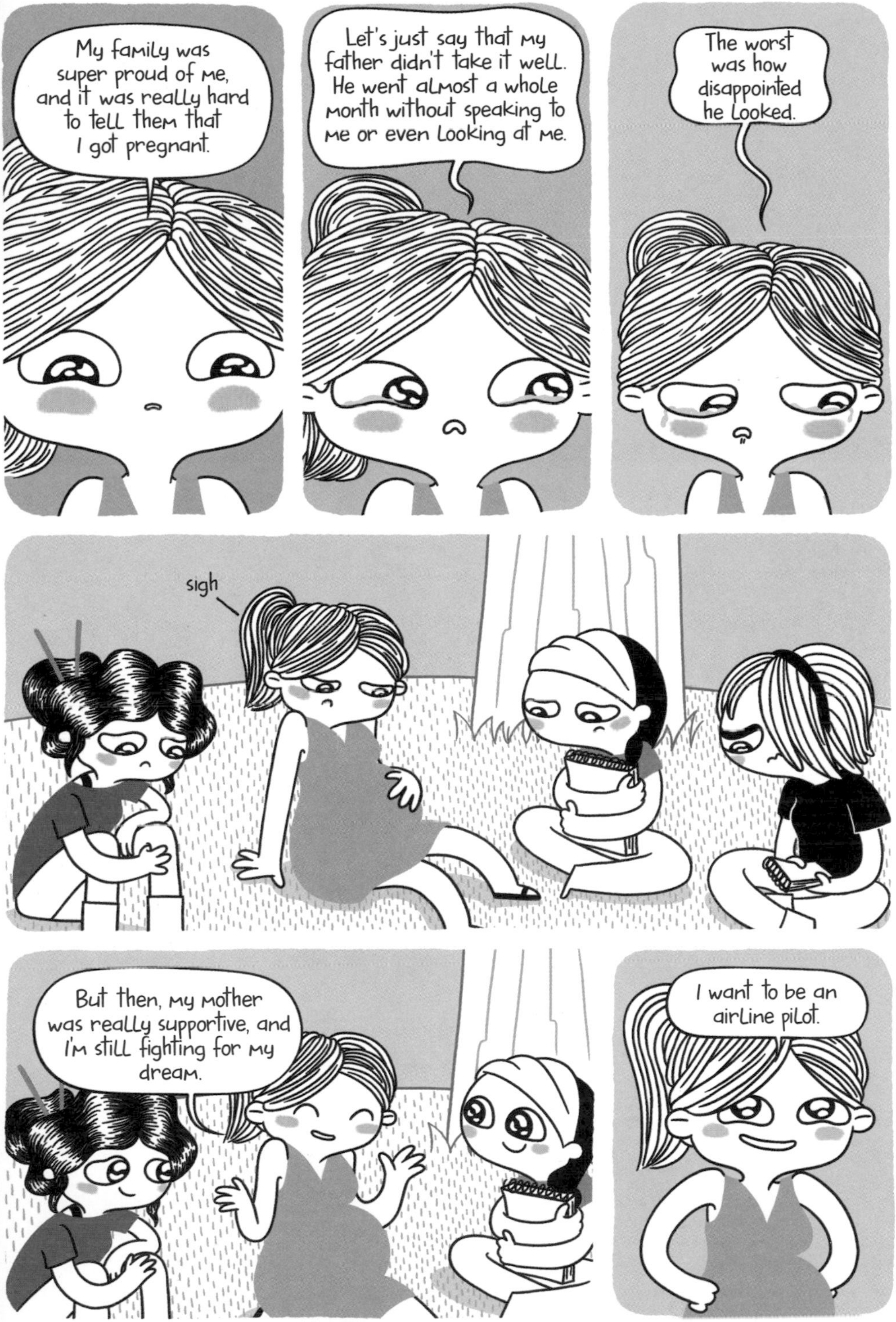

My family was super proud of me, and it was really hard to tell them that I got pregnant.
Let's just say that my father didn't take it well. He went almost a whole month without speaking to me or even looking at me.
The worst was how disappointed he looked.
sigh
But then, my mother was really supportive, and I'm still fighting for my dream.
I want to be an airline pilot.

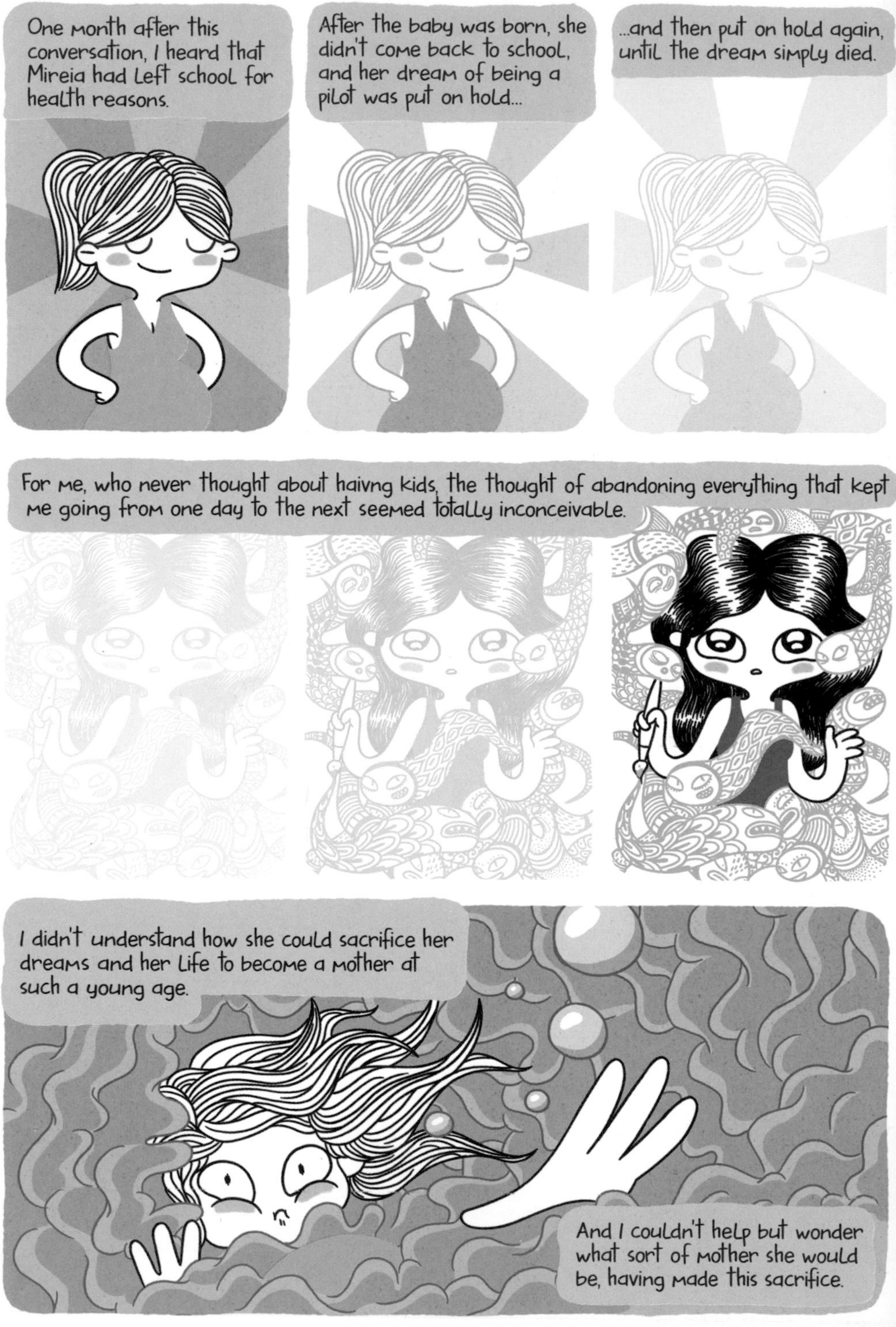
One month after this conversation, I heard that Mireia had left school for health reasons.
After the baby was born, she didn't come back to school, and her dream of being a pilot was put on hold...
...and then put on hold again, until the dream simply died.
For me, who never thought about haivng kids, the thought of abandoning everything that kept me going from one day to the next seemed totally inconceivable.
I didn't understand how she could sacrifice her dreams and her life to become a mother at such a young age.
And I couldn't help but wonder what sort of mother she would be, having made this sacrifice.

CHAPTER 3

Everything in Its Own Time

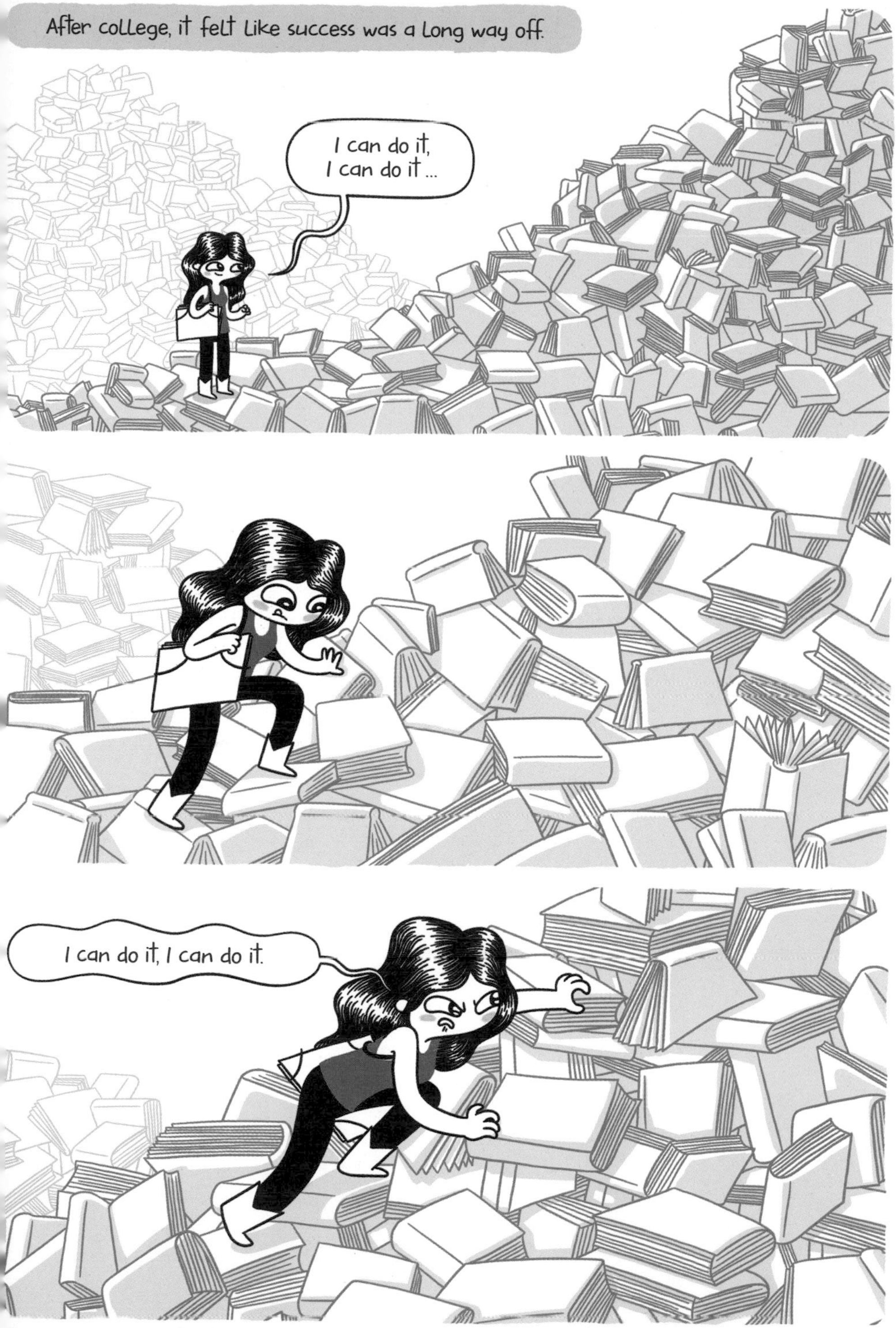
After college, it felt like success was a long way off.
I can do it, I can do it...
I can do it, I can do it.

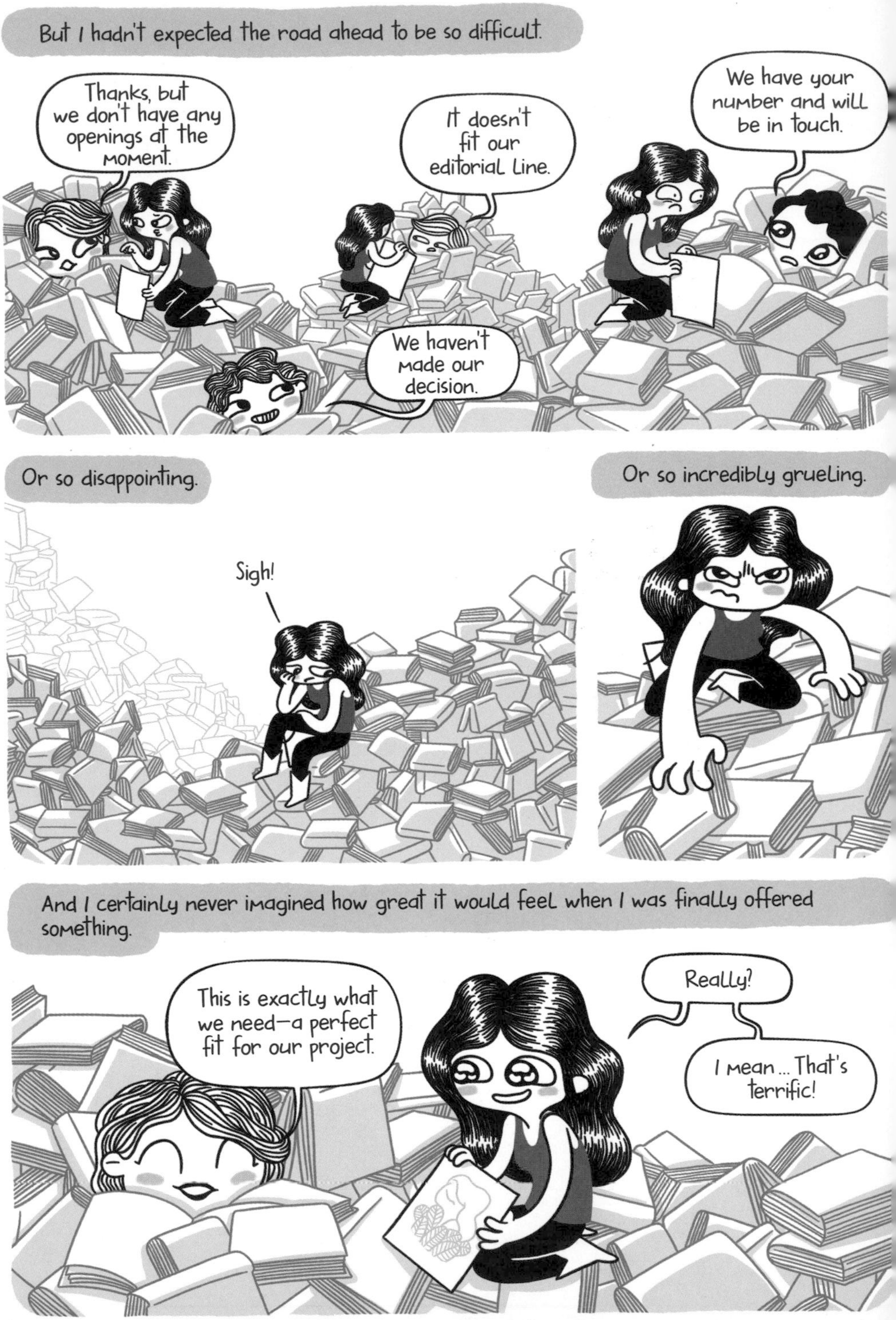
But I hadn't expected the road ahead to be so difficult.
Thanks, but we don't have any openings at the moment.
It doesn't fit our editorial line.
We have your number and will be in touch.
We haven't made our decision.
Or so disappointing.
Sigh!
Or so incredibly grueling.
And I certainly never imagined how great it would feel when I was finally offered something.
This is exactly what we need—a perfect fit for our project.
Really?
I mean... That's terrific!

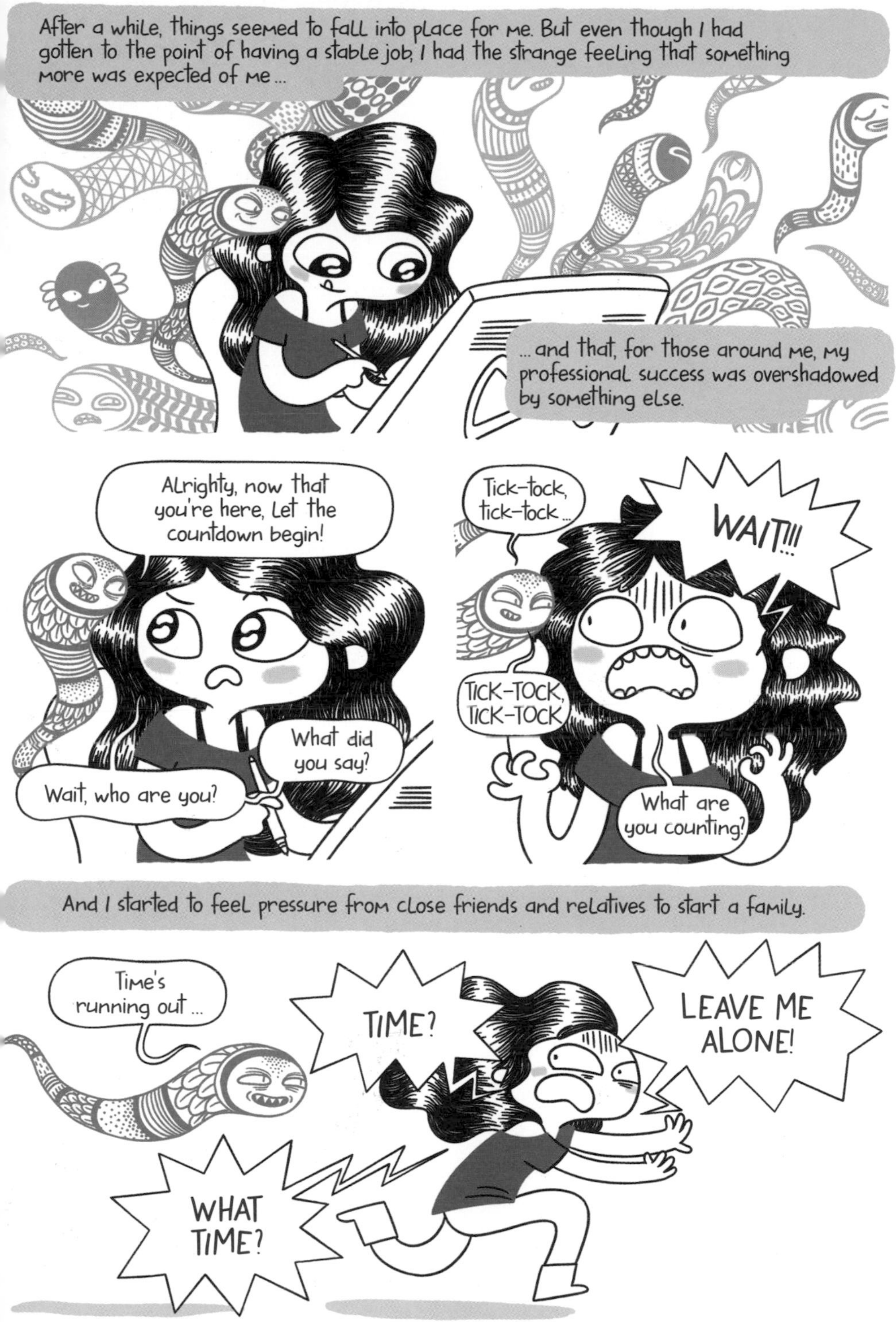

After a while, things seemed to fall into place for me. But even though I had gotten to the point of having a stable job, I had the strange feeling that something more was expected of me...
... and that, for those around me, my professional success was overshadowed by something else.
Alrighty, now that you're here, let the countdown begin!
What did you say?
Wait, who are you?
Tick-tock, tick-tock...
WAIT!!!
TICK-TOCK, TICK-TOCK
What are you counting?
And I started to feel pressure from close friends and relatives to start a family.
Time's running out...
TIME?
LEAVE ME ALONE!
WHAT TIME?

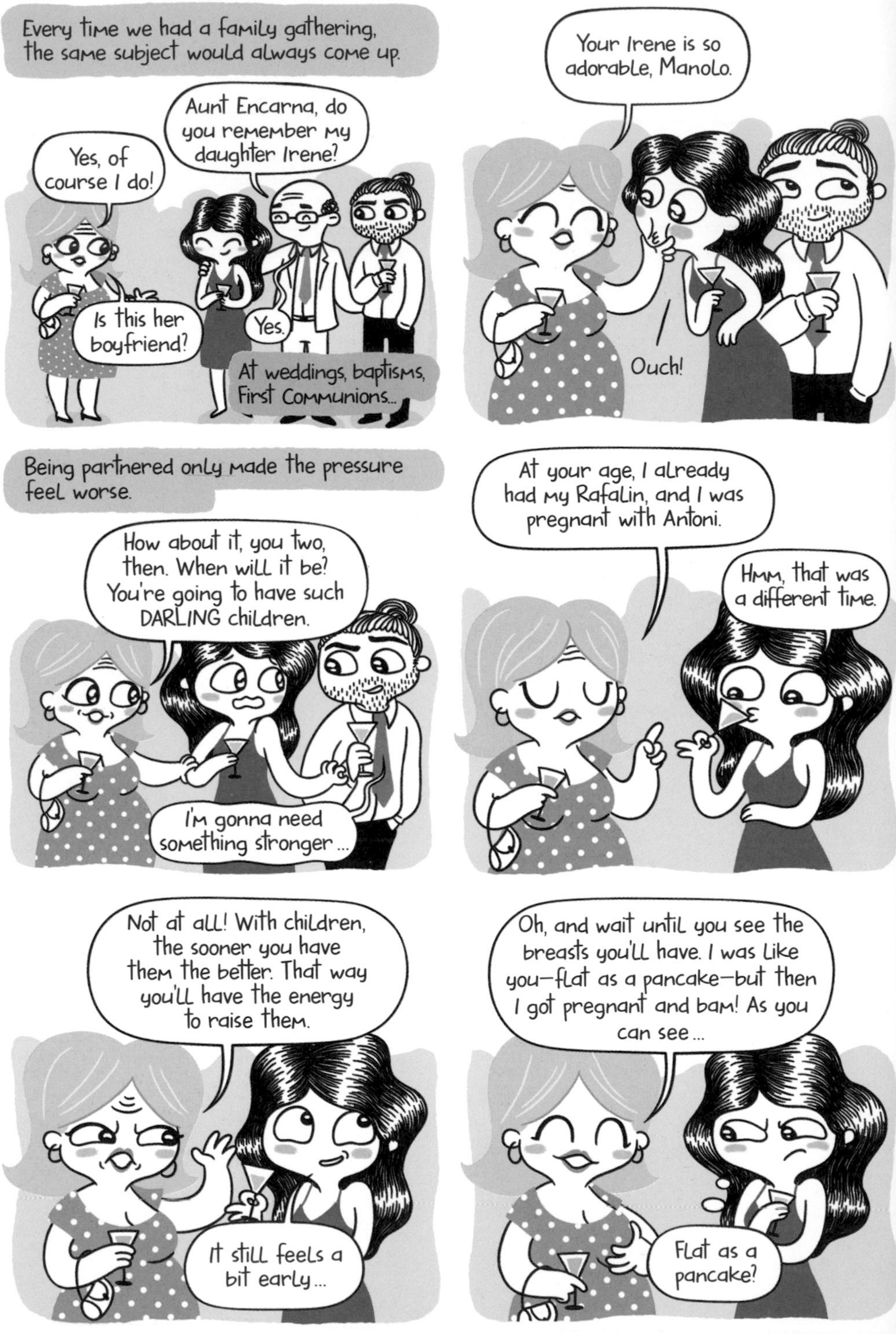

Every time we had a family gathering, the same subject would always come up.
Aunt Encarna, do you remember my daughter Irene?
Yes, of course I do!
Is this her boyfriend?
Yes.
At weddings, baptisms, First Communions...
Your Irene is so adorable, Manolo.
Ouch!
Being partnered only made the pressure feel worse.
How about it, you two, then. When will it be? You're going to have such DARLING children.
I'm gonna need something stronger ...
At your age, I already had my Rafalin, and I was pregnant with Antoni.
Hmm, that was a different time.
Not at all! With children, the sooner you have them the better. That way you'll have the energy to raise them.
It still feels a bit early...
Oh, and wait until you see the breasts you'll have. I was like you—flat as a pancake—but then I got pregnant and bam! As you can see...
Flat as a pancake?

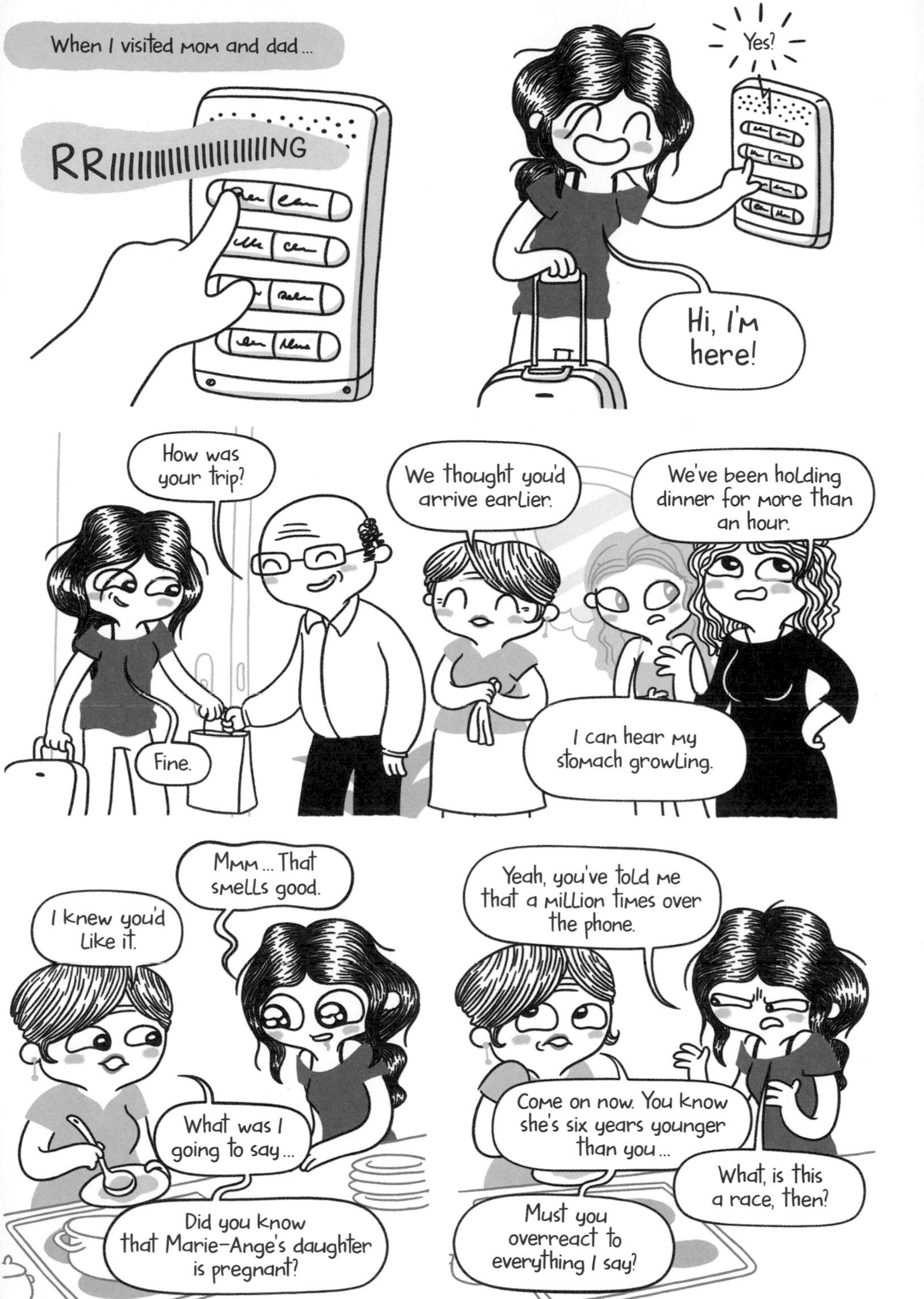
When I visited mom and dad...
RRIIIIIIIIIIIIIIIIIIIIIING
Yes?
Hi, I'm here!
How was your trip?
Fine.
We thought you'd arrive earlier.
We've been holding dinner for more than an hour.
I can hear my stomach growling.
Mmm... That smells good.
I knew you'd like it.
What was I going to say...
Did you know that Marie-Ange's daughter is pregnant?
Yeah, you've told me that a million times over the phone.
Come on now. You know she's six years younger than you...
What, is this a race, then?
Must you overreact to everything I say?

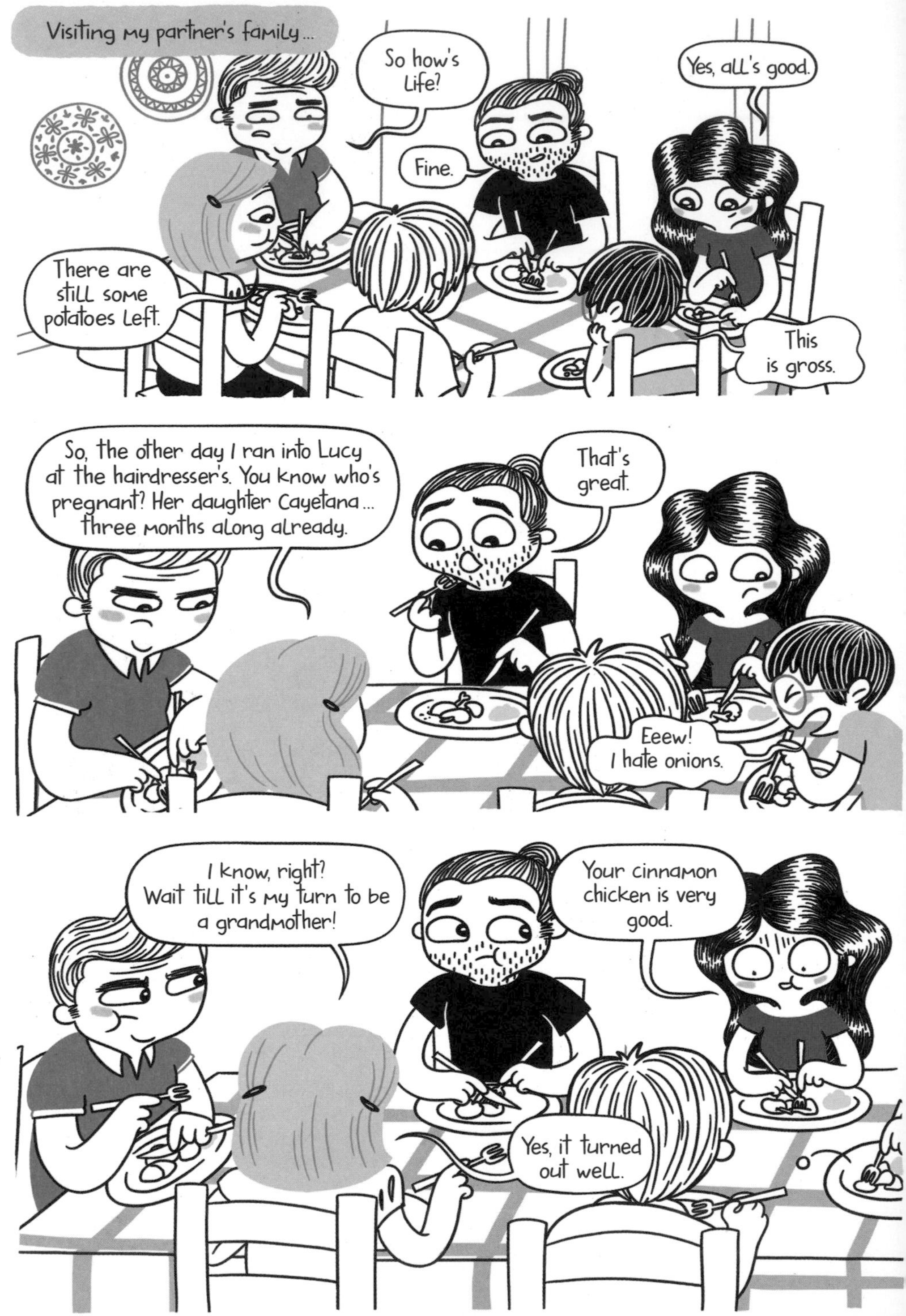
Visiting my partner's family...
So how's life?
Fine.
Yes, all's good.
There are still some potatoes left.
This is gross.
So, the other day I ran into Lucy at the hairdresser's. You know who's pregnant? Her daughter Cayetana... three months along already.
That's great.
Eeew! I hate onions.
I know, right? Wait till it's my turn to be a grandmother!
Your cinnamon chicken is very good.
Yes, it turned out well.

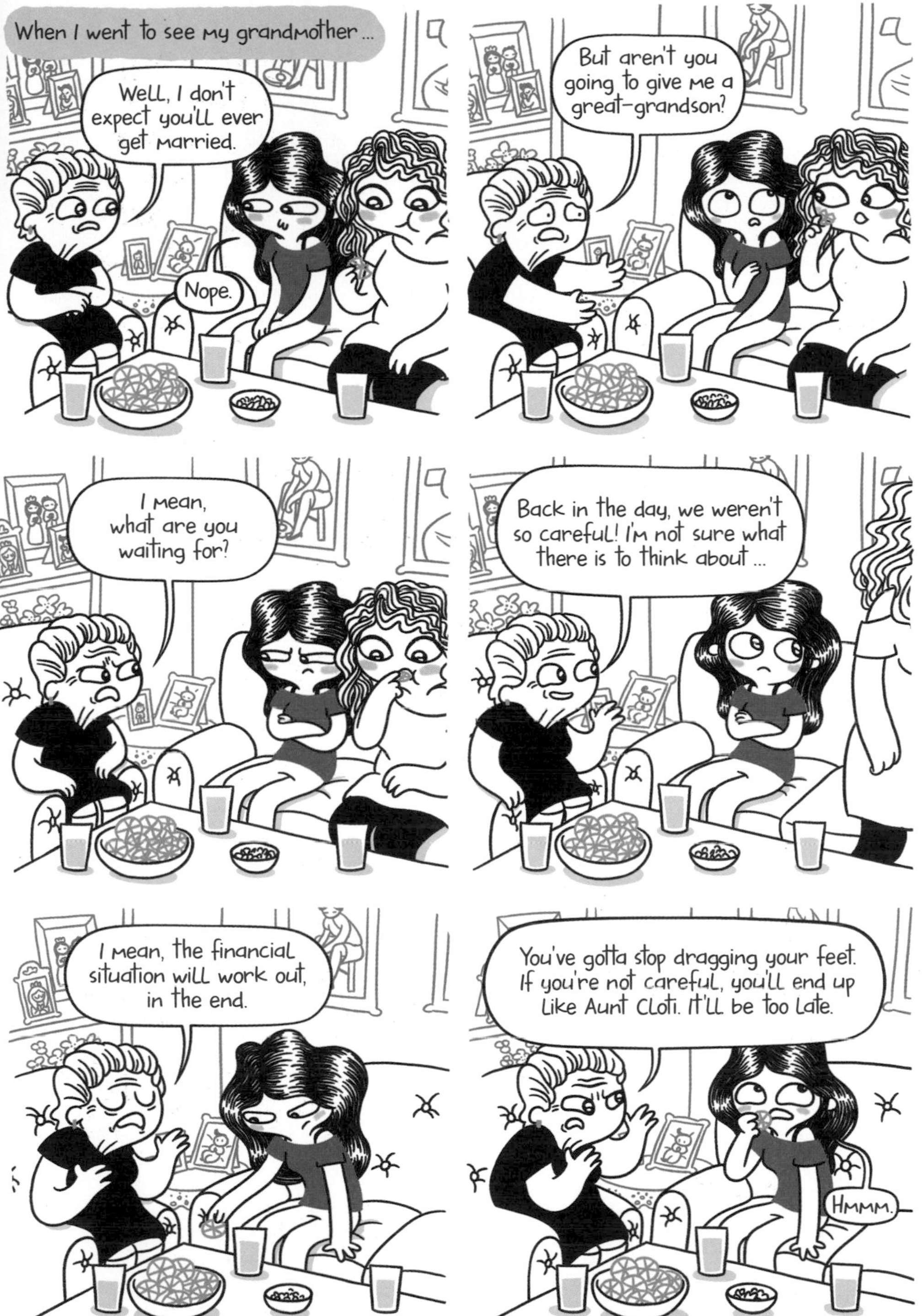
When I went to see my grandmother ...
Well, I don't expect you'll ever get married.
Nope.
But aren't you going to give me a great-grandson?
I mean, what are you waiting for?
Back in the day, we weren't so careful! I'm not sure what there is to think about ...
I mean, the financial situation will work out, in the end.
You've gotta stop dragging your feet. If you're not careful, you'll end up like Aunt Cloti. It'll be too late.
Hmmm.

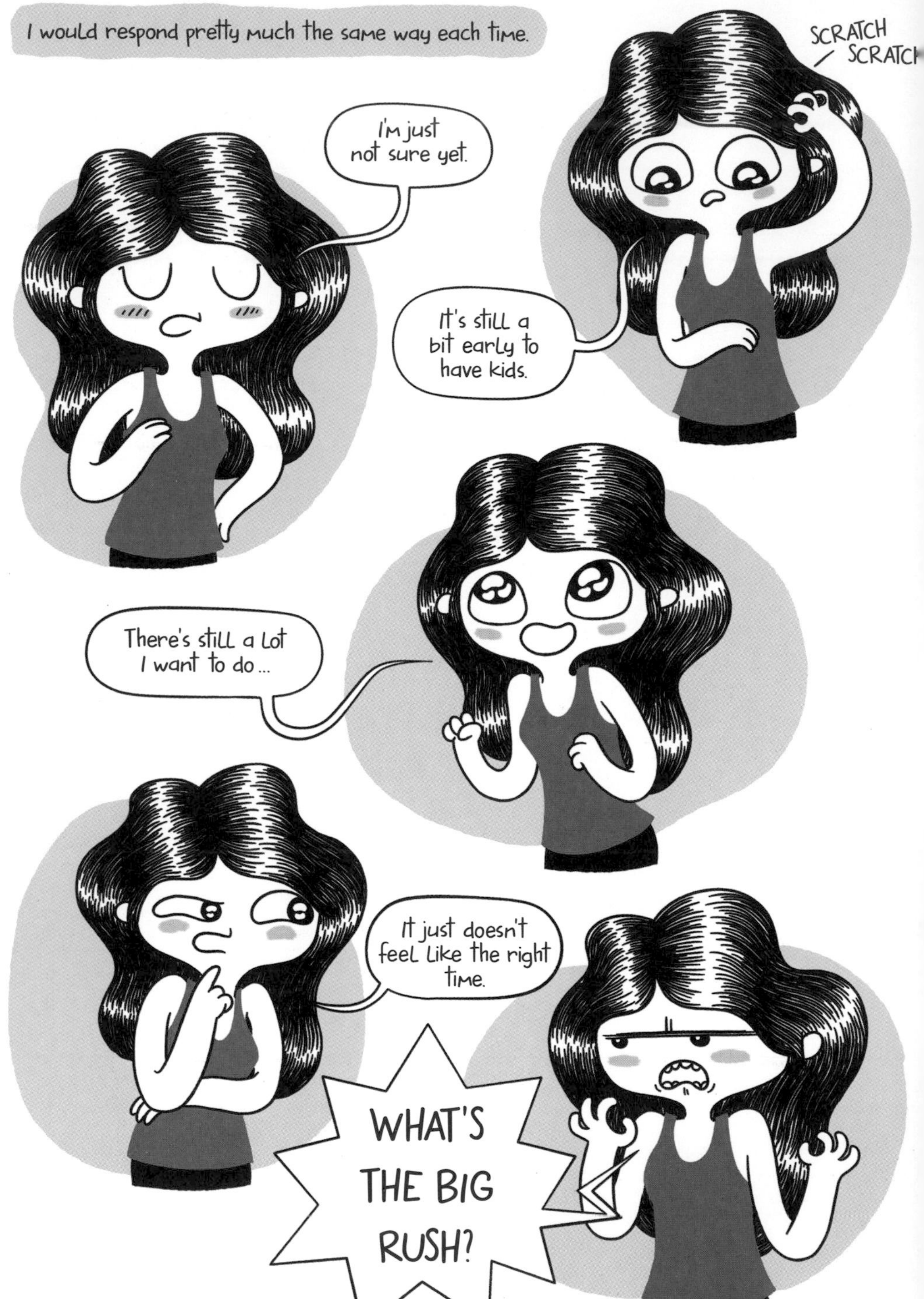
I would respond pretty much the same way each time.
I'm just not sure yet.
SCRATCH SCRATCH
It's still a bit early to have kids.
There's still a lot I want to do...
It just doesn't feel like the right time.
WHAT'S THE BIG RUSH?

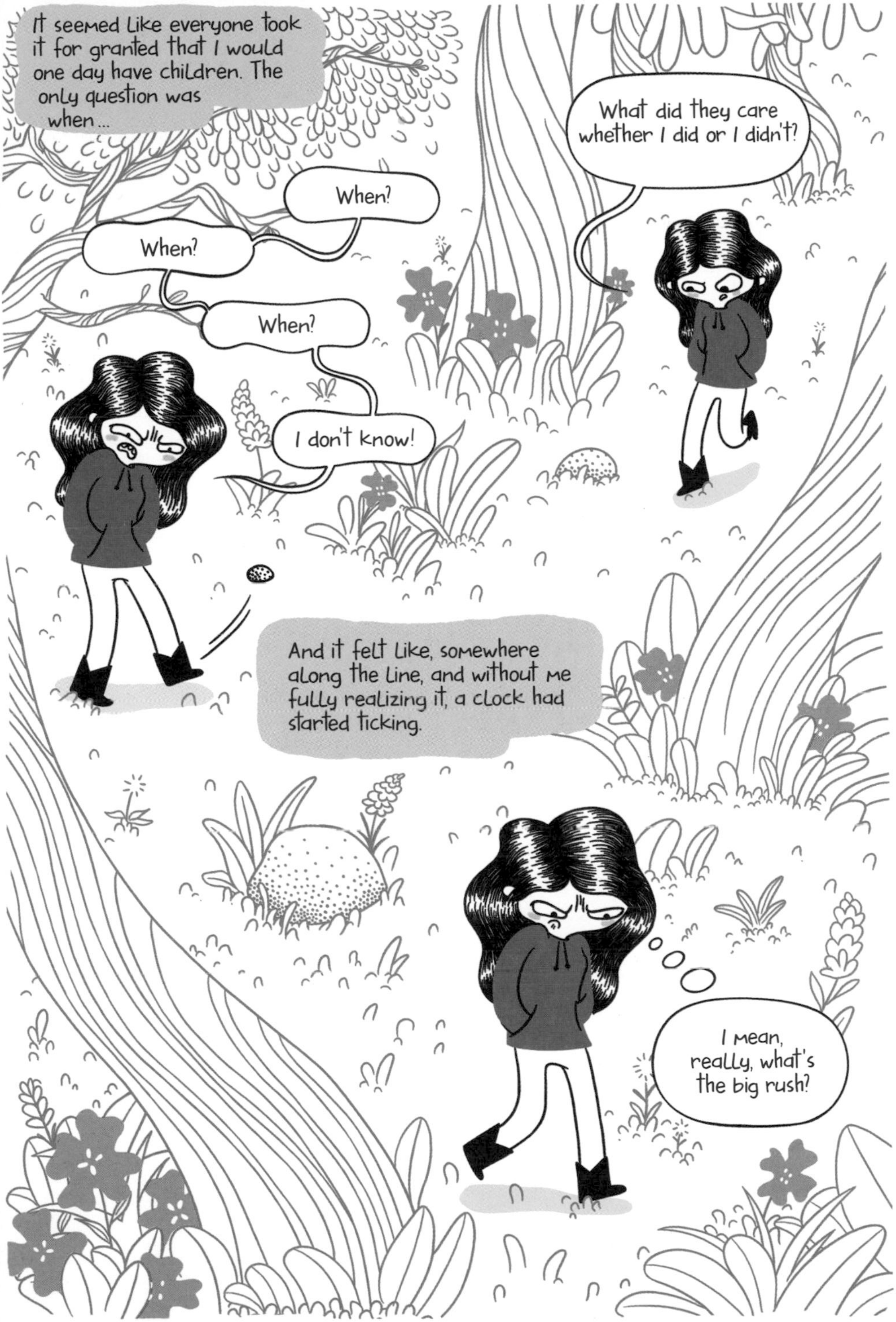
It seemed like everyone took it for granted that I would one day have children. The only question was when...
When?
When?
When?
I don't know!
What did they care whether I did or I didn't?
And it felt like, somewhere along the line, and without me fully realizing it, a clock had started ticking.
I mean, really, what's the big rush?

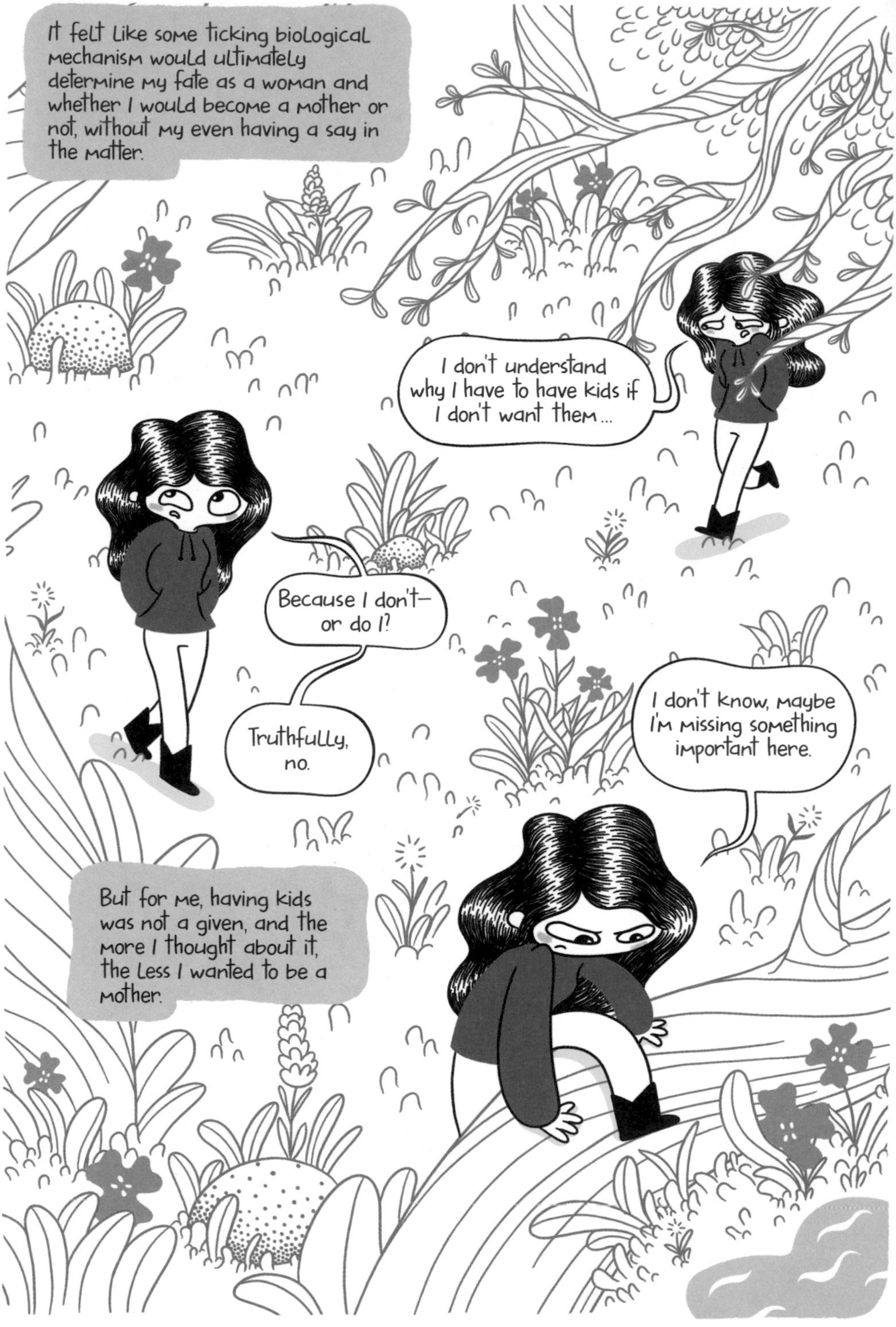
It felt like some ticking biological mechanism would ultimately determine my fate as a woman and whether I would become a mother or not, without my even having a say in the matter.
I don't understand why I have to have kids if I don't want them...
Because I don't— or do I?
Truthfully, no.
I don't know, maybe I'm missing something important here.
But for me, having kids was not a given, and the more I thought about it, the less I wanted to be a mother.

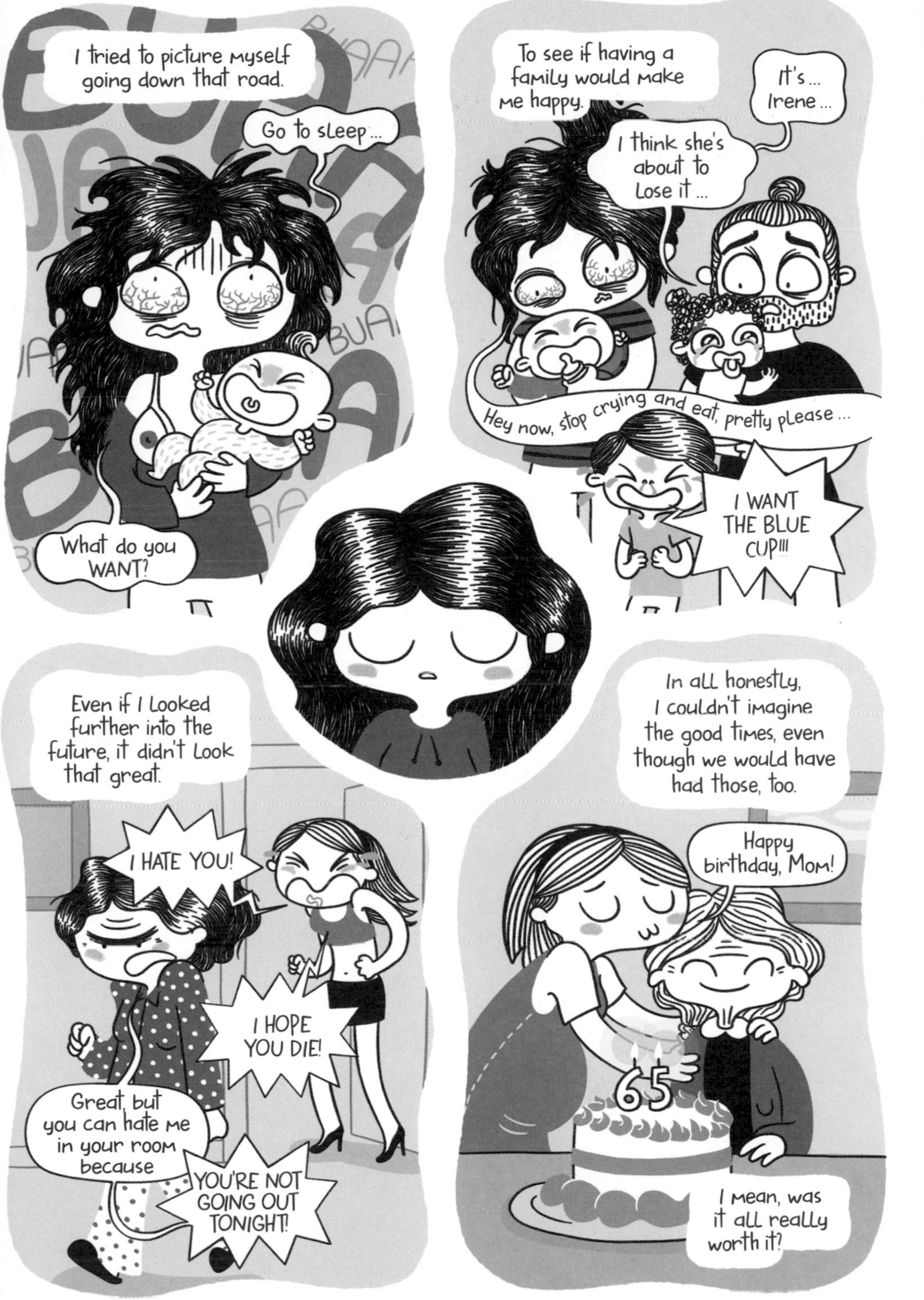
I tried to picture myself going down that road.
Go to sleep...
What do you WANT?
To see if having a family would make me happy.
It's... Irene...
I think she's about to lose it ...
Hey now, stop crying and eat, pretty please ...
I WANT THE BLUE CUP!!!
Even if I looked further into the future, it didn't look that great.
I HATE YOU!
I HOPE YOU DIE!
Great, but you can hate me in your room because
YOU'RE NOT GOING OUT TONIGHT!
In all honestly, I couldn't imagine the good times, even though we would have had those, too.
Happy birthday, Mom!
65
I mean, was it all really worth it?

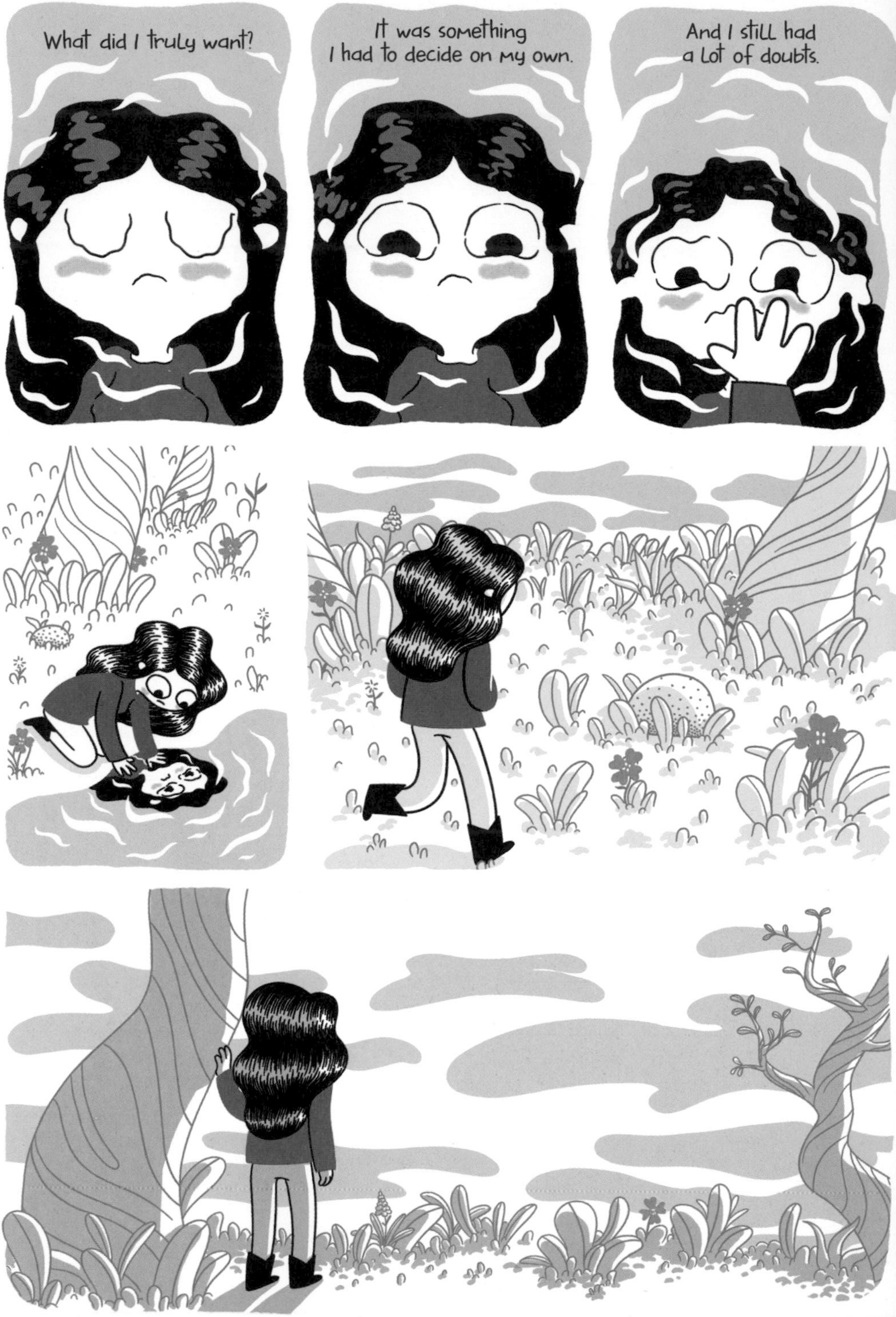
What did I truly want?
It was something I had to decide on my own.
And I still had a lot of doubts.

Even though it was a decision that only I could make, I thought it would be helpful to hear why other women chose to have kids—or wanted to have them. So I asked my friends and family.

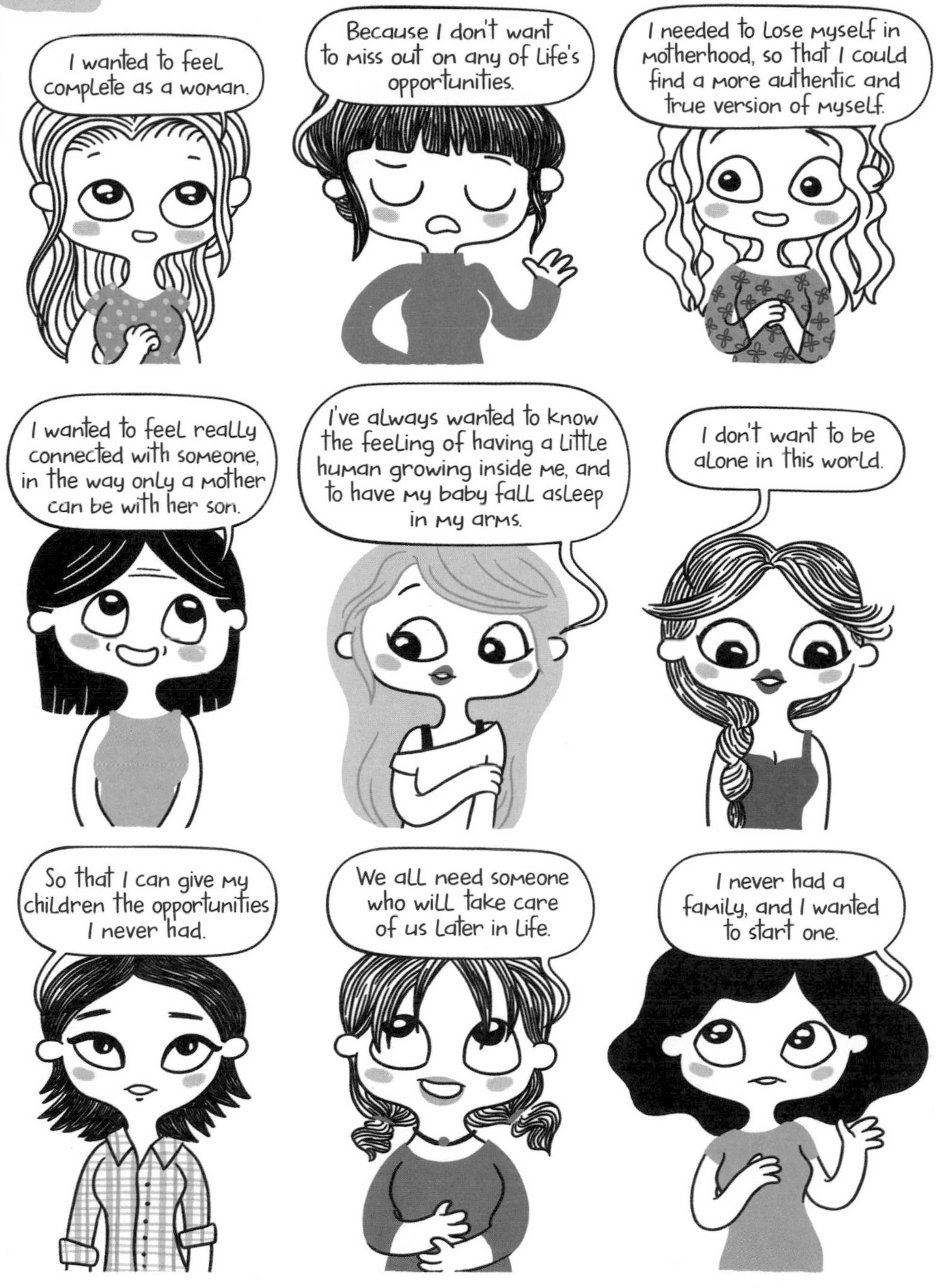
I wanted to feel complete as a woman.
Because I don't want to miss out on any of life's opportunities.
I needed to lose myself in motherhood, so that I could find a more authentic and true version of myself.
I wanted to feel really connected with someone, in the way only a mother can be with her son.
I've always wanted to know the feeling of having a little human growing inside me, and to have my baby fall asleep in my arms.
I don't want to be alone in this world.
So that I can give my children the opportunities I never had.
We all need someone who will take care of us later in life.
I never had a family, and I wanted to start one.

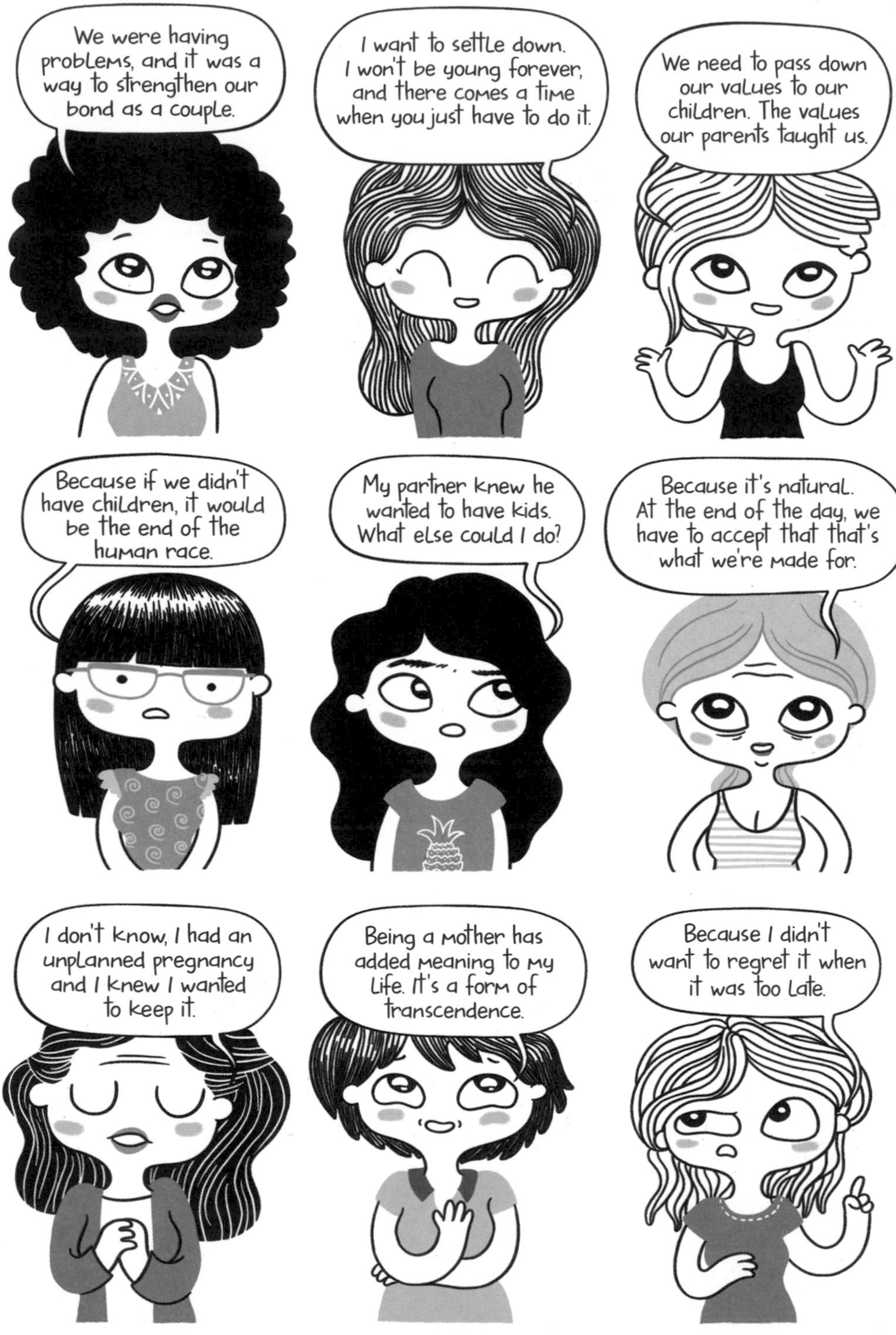
We were having problems, and it was a way to strengthen our bond as a couple.
I want to settle down. I won't be young forever, and there comes a time when you just have to do it.
We need to pass down our values to our children. The values our parents taught us.
Because if we didn't have children, it would be the end of the human race.
My partner knew he wanted to have kids. What else could I do?
Because it's natural. At the end of the day, we have to accept that that's what we're made for.
I don't know, I had an unplanned pregnancy and I knew I wanted to keep it.
Being a mother has added meaning to my life. It's a form of transcendence.
Because I didn't want to regret it when it was too late.

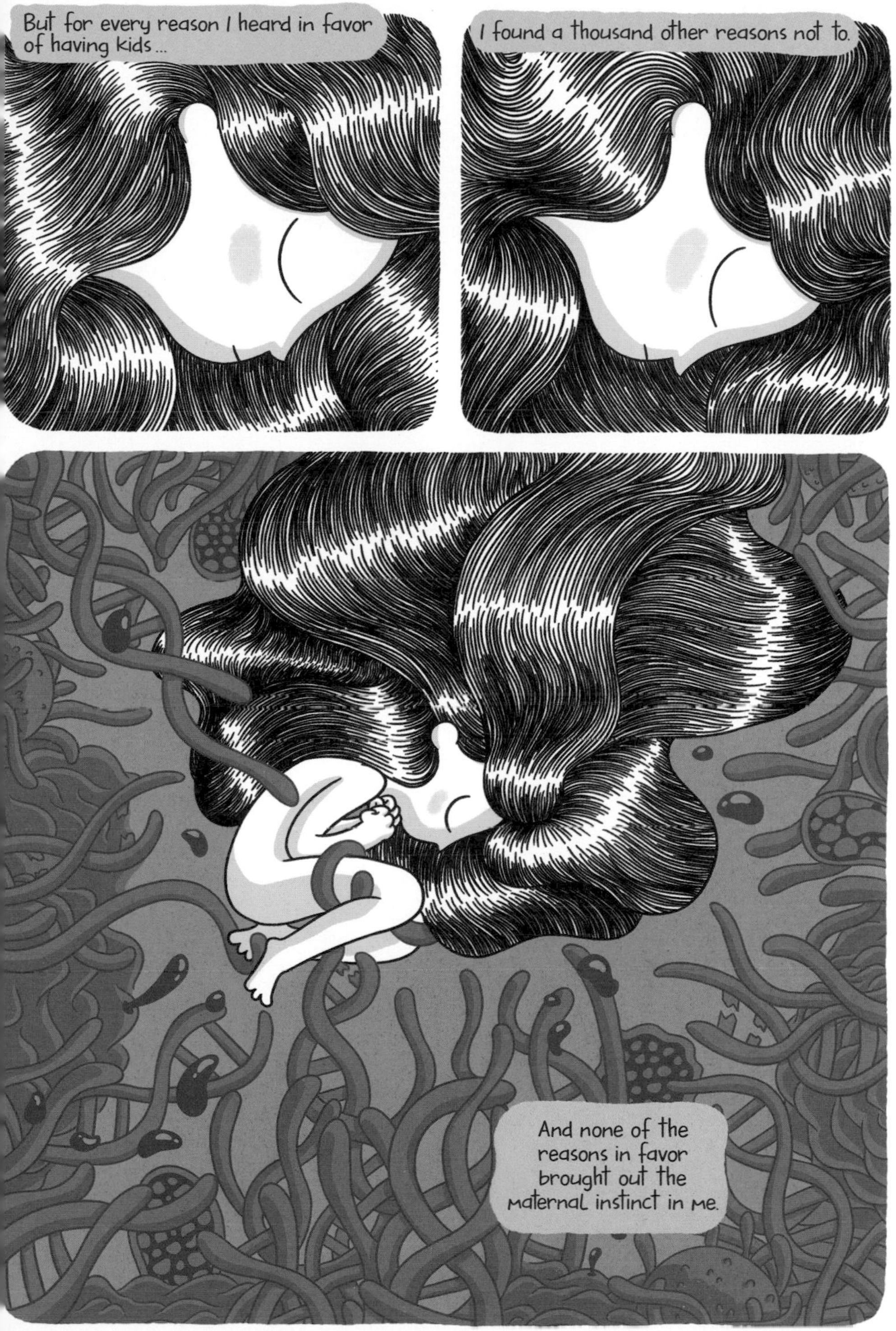
But for every reason I heard in favor of having kids...
I found a thousand other reasons not to.
And none of the reasons in favor brought out the maternal instinct in me.

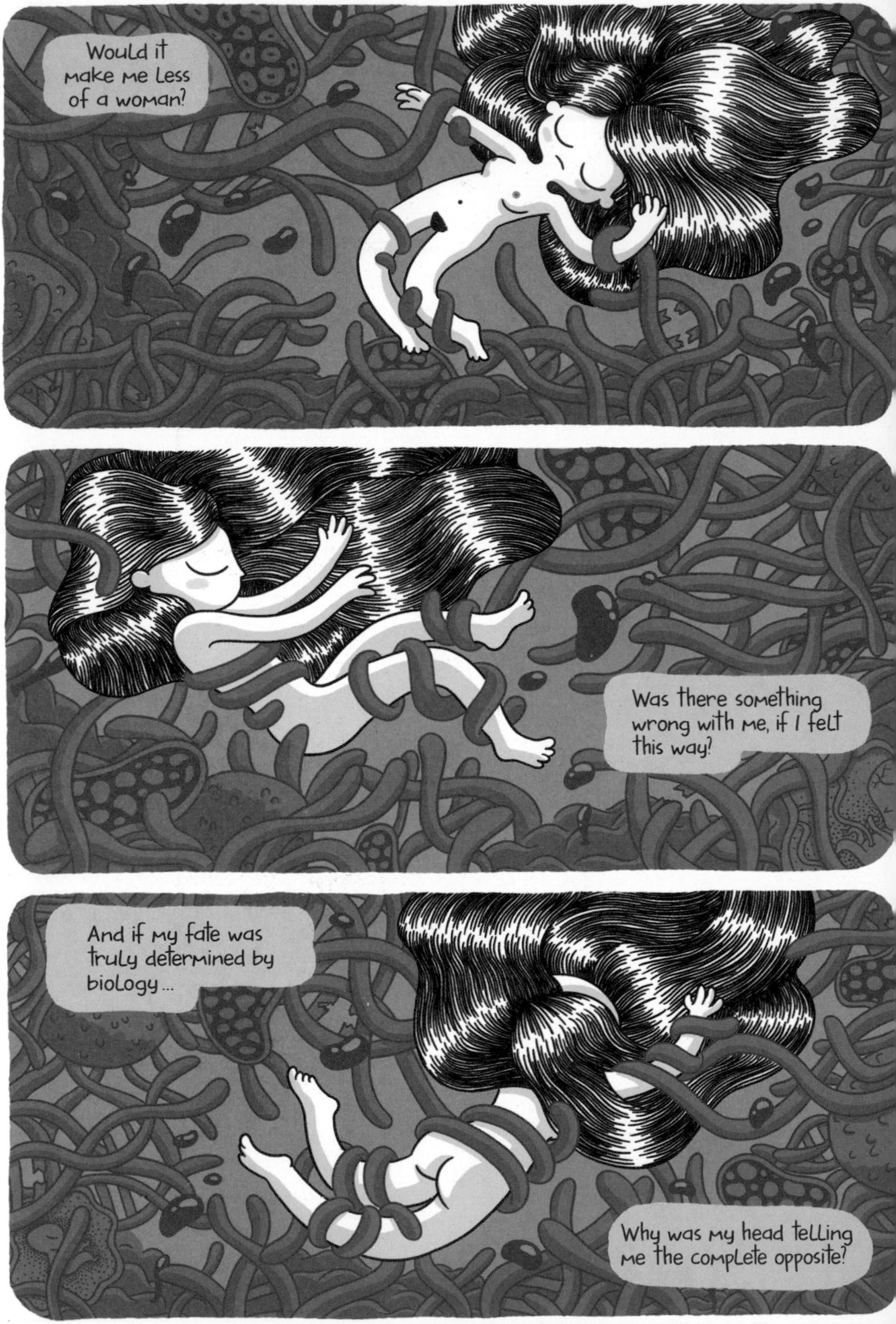
Would it make me less of a woman?
Was there something wrong with me, if I felt this way?
And if my fate was truly determined by biology...
Why was my head telling me the complete opposite?

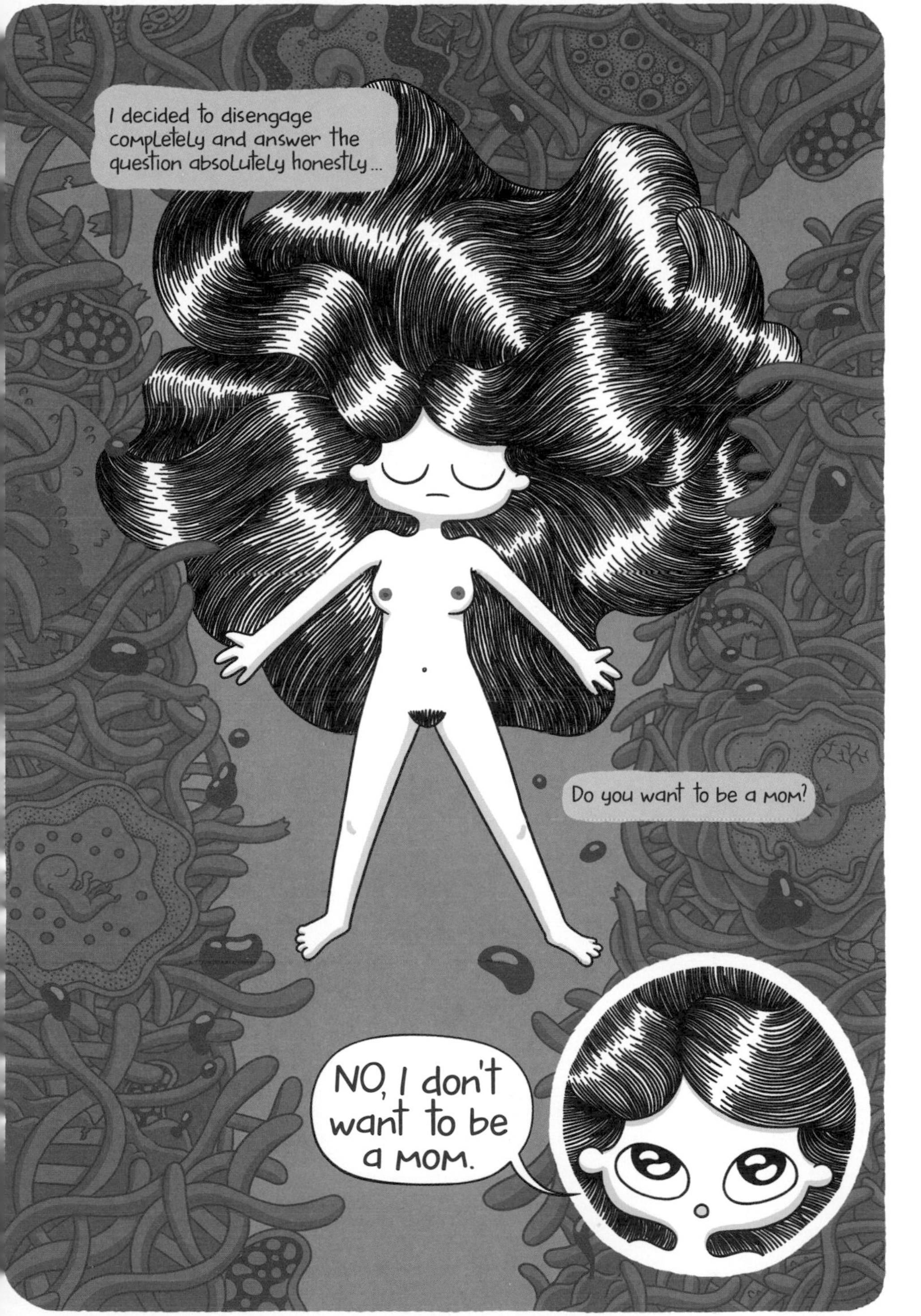
I decided to disengage completely and answer the question absolutely honestly...
Do you want to be a MOM?
NO, I don't want to be a MOM.

CHAPTER 4

Drawing the Line at No

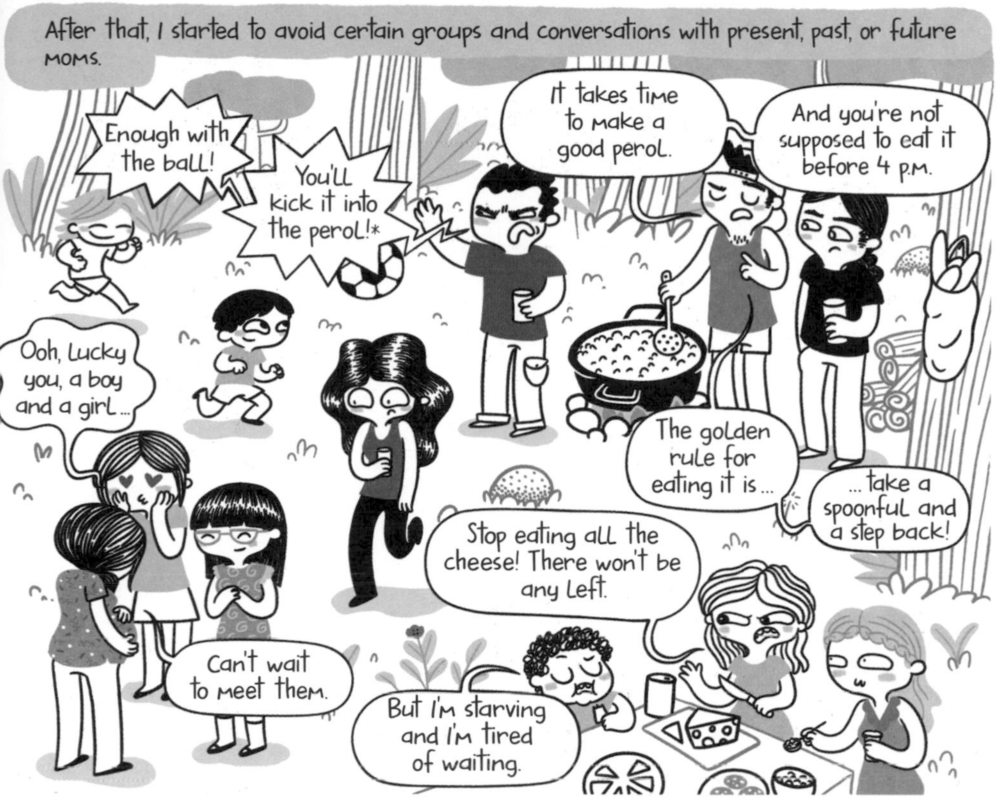
After that, I started to avoid certain groups and conversations with present, past, or future moms.
Enough with the ball!
You'll kick it into the perol!*
It takes time to make a good perol.
And you're not supposed to eat it before 4 p.m.
Ooh, lucky you, a boy and a girl...
The golden rule for eating it is...
... take a spoonful and a step back!
Stop eating all the cheese! There won't be any left.
Can't wait to meet them.
But I'm starving and I'm tired of waiting.

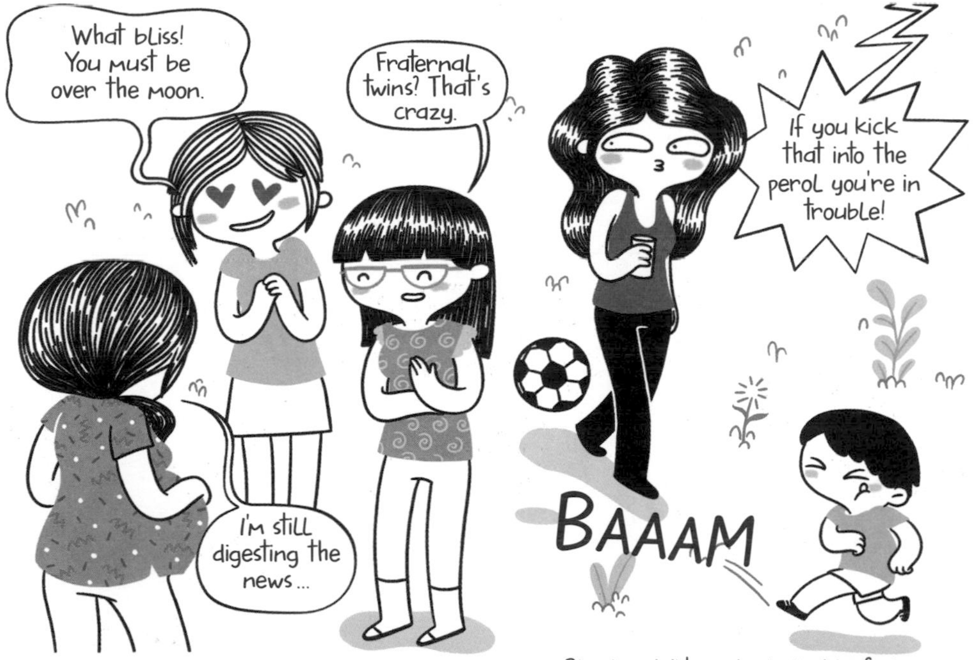
What bliss! You must be over the moon.
Fraternal twins? That's crazy.
I'm still digesting the news...
If you kick that into the perol you're in trouble!
BAAAM

*Rice-based dish popular in Cordoba, Spain.

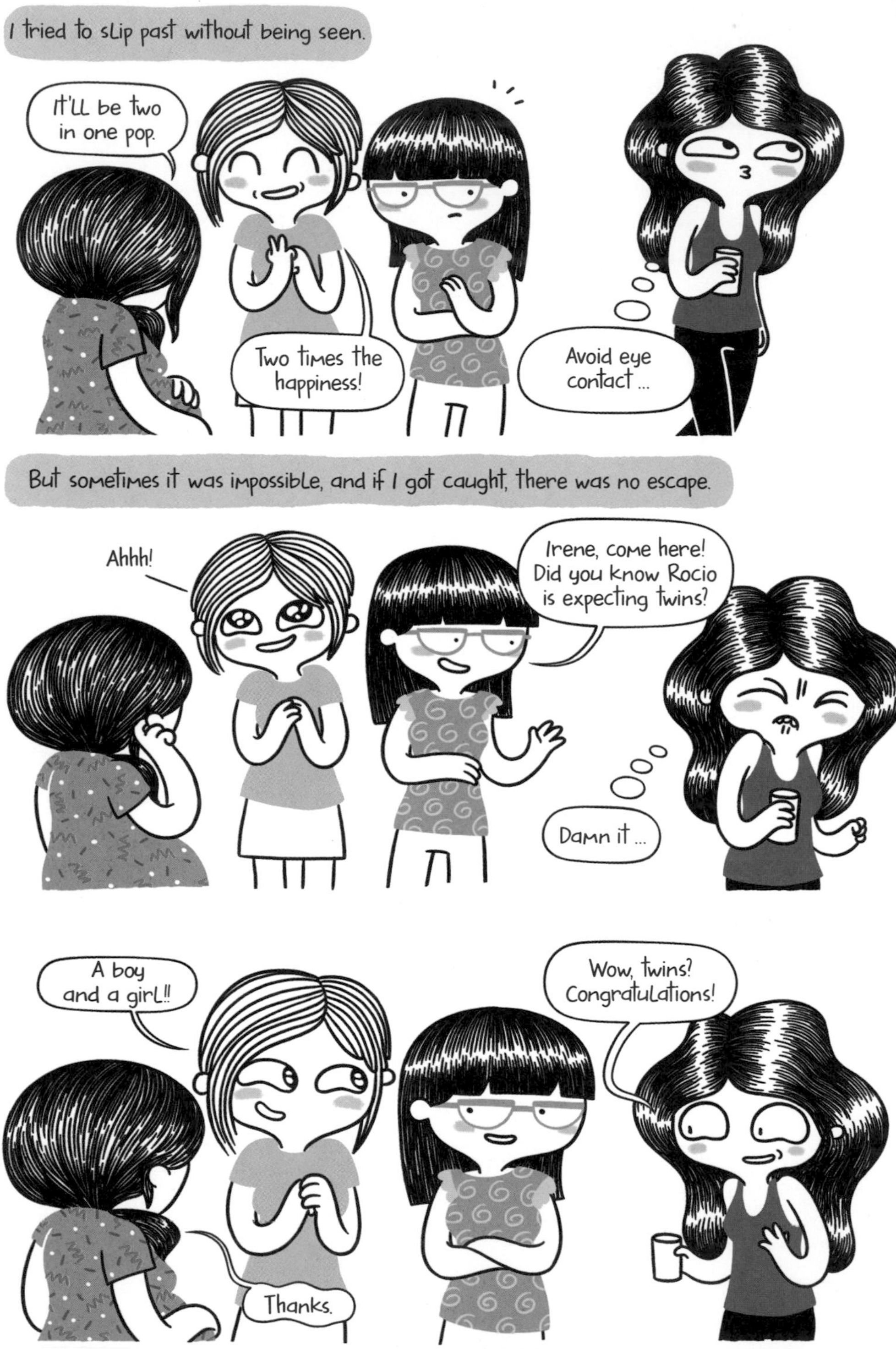

I tried to slip past without being seen.
It'll be two in one pop.
Two times the happiness!
Avoid eye contact ...
But sometimes it was impossible, and if I got caught, there was no escape.
Ahhh!
Irene, come here! Did you know Rocio is expecting twins?
Damn it ...
A boy and a girl!!
Wow, twins? Congratulations!
Thanks.

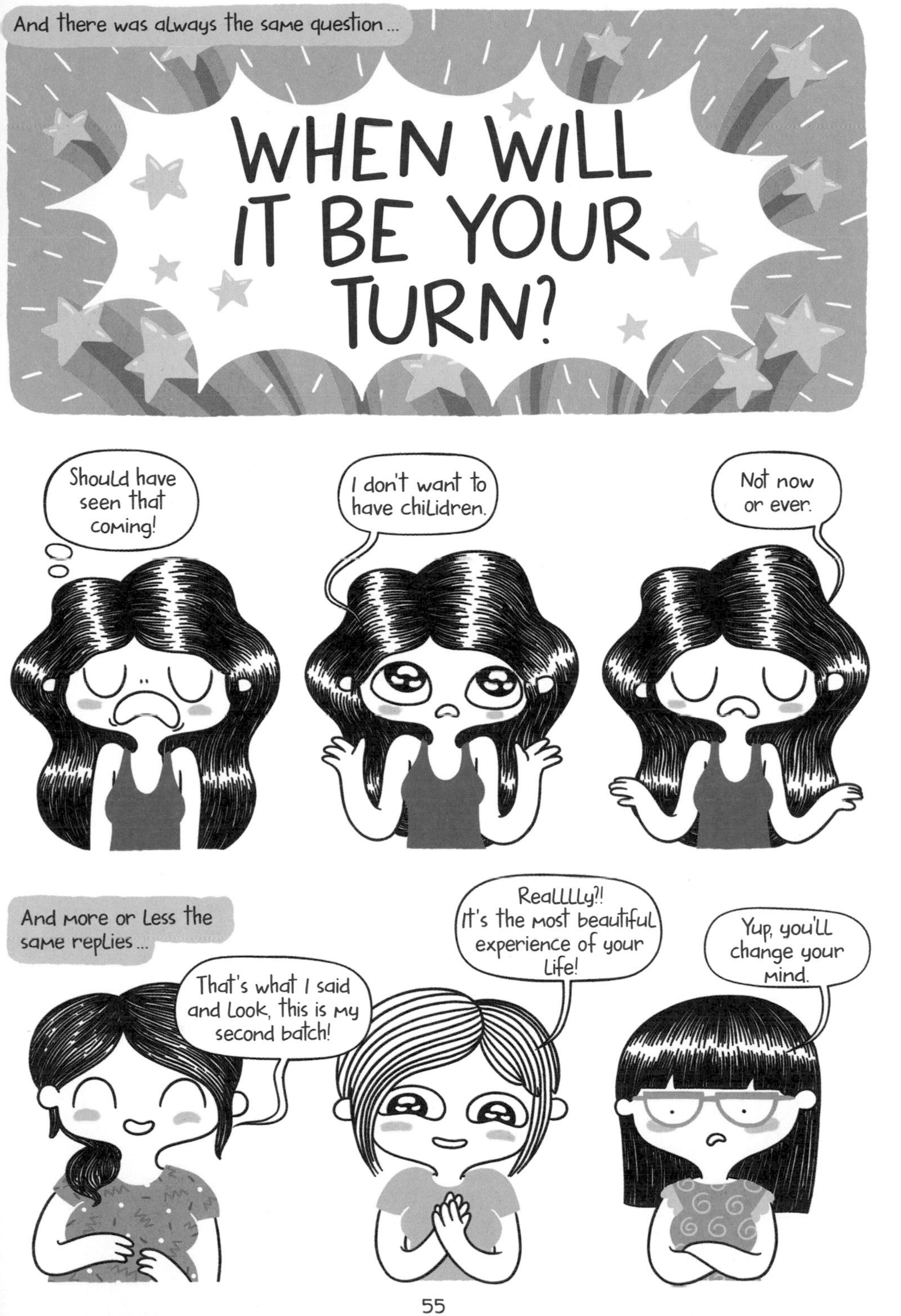

And there was always the same question ...
WHEN WILL IT BE YOUR TURN?
Should have seen that coming!
I don't want to have chilidren.
Not now or ever.
And more or less the same replies ...
That's what I said and look, this is my second batch!
Realllly?! It's the most beautiful experience of your life!
Yup, you'll change your mind.

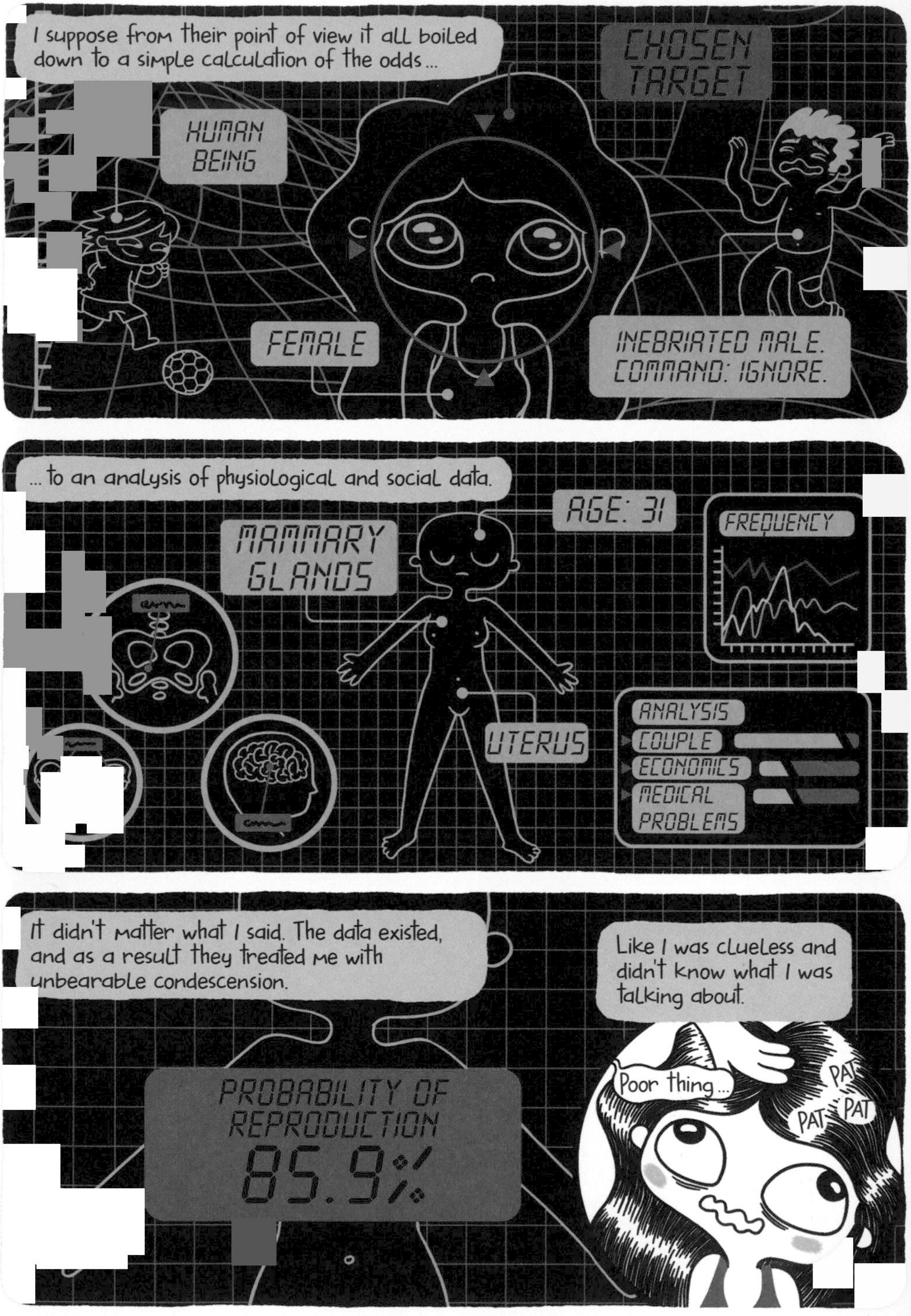
I suppose from their point of view it all boiled down to a simple calculation of the odds...
CHOSEN TARGET
HUMAN BEING
FEMALE
INEBRIATED MALE. COMMAND: IGNORE.
... to an analysis of physiological and social data.
AGE: 31
MAMMARY GLANDS
FREQUENCY
UTERUS
ANALYSIS
COUPLE
ECONOMICS
MEDICAL PROBLEMS
It didn't matter what I said. The data existed, and as a result they treated me with unbearable condescension.
Like I was clueless and didn't know what I was talking about.
PROBABILITY OF REPRODUCTION 85.9%
Poor thing...
PAT PAT PAT

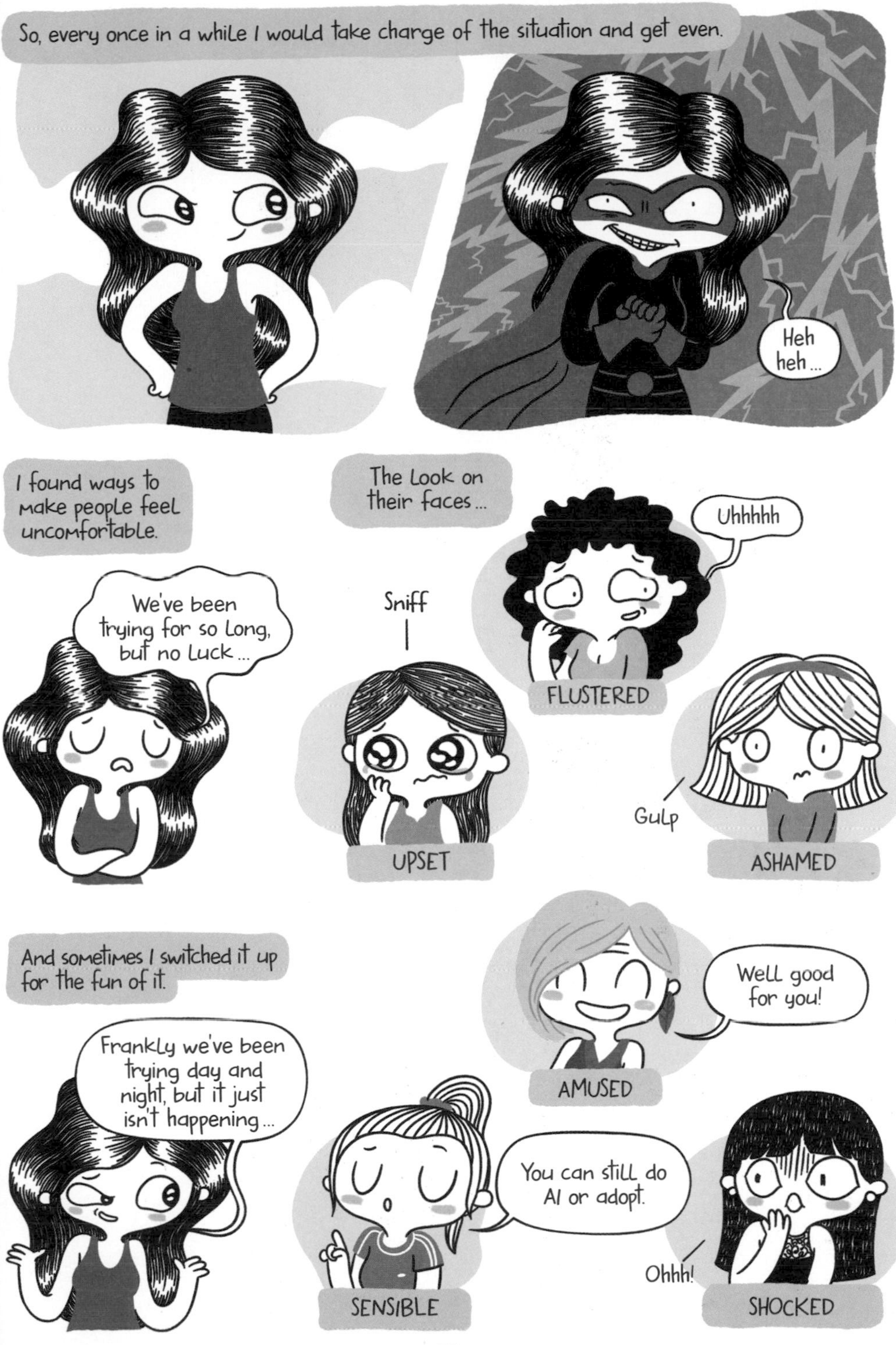
So, every once in a while I would take charge of the situation and get even.
Heh heh...
I found ways to make people feel uncomfortable.
The look on their faces...
We've been trying for so long, but no luck...
Sniff
Uhhhhh
FLUSTERED
UPSET
Gulp
ASHAMED
And sometimes I switched it up for the fun of it.
Frankly we've been trying day and night, but it just isn't happening...
Well good for you!
AMUSED
You can still do AI or adopt.
Ohhh!
SENSIBLE
SHOCKED

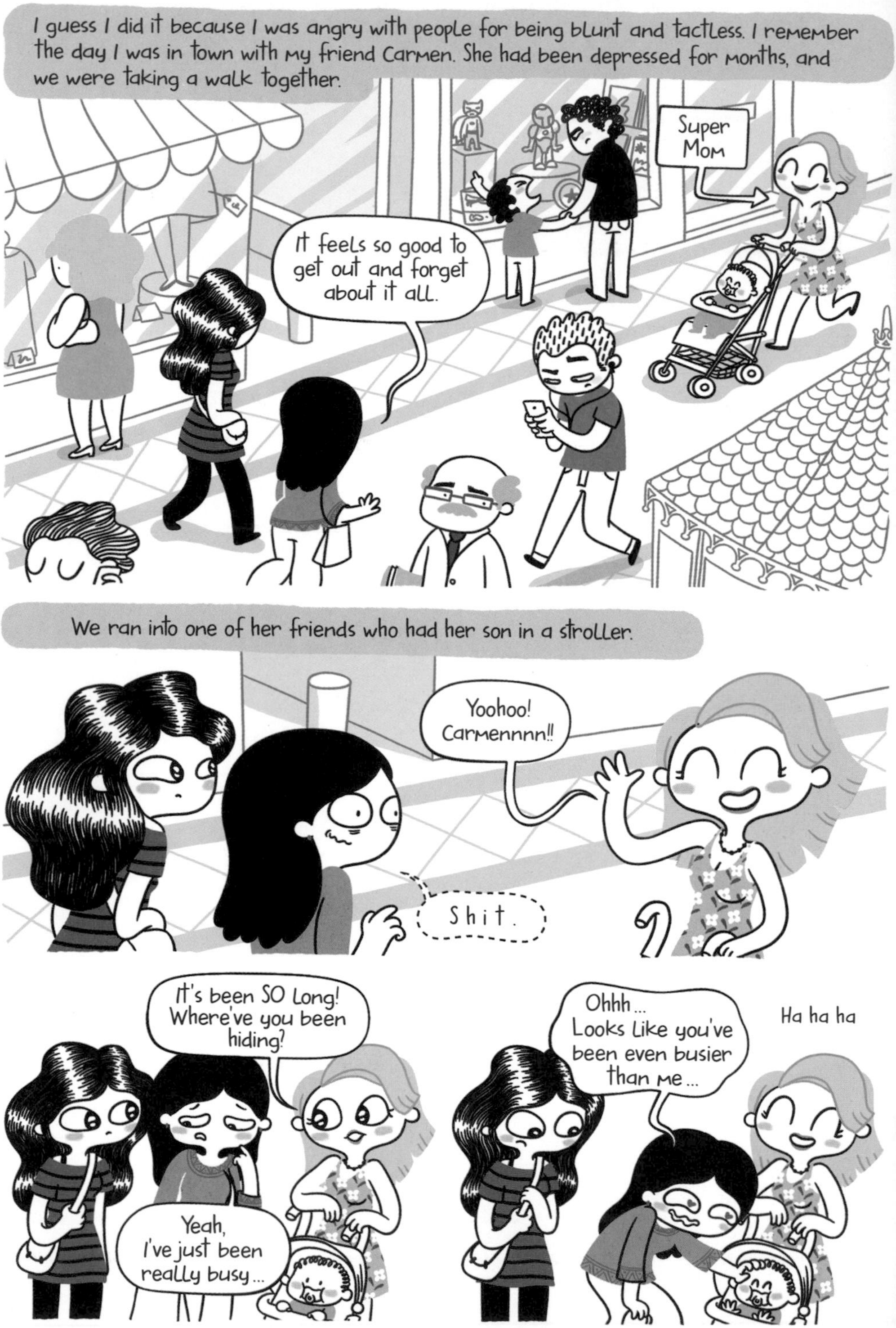
I guess I did it because I was angry with people for being blunt and tactless. I remember the day I was in town with my friend Carmen. She had been depressed for months, and we were taking a walk together.
Super Mom
It feels so good to get out and forget about it all.
We ran into one of her friends who had her son in a stroller.
Yoohoo! Carmennnn!!
Shit.
It's been SO long! Where've you been hiding?
Yeah, I've just been really busy...
Ohhh... Looks like you've been even busier than me...
Ha ha ha

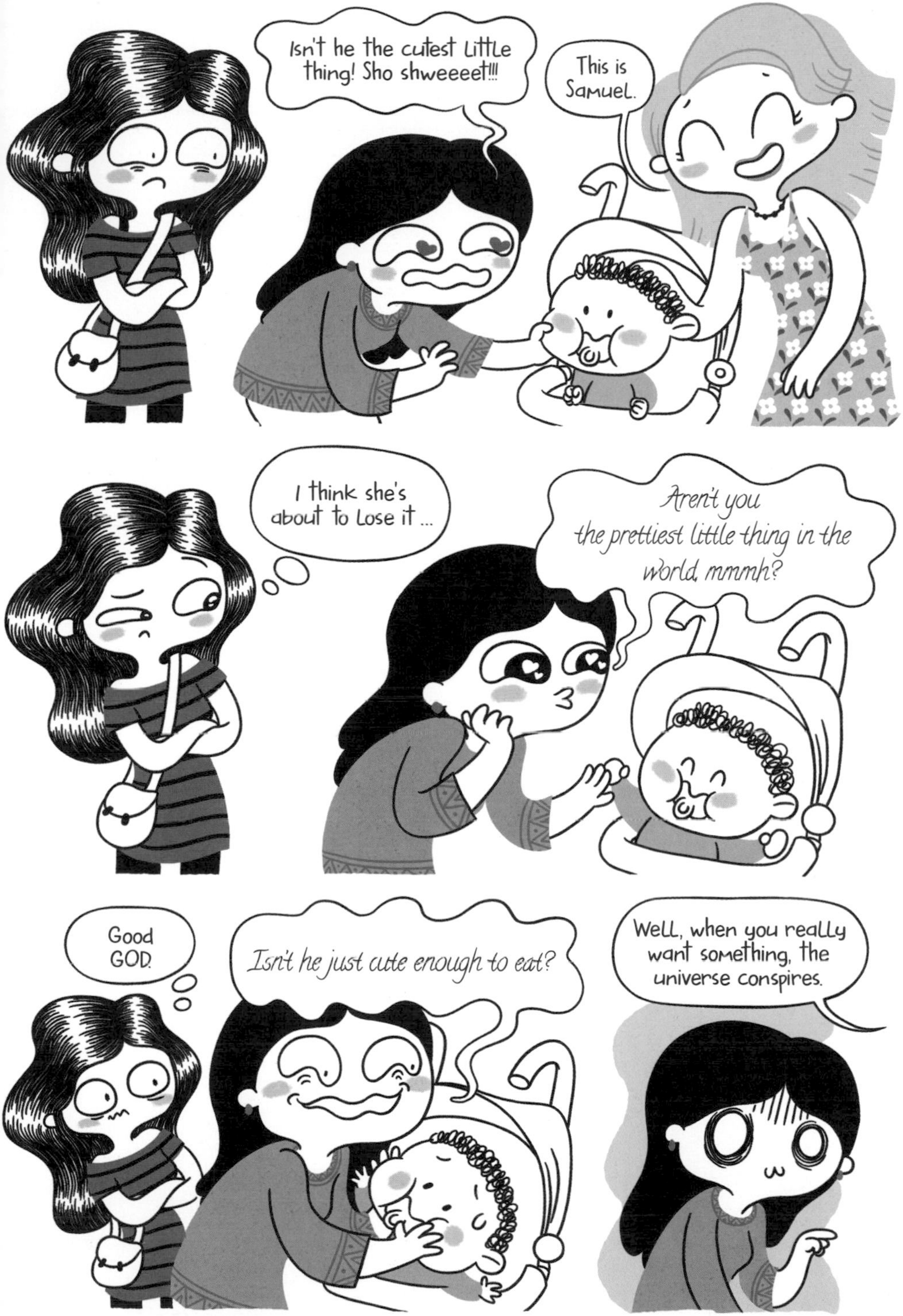
Isn't he the cutest Little thing! Sho shweeeet!!!
This is Samuel.
I think she's about to Lose it ...
Aren't you the prettiest little thing in the world, mmmh?
Good GOD.
Isn't he just cute enough to eat?
WeLL, when you reaLLy want something, the universe conspires.

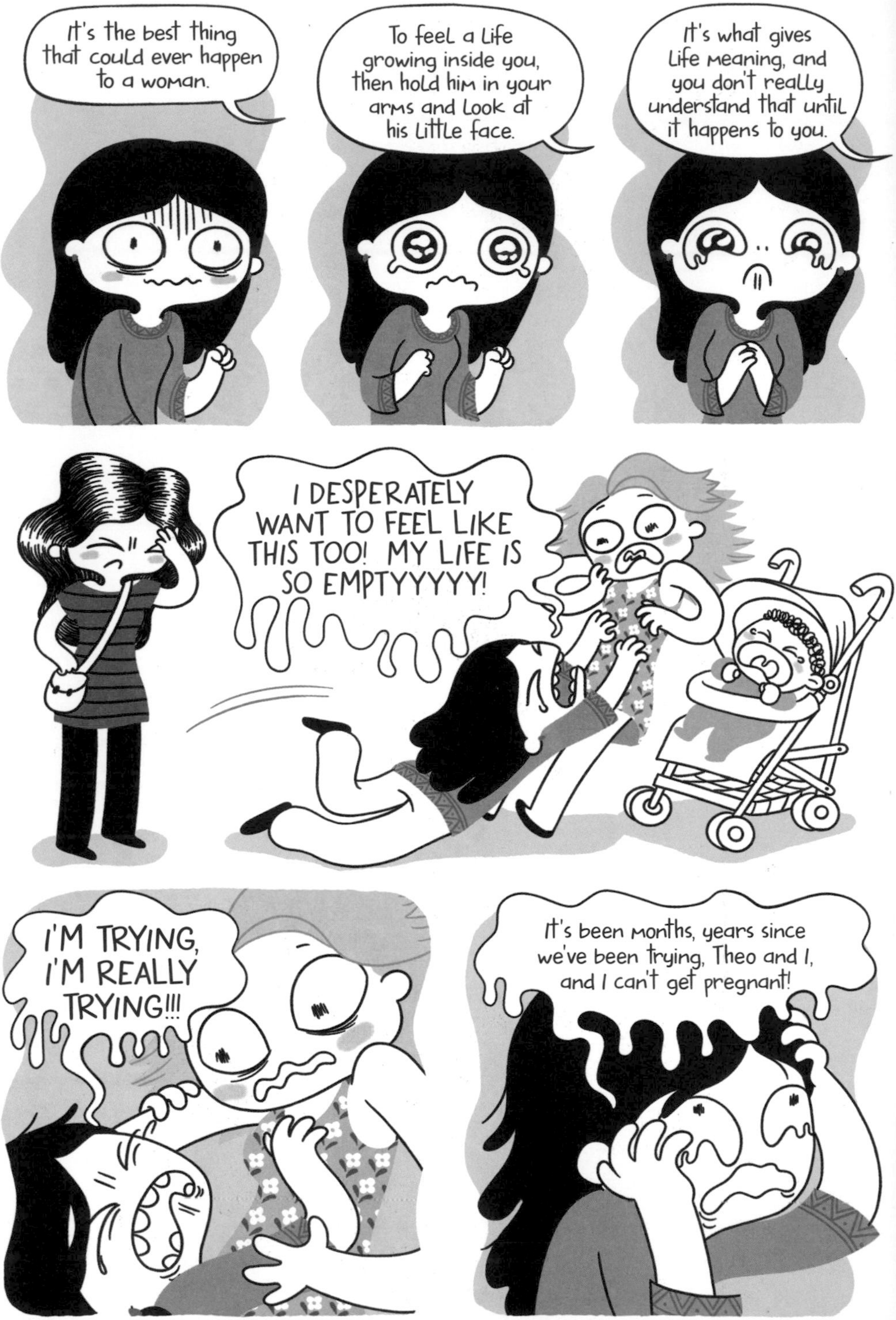
It's the best thing that could ever happen to a woman.
To feel a life growing inside you, then hold him in your arms and look at his little face.
It's what gives life meaning, and you don't really understand that until it happens to you.
I DESPERATELY WANT TO FEEL LIKE THIS TOO! MY LIFE IS SO EMPTYYYYY!
I'M TRYING, I'M REALLY TRYING!!!
It's been months, years since we've been trying, Theo and I, and I can't get pregnant!

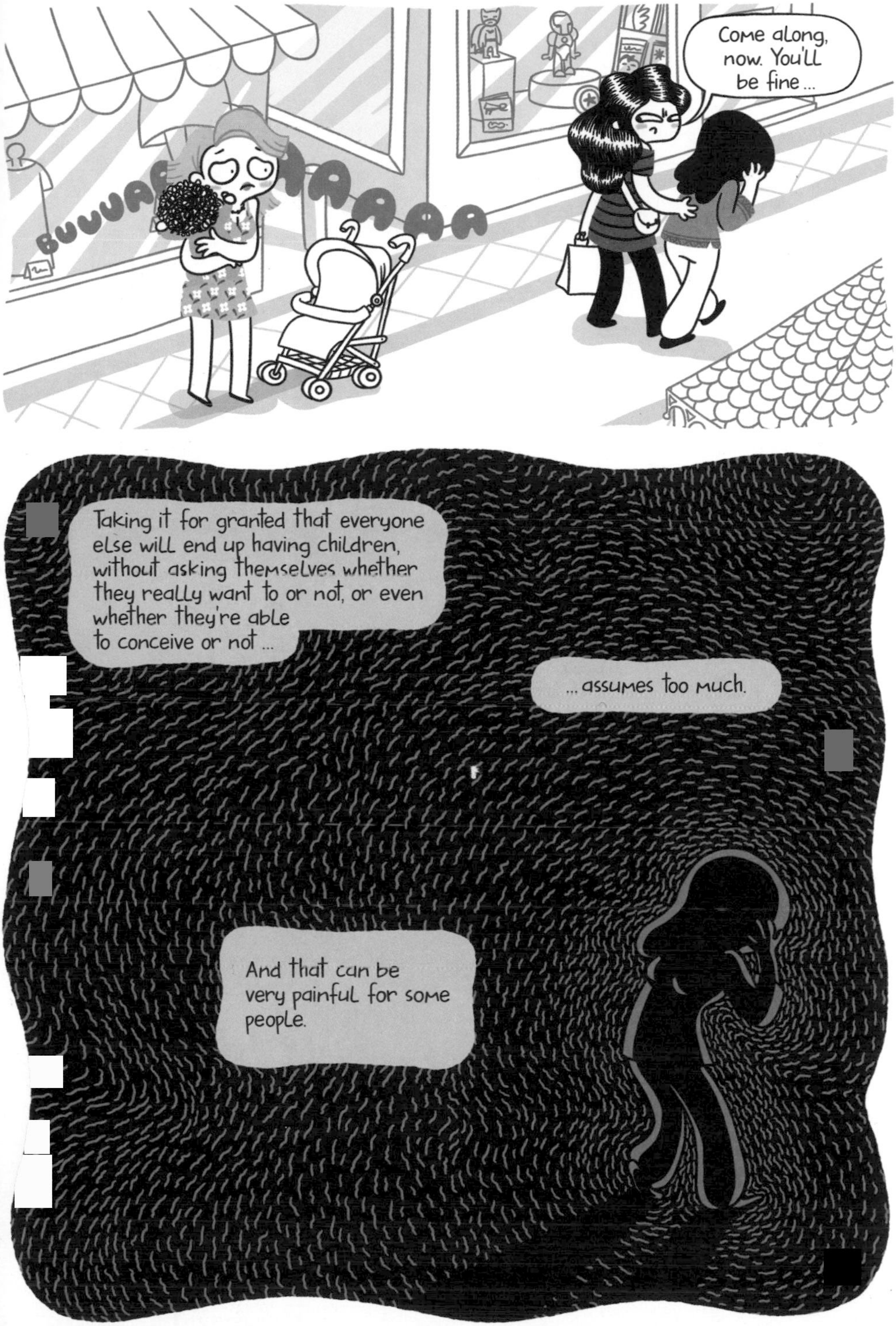

Come along, now. You'll be fine ...
Taking it for granted that everyone else will end up having children, without asking themselves whether they really want to or not, or even whether they're able to conceive or not ...
... assumes too much.
And that can be very painful for some people.

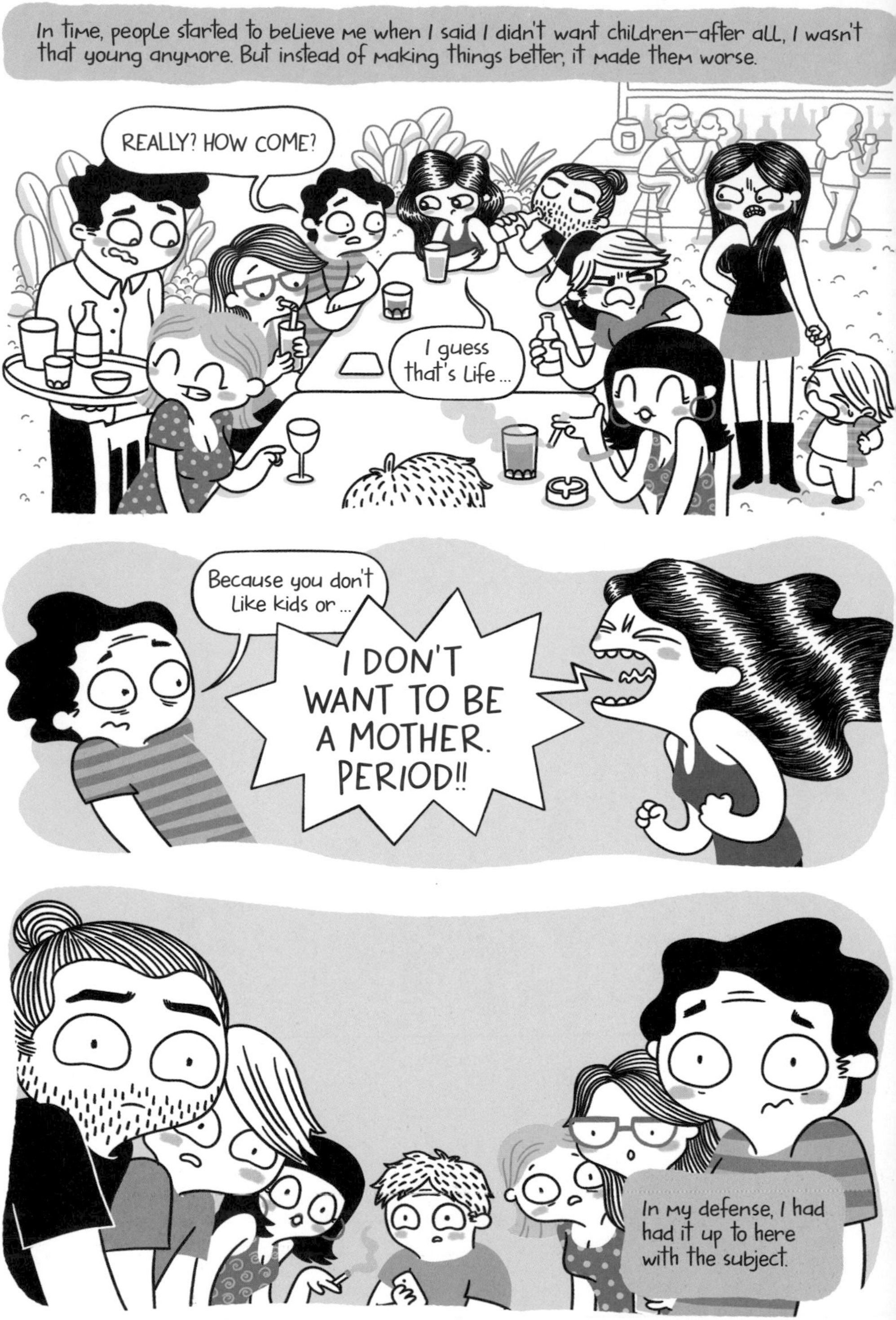
In time, people started to believe me when I said I didn't want children—after all, I wasn't that young anymore. But instead of making things better, it made them worse.
REALLY? HOW COME?
I guess that's life...
Because you don't like kids or ...
I DON'T WANT TO BE A MOTHER. PERIOD!!
In my defense, I had had it up to here with the subject.

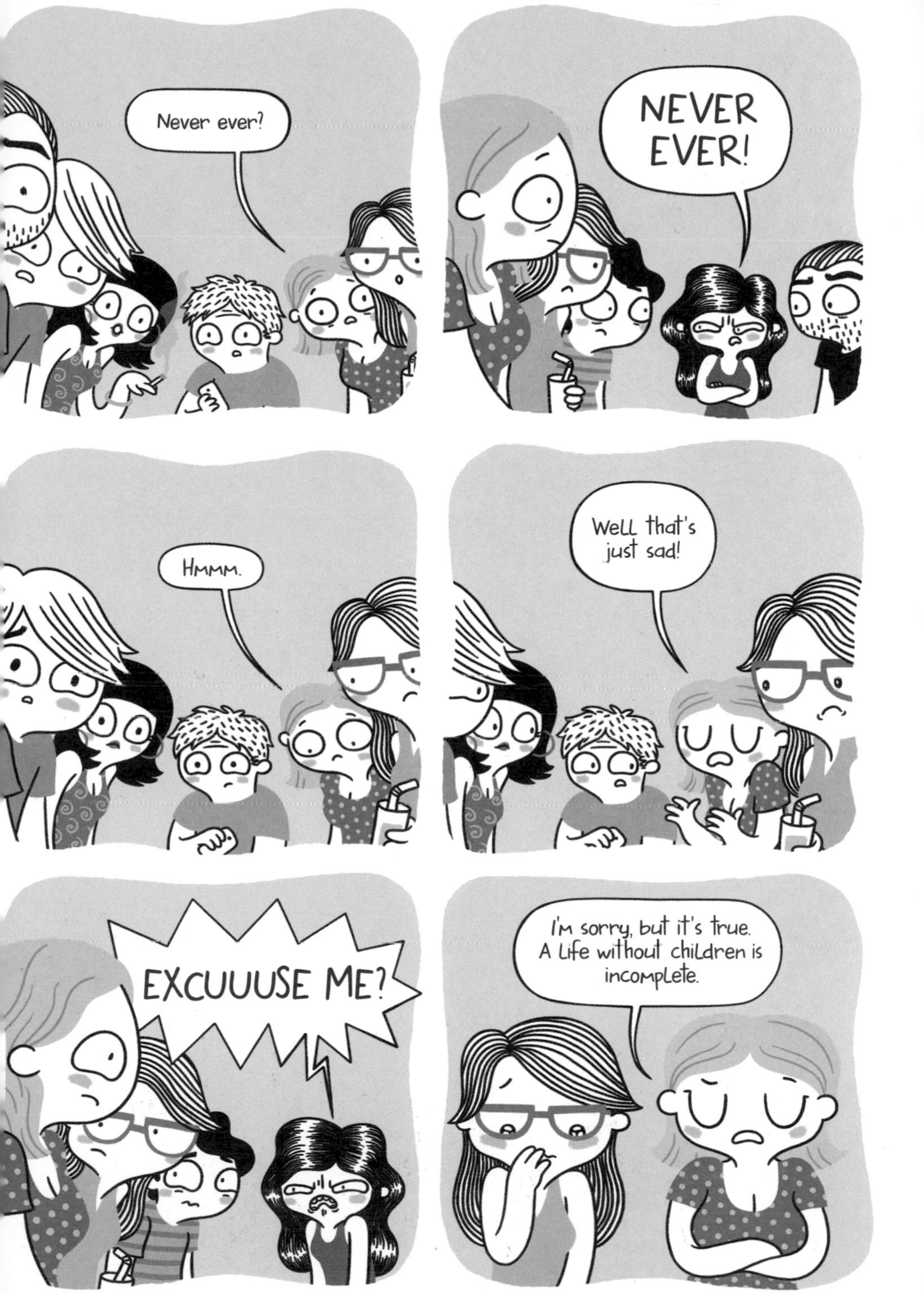

Never ever?
NEVER EVER!
HMMM.
WeLL that's just sad!
EXCUUUSE ME?
I'M sorry, but it's true. A Life without chiLdren is incompLete.

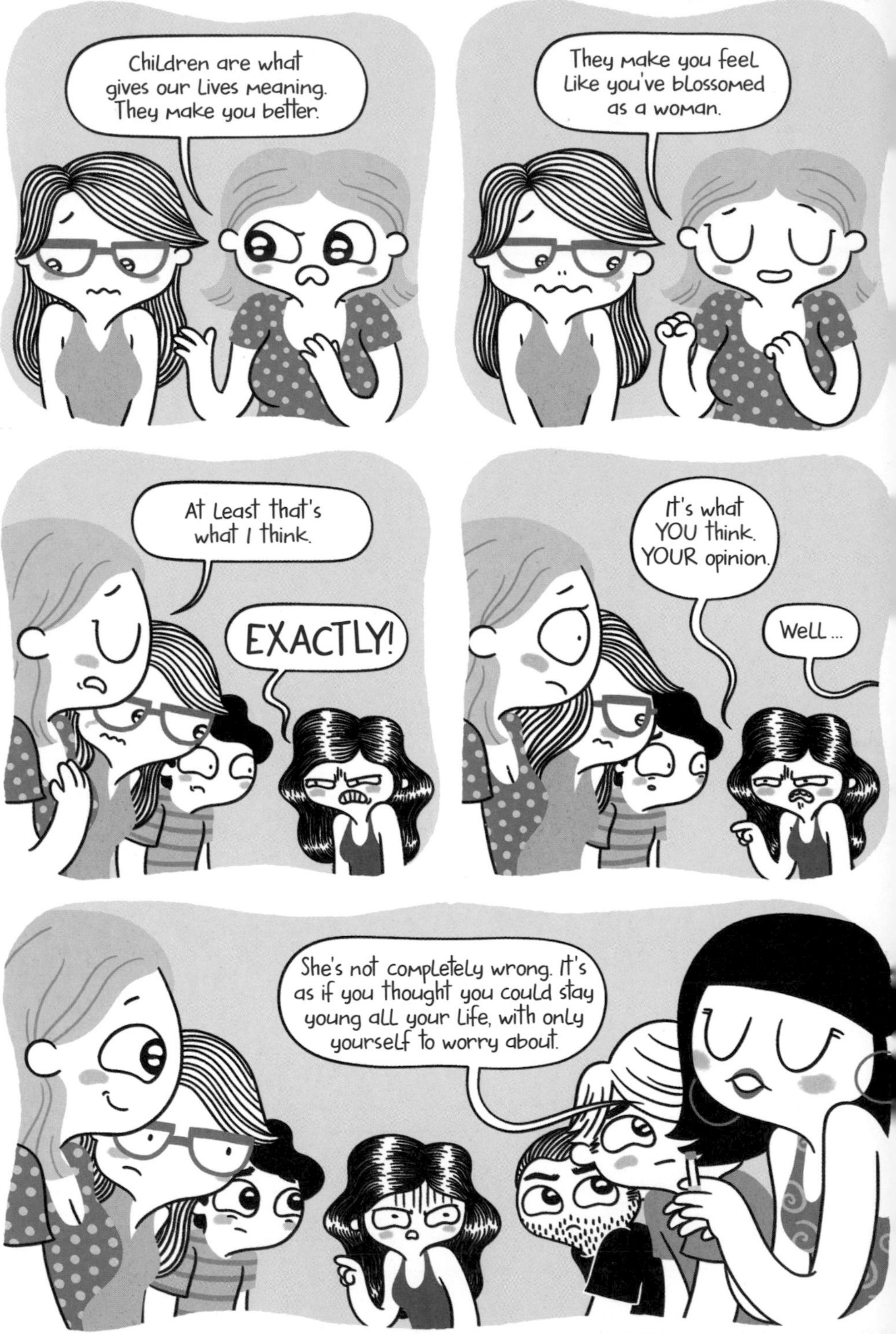

Children are what gives our lives meaning. They make you better.
They make you feel like you've blossomed as a woman.
At least that's what I think.
EXACTLY!
It's what YOU think. YOUR opinion.
Well ...
She's not completely wrong. It's as if you thought you could stay young all your life, with only yourself to worry about.

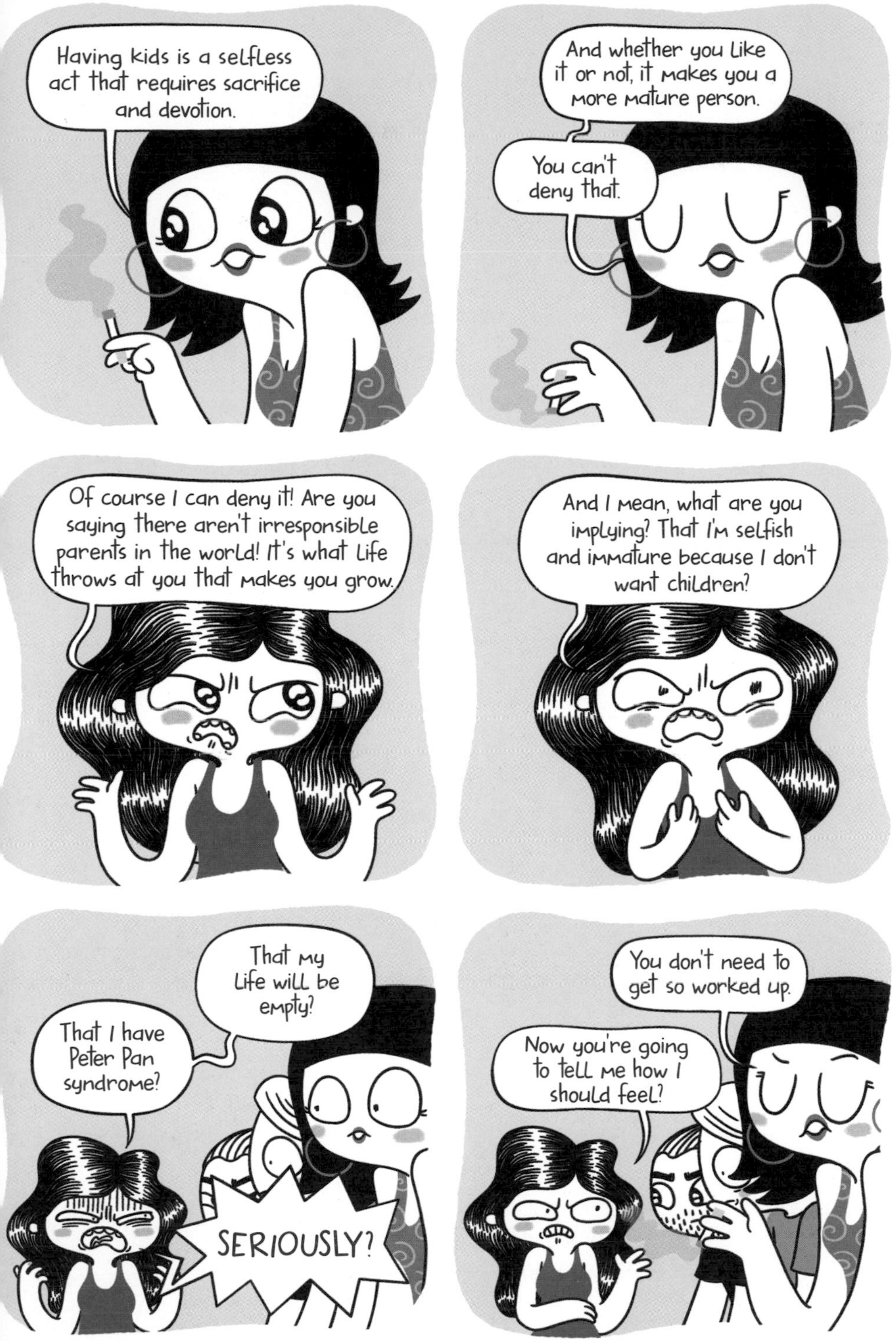
Having kids is a selfless act that requires sacrifice and devotion.
And whether you like it or not, it makes you a more mature person.
You can't deny that.
Of course I can deny it! Are you saying there aren't irresponsible parents in the world! It's what life throws at you that makes you grow.
And I mean, what are you implying? That I'm selfish and immature because I don't want children?
That I have Peter Pan syndrome?
That my life will be empty?
SERIOUSLY?
You don't need to get so worked up.
Now you're going to tell me how I should feel?

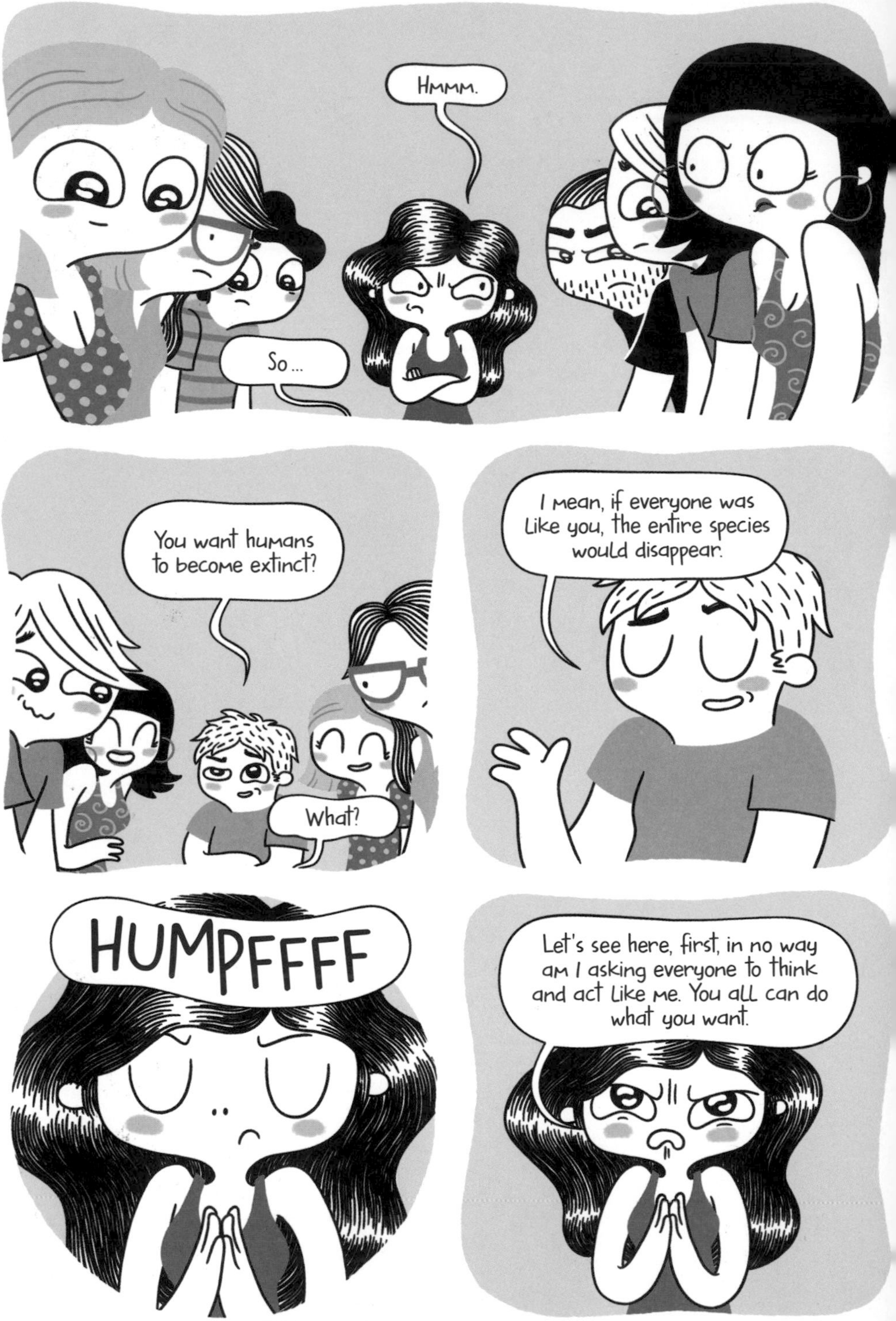
Hmmm.
So...
You want humans to become extinct?
What?
I mean, if everyone was like you, the entire species would disappear.
HUMPFFFF
Let's see here, first, in no way am I asking everyone to think and act like me. You all can do what you want.

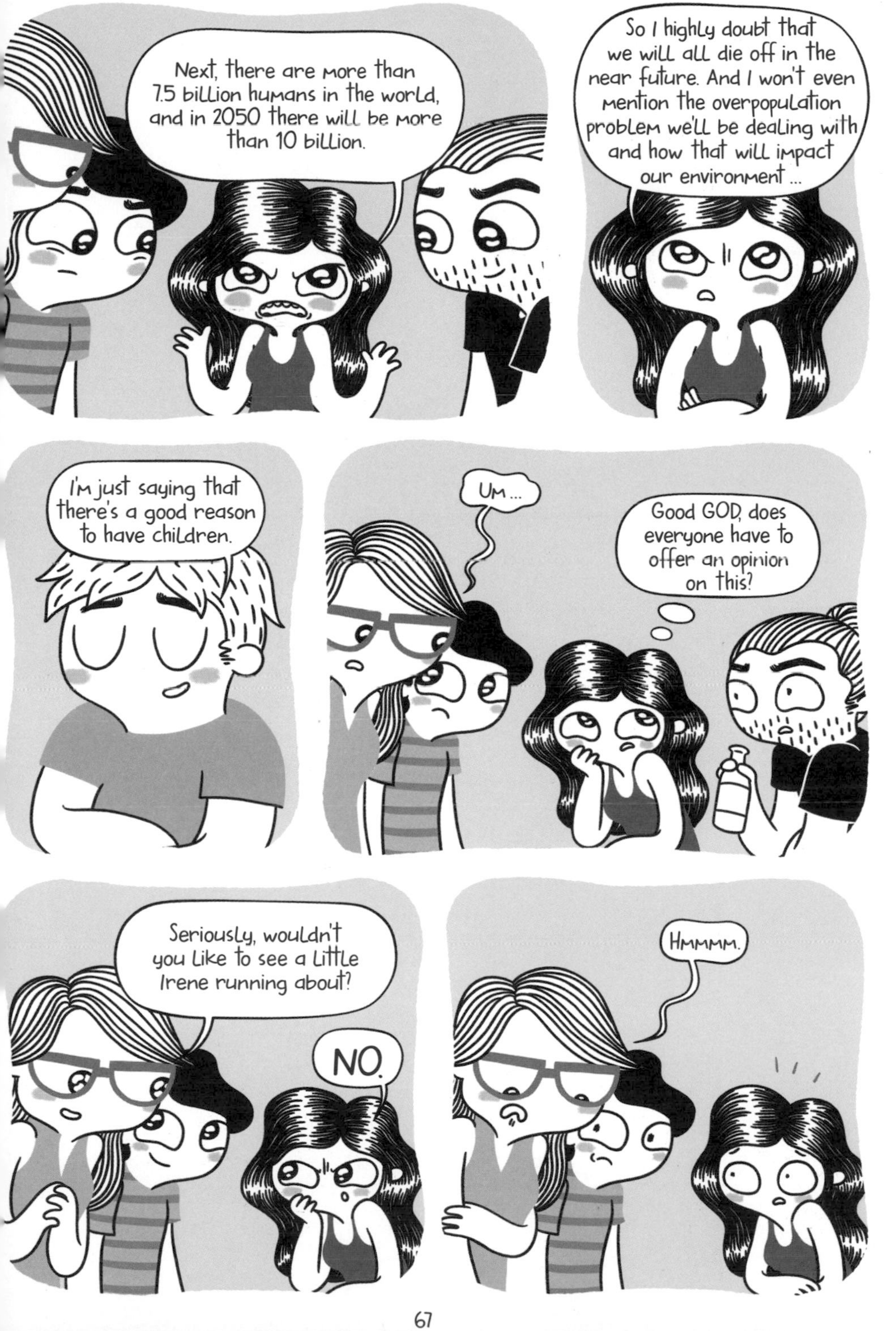
Next, there are more than 7.5 billion humans in the world, and in 2050 there will be more than 10 billion.
So I highly doubt that we will all die off in the near future. And I won't even mention the overpopulation problem we'll be dealing with and how that will impact our environment ...
I'm just saying that there's a good reason to have children.
Um ...
Good GOD, does everyone have to offer an opinion on this?
Seriously, wouldn't you like to see a little Irene running about?
NO.
Hmmmm.

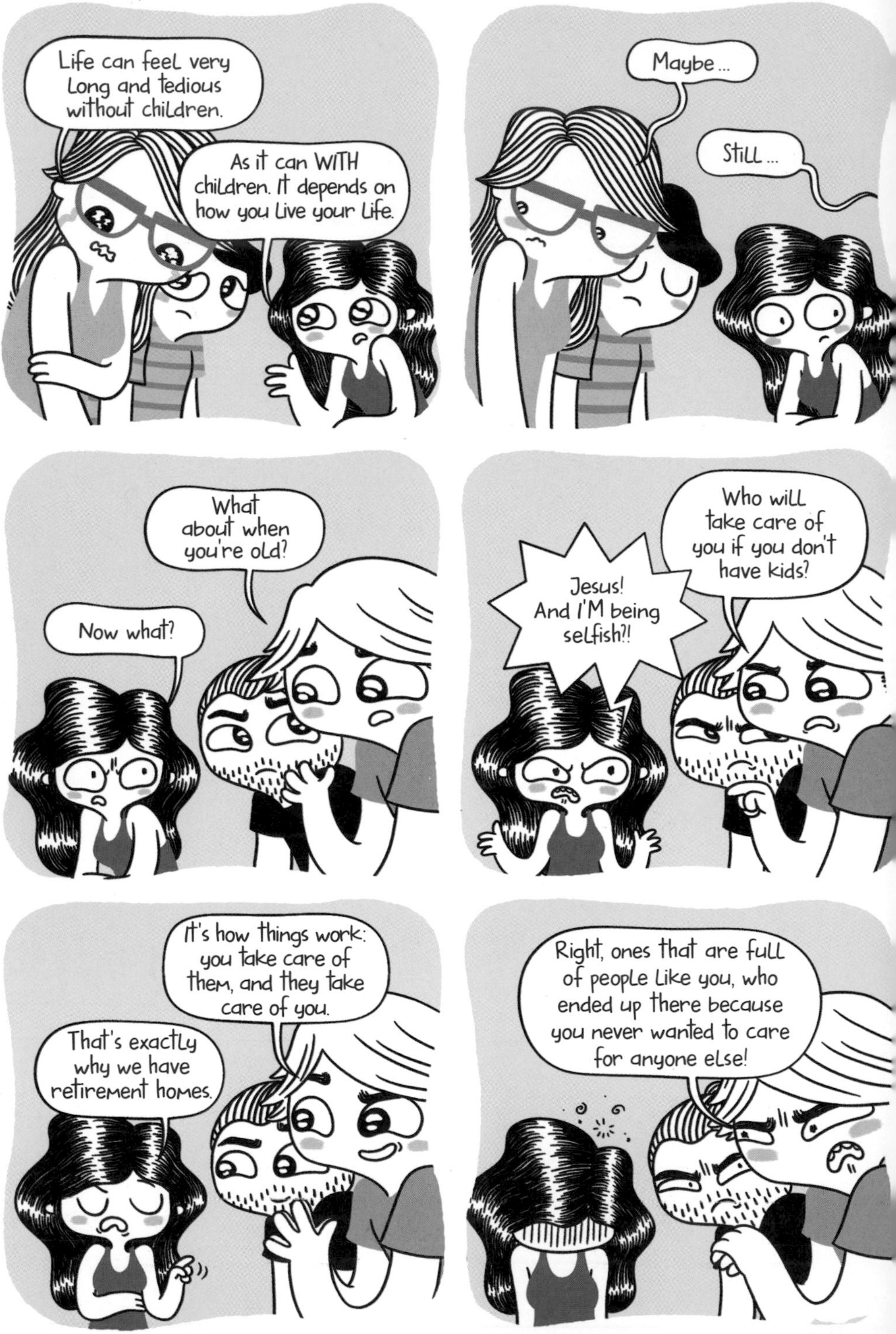
Life can feel very long and tedious without children.
As it can WITH children. It depends on how you live your life.
Maybe...
Still...
Now what?
What about when you're old?
Who will take care of you if you don't have kids?
Jesus! And I'M being selfish?!
That's exactly why we have retirement homes.
It's how things work: you take care of them, and they take care of you.
Right, ones that are full of people like you, who ended up there because you never wanted to care for anyone else!

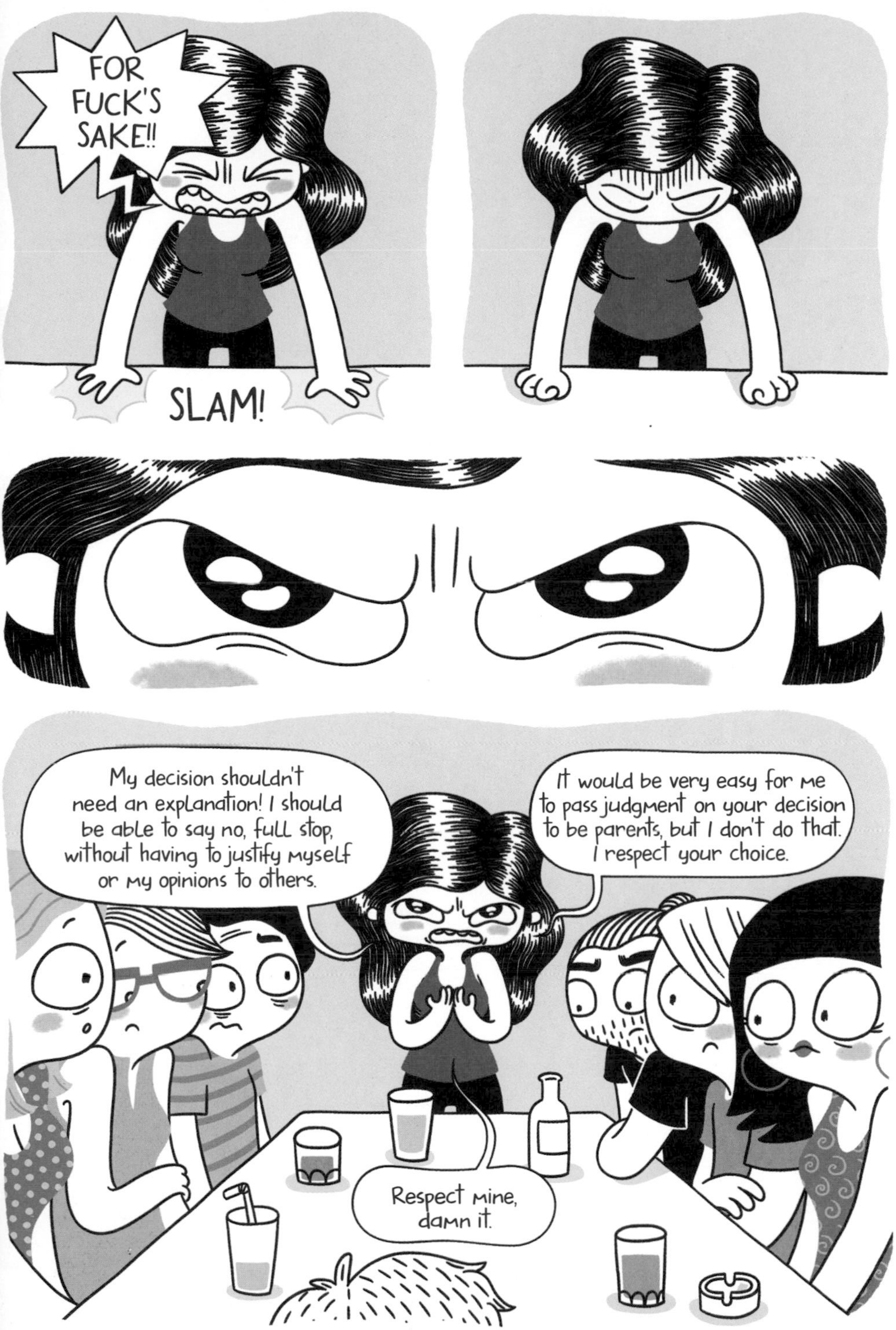
FOR FUCK'S SAKE!!
SLAM!
My decision shouldn't need an explanation! I should be able to say no, full stop, without having to justify myself or my opinions to others.
It would be very easy for me to pass judgment on your decision to be parents, but I don't do that. I respect your choice.
Respect mine, damn it.

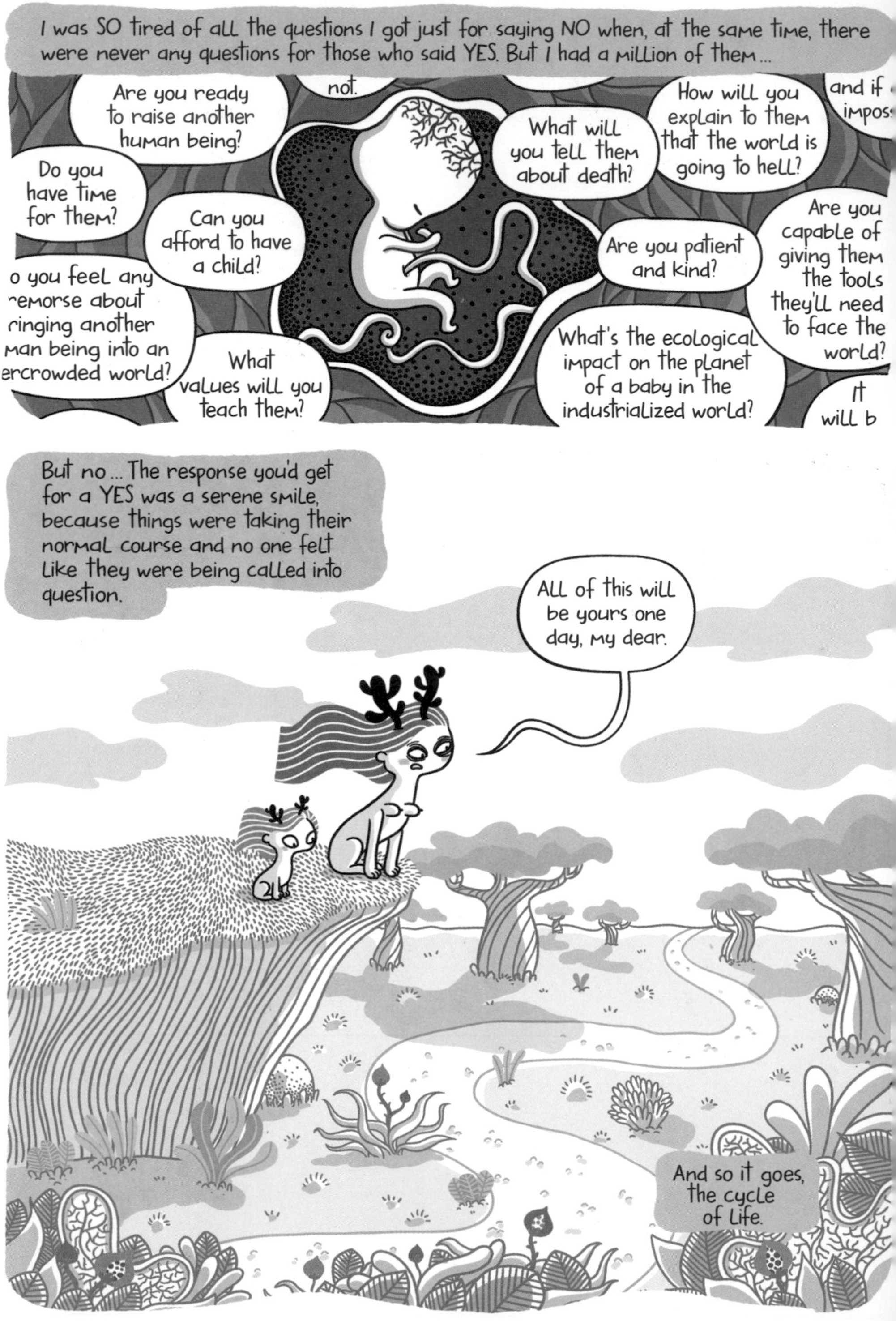
I was SO tired of all the questions I got just for saying NO when, at the same time, there were never any questions for those who said YES. But I had a million of them...
not.
Are you ready to raise another human being?
What will you tell them about death?
How will you explain to them that the world is going to hell?
and if
impos
Do you have time for them?
Can you afford to have a child?
Are you patient and kind?
Are you capable of giving them the tools they'll need to face the world?
o you feel any
remorse about
ringing another
man being into an
ercrowded world?
What values will you teach them?
What's the ecological impact on the planet of a baby in the industrialized world?
It
will b
But no... The response you'd get for a YES was a serene smile, because things were taking their normal course and no one felt like they were being called into question.
All of this will be yours one day, my dear.
And so it goes, the cycle of life.

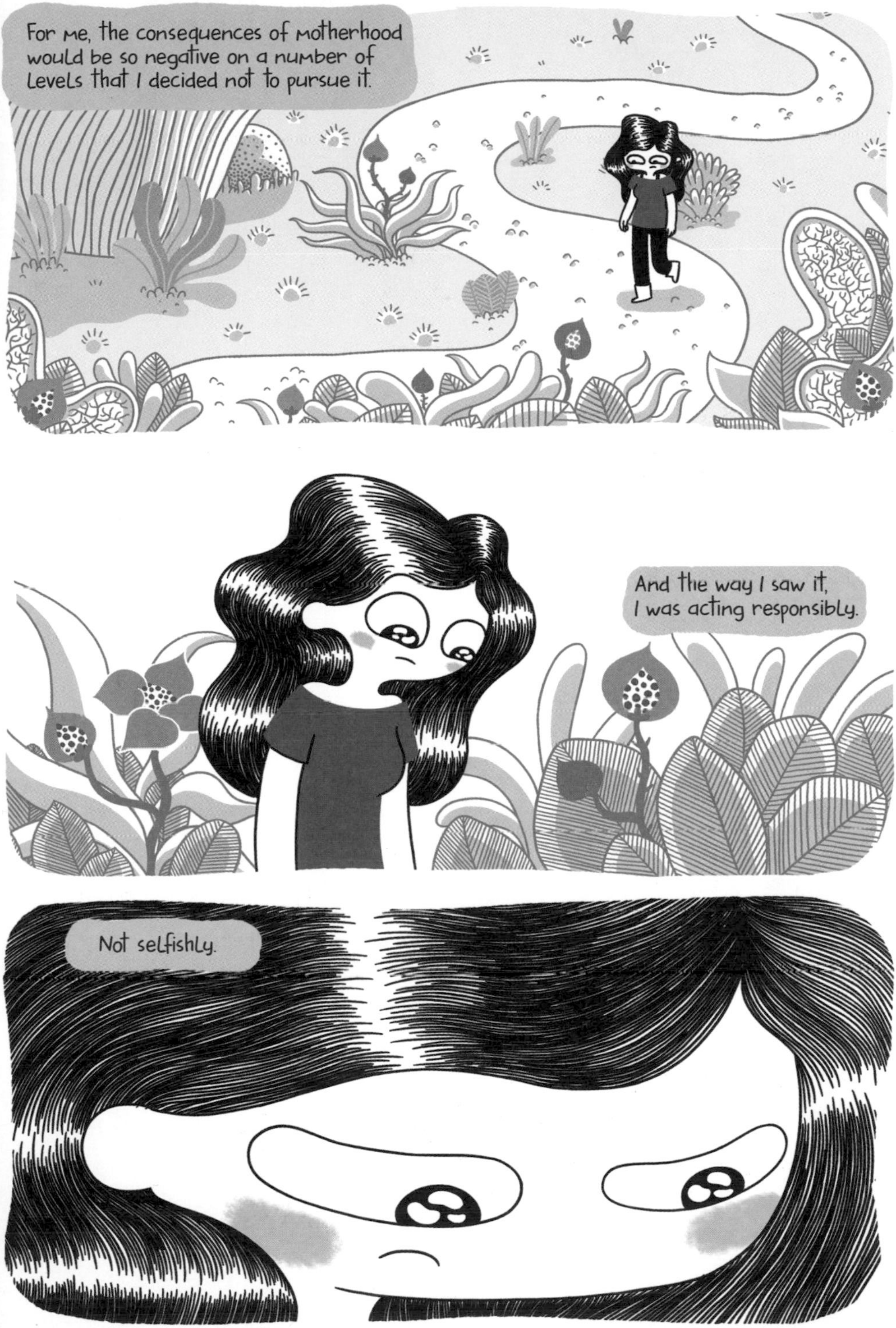
For me, the consequences of motherhood would be so negative on a number of levels that I decided not to pursue it.
And the way I saw it, I was acting responsibly.
Not selfishly.

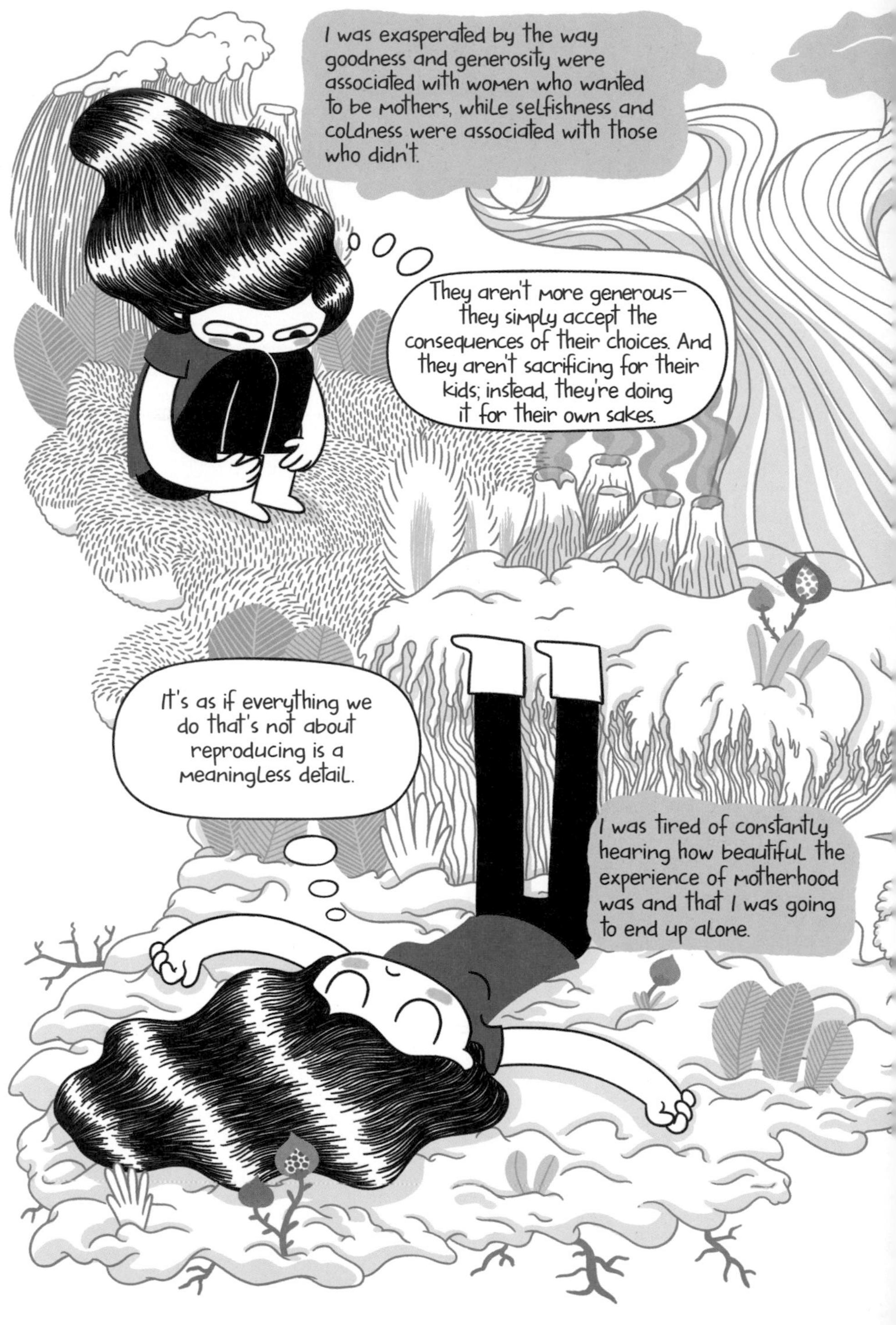
I was exasperated by the way goodness and generosity were associated with women who wanted to be mothers, while selfishness and coldness were associated with those who didn't.
They aren't more generous—they simply accept the consequences of their choices. And they aren't sacrificing for their kids; instead, they're doing it for their own sakes.
It's as if everything we do that's not about reproducing is a meaningless detail.
I was tired of constantly hearing how beautiful the experience of motherhood was and that I was going to end up alone.

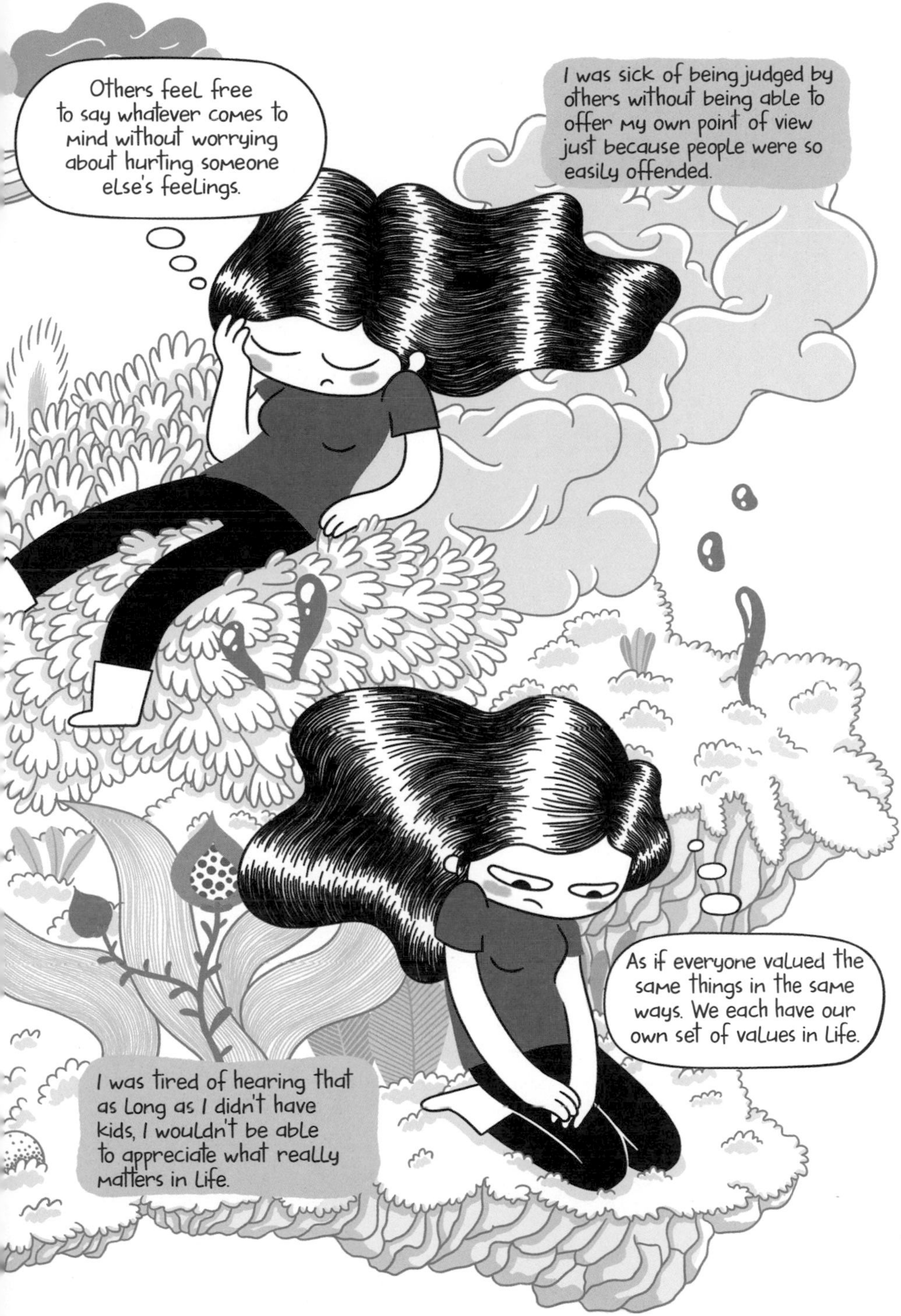

Others feel free to say whatever comes to mind without worrying about hurting someone else's feelings.
I was sick of being judged by others without being able to offer my own point of view just because people were so easily offended.
As if everyone valued the same things in the same ways. We each have our own set of values in life.
I was tired of hearing that as long as I didn't have kids, I wouldn't be able to appreciate what really matters in life.

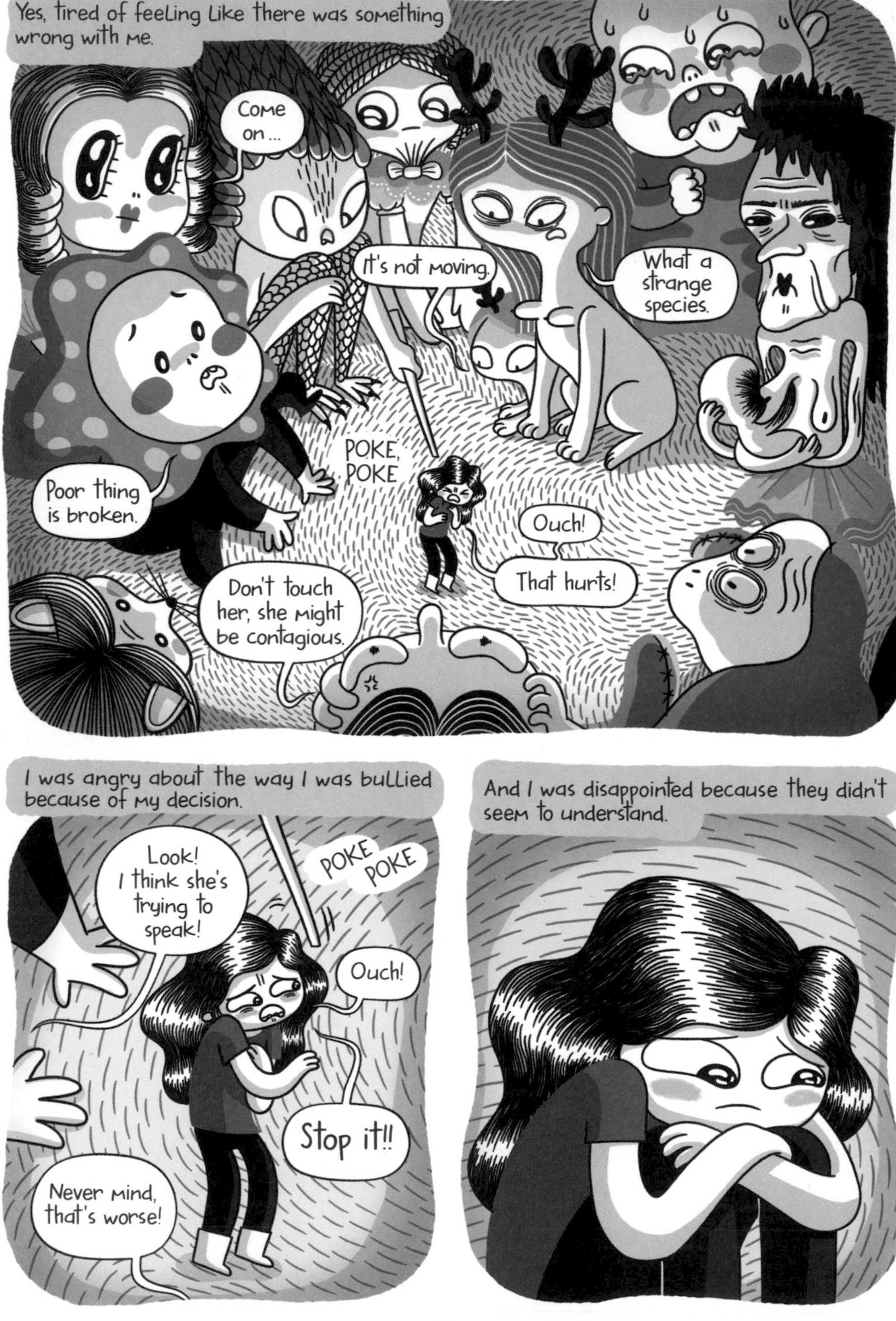
Yes, tired of feeling like there was something wrong with me.
Come on...
It's not moving.
What a strange species.
POKE, POKE
Poor thing is broken.
Ouch!
That hurts!
Don't touch her, she might be contagious.
I was angry about the way I was bullied because of my decision.
Look! I think she's trying to speak!
POKE POKE
Ouch!
Stop it!!
Never mind, that's worse!
And I was disappointed because they didn't seem to understand.

CHAPTER 5

● An Island in an Ocean ●

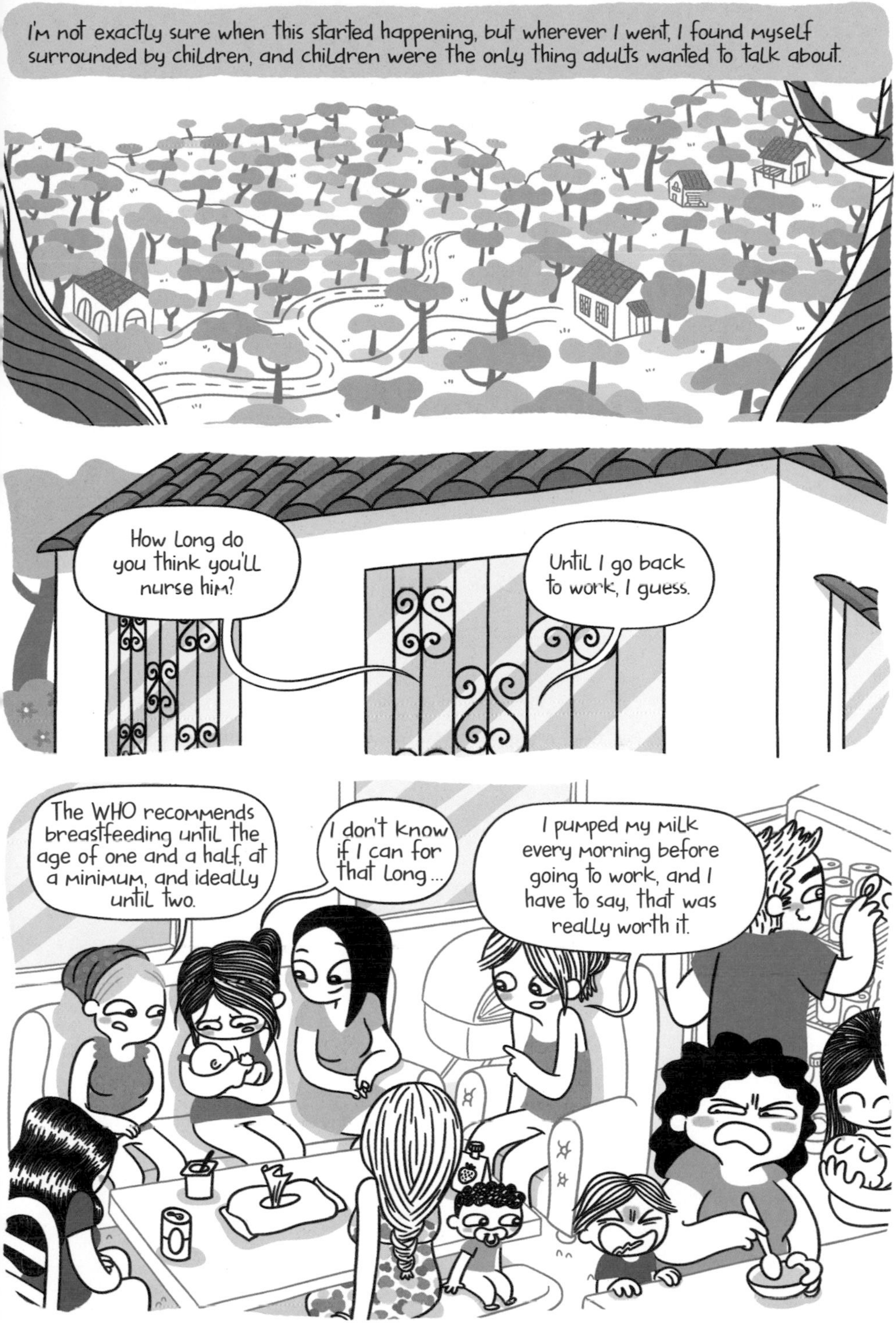

I'm not exactly sure when this started happening, but wherever I went, I found myself surrounded by children, and children were the only thing adults wanted to talk about.
How long do you think you'll nurse him?
Until I go back to work, I guess.
The WHO recommends breastfeeding until the age of one and a half, at a minimum, and ideally until two.
I don't know if I can for that long...
I pumped my milk every morning before going to work, and I have to say, that was really worth it.

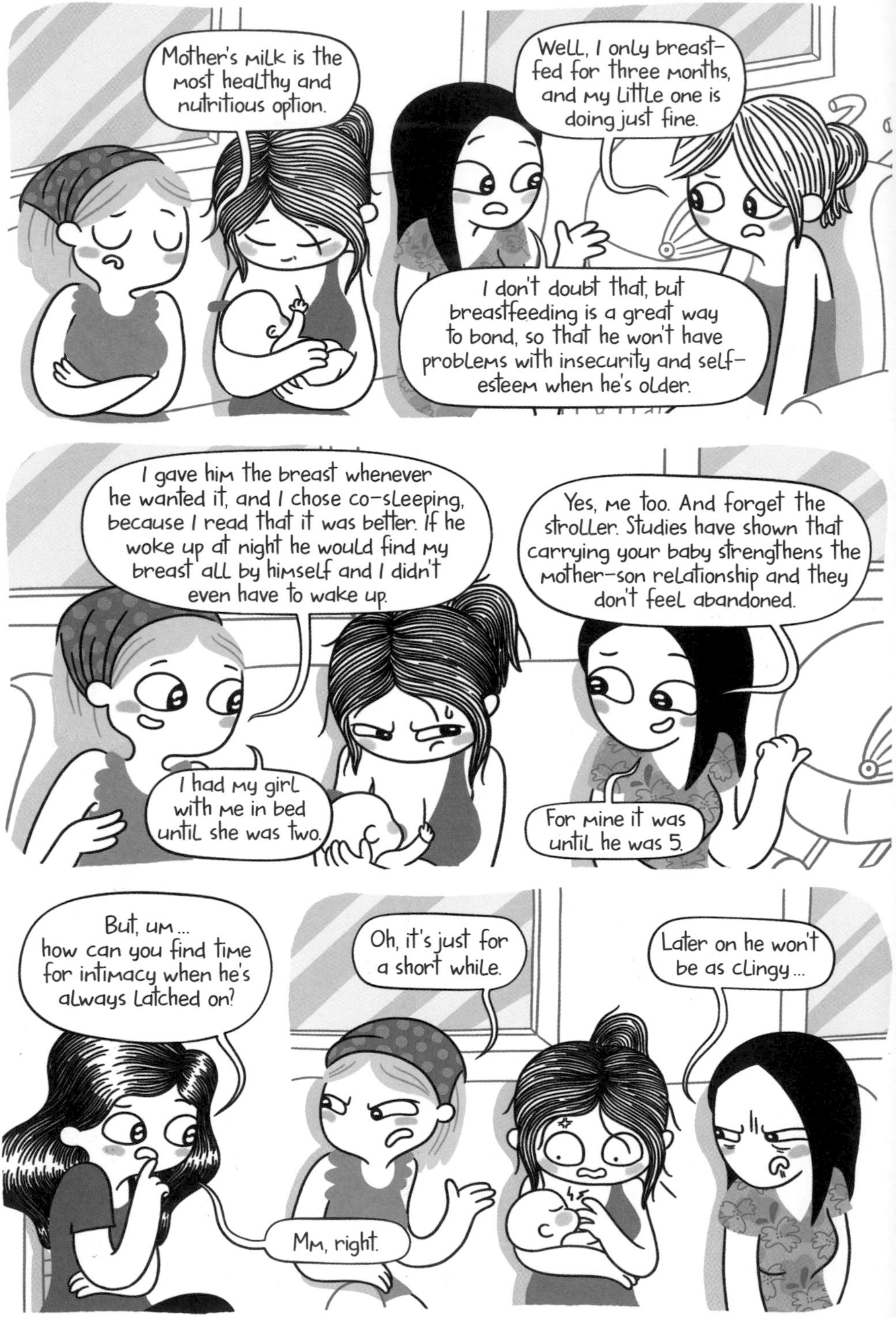
Mother's milk is the most healthy and nutritious option.
Well, I only breast-fed for three months, and my little one is doing just fine.
I don't doubt that, but breastfeeding is a great way to bond, so that he won't have problems with insecurity and self-esteem when he's older.
I gave him the breast whenever he wanted it, and I chose co-sleeping, because I read that it was better. If he woke up at night he would find my breast all by himself and I didn't even have to wake up.
I had my girl with me in bed until she was two.
Yes, me too. And forget the stroller. Studies have shown that carrying your baby strengthens the mother-son relationship and they don't feel abandoned.
For mine it was until he was 5.
But, um... how can you find time for intimacy when he's always latched on?
Mm, right.
Oh, it's just for a short while.
Later on he won't be as clingy...

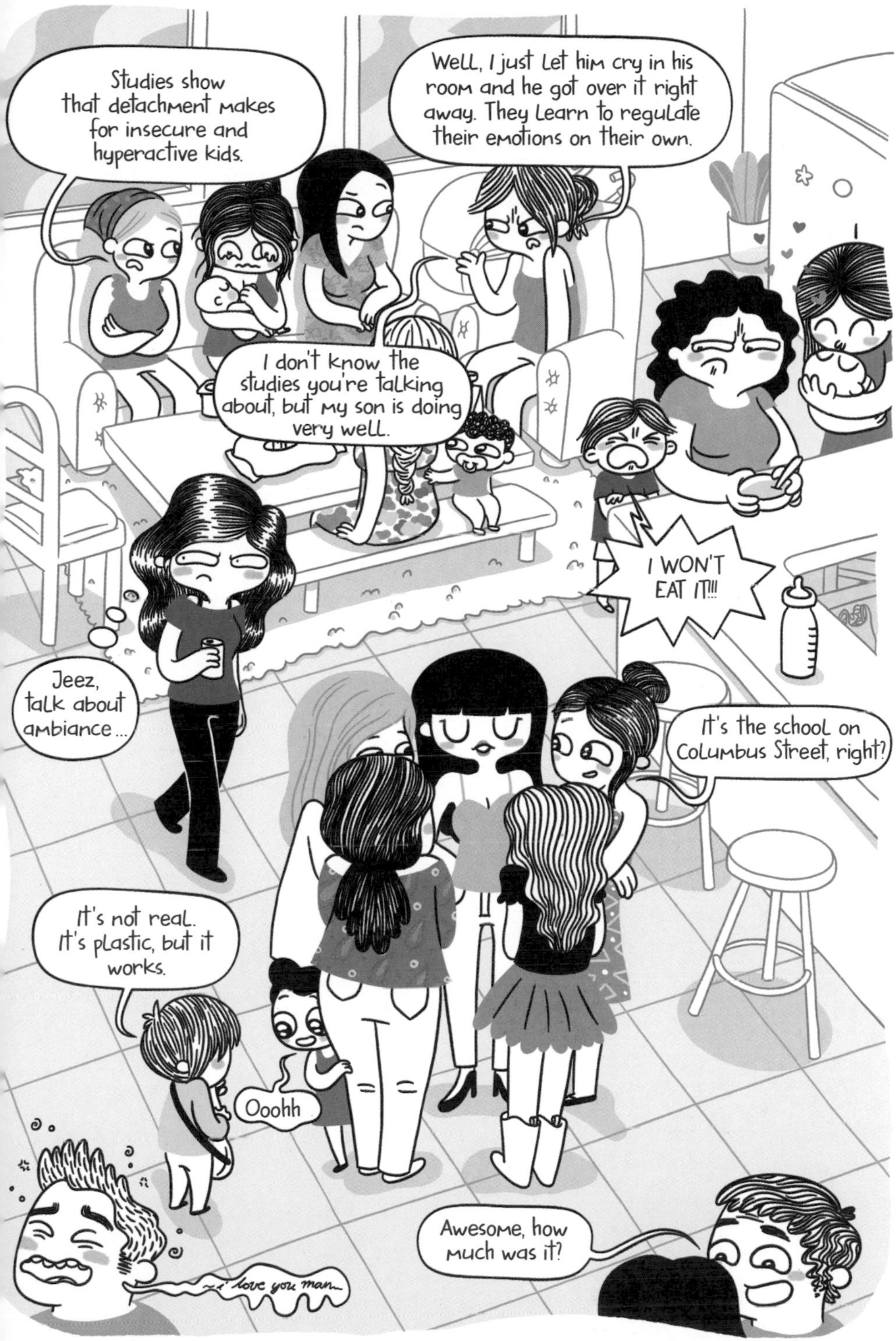
Studies show that detachment makes for insecure and hyperactive kids.
Well, I just let him cry in his room and he got over it right away. They learn to regulate their emotions on their own.
I don't know the studies you're talking about, but my son is doing very well.
I WON'T EAT IT!!!
Jeez, talk about ambiance...
It's the school on Columbus Street, right?
It's not real. It's plastic, but it works.
Ooohh
Awesome, how much was it?
I love you man

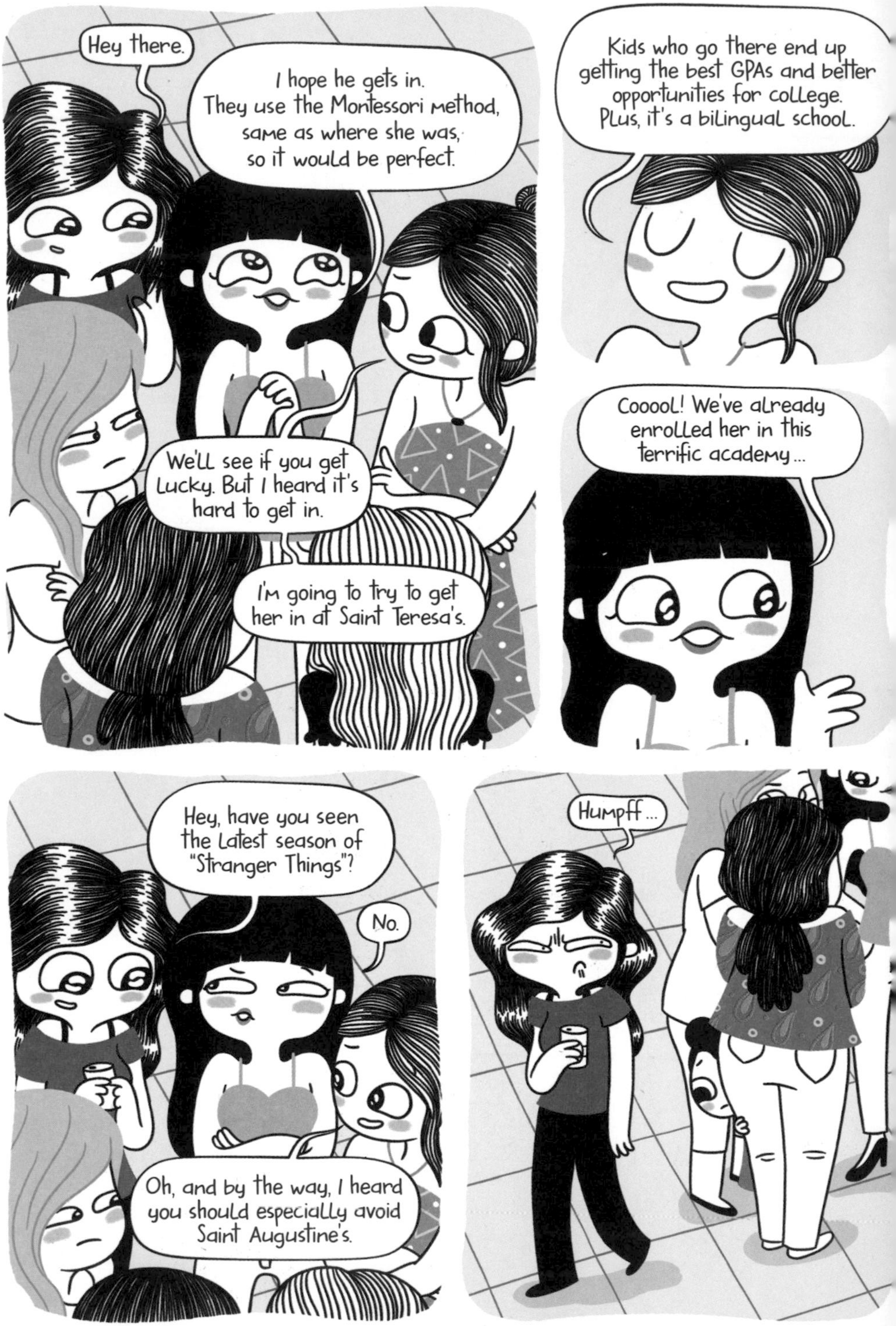
Hey there.
I hope he gets in. They use the Montessori method, same as where she was, so it would be perfect.
We'll see if you get lucky. But I heard it's hard to get in.
I'm going to try to get her in at Saint Teresa's.
Kids who go there end up getting the best GPAs and better opportunities for college. Plus, it's a bilingual school.
Cooool! We've already enrolled her in this terrific academy...
Hey, have you seen the latest season of "Stranger Things"?
No.
Oh, and by the way, I heard you should especially avoid Saint Augustine's.
Humpff...

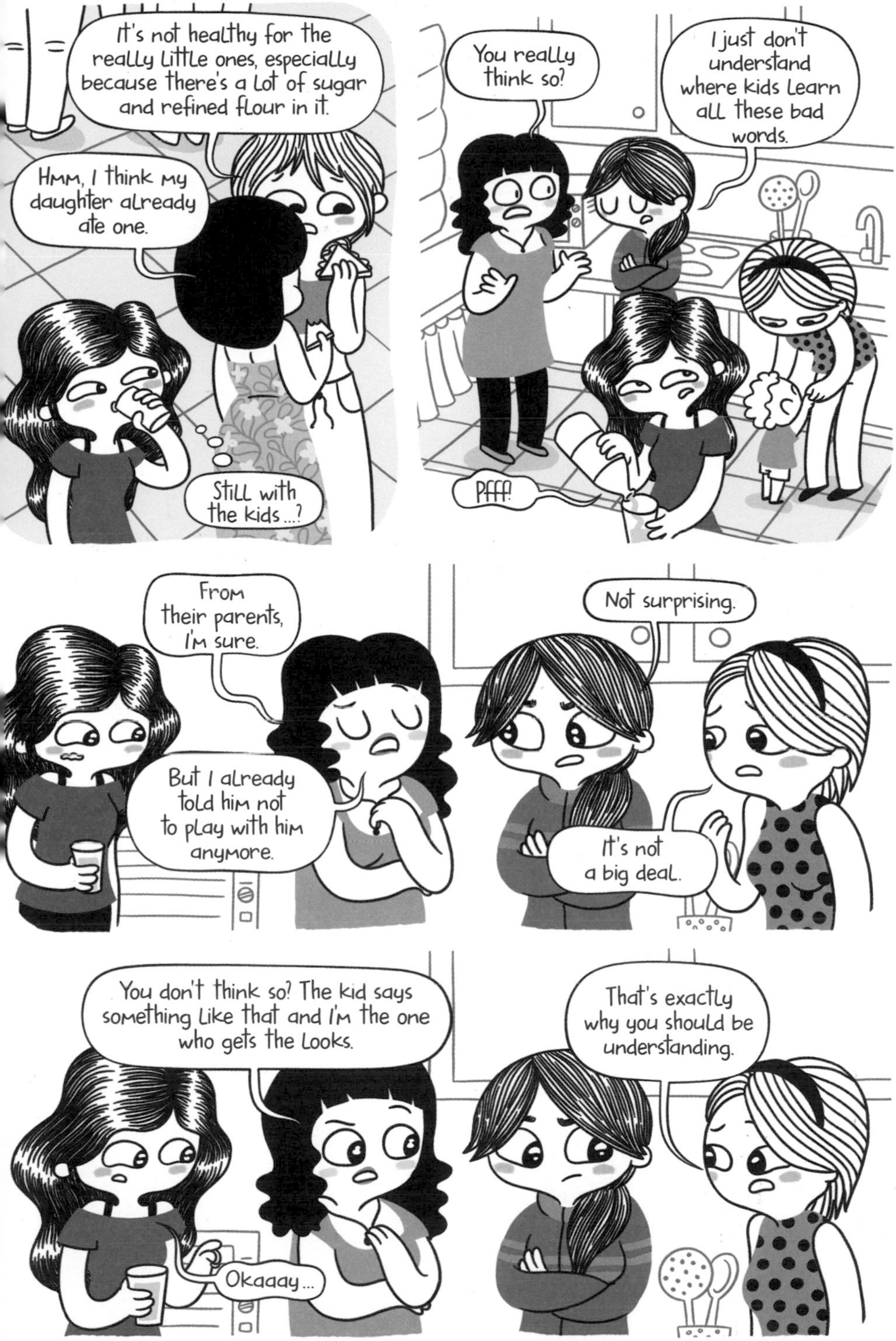
It's not healthy for the really little ones, especially because there's a lot of sugar and refined flour in it.
Hmm, I think my daughter already ate one.
Still with the kids...?
You really think so?
I just don't understand where kids learn all these bad words.
Pfff!
From their parents, I'm sure.
But I already told him not to play with him anymore.
Not surprising.
It's not a big deal.
You don't think so? The kid says something like that and I'm the one who gets the looks.
Okaaay...
That's exactly why you should be understanding.

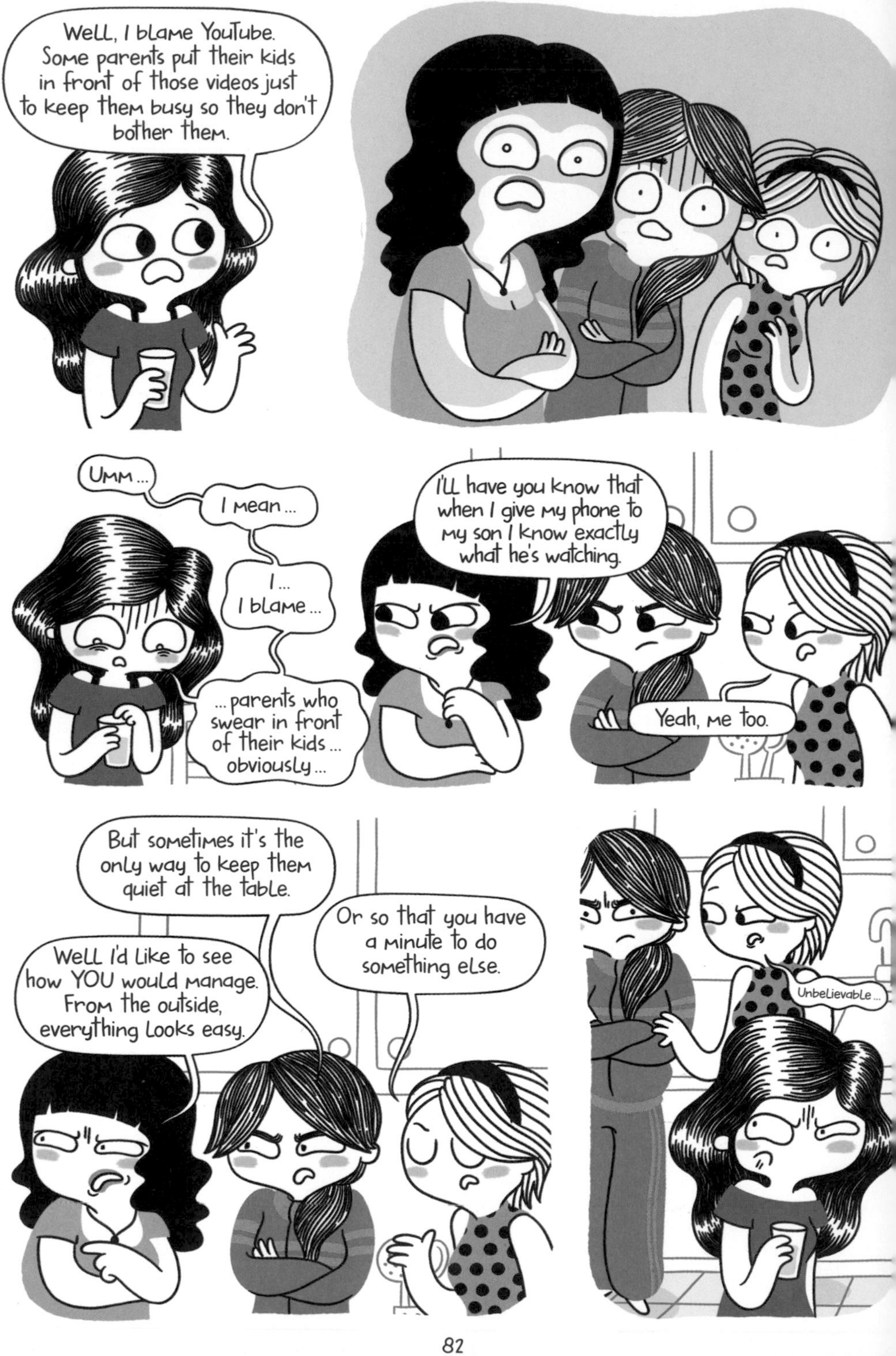
Well, I blame YouTube. Some parents put their kids in front of those videos just to keep them busy so they don't bother them.
Umm...
I mean...
I... I blame...
...parents who swear in front of their kids... obviously...
I'll have you know that when I give my phone to my son I know exactly what he's watching.
Yeah, me too.
But sometimes it's the only way to keep them quiet at the table.
Well I'd like to see how YOU would manage. From the outside, everything looks easy.
Or so that you have a minute to do something else.
Unbelievable...

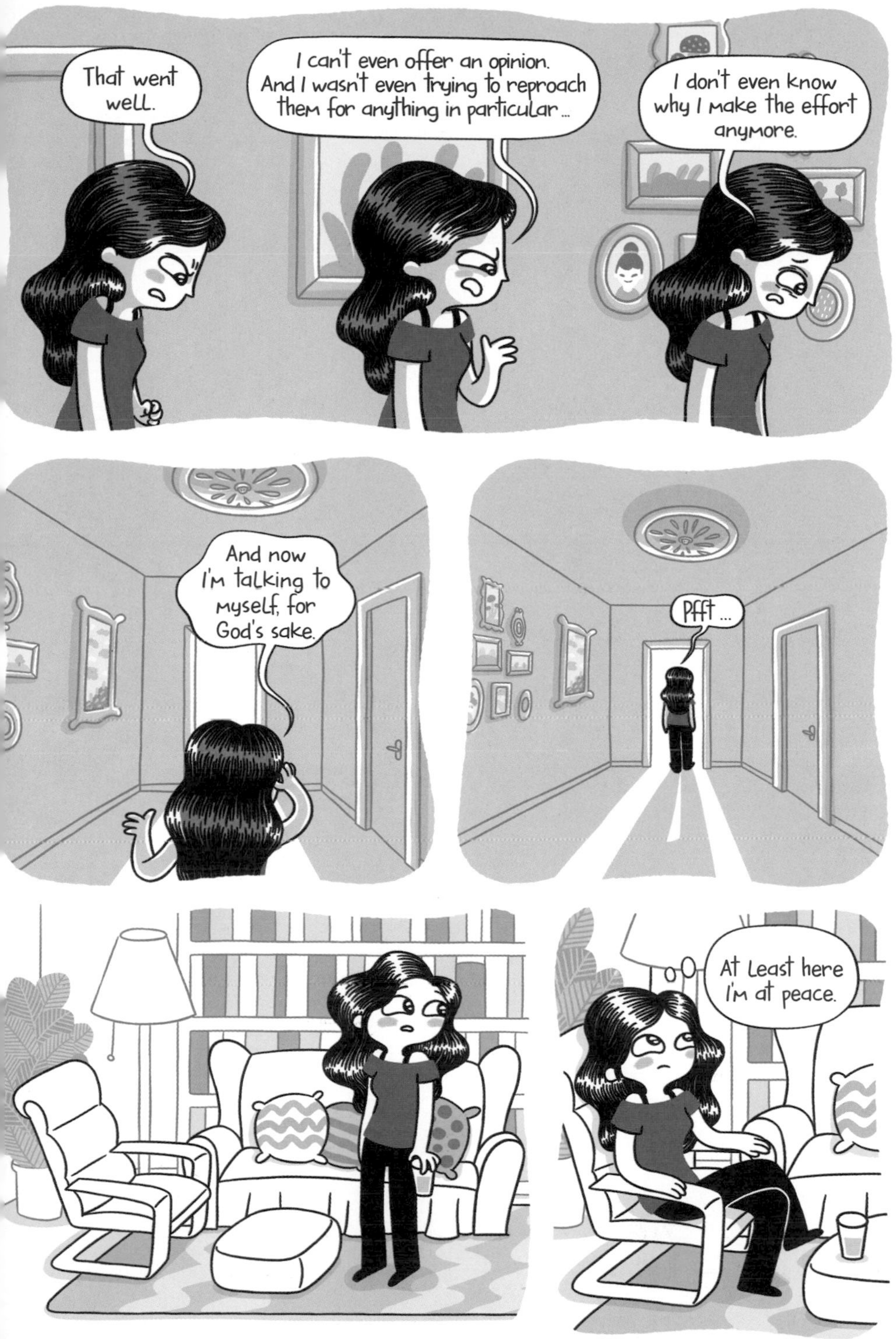
That went well.
I can't even offer an opinion. And I wasn't even trying to reproach them for anything in particular ...
I don't even know why I make the effort anymore.
And now I'm talking to myself, for God's sake.
Pfft ...
At least here I'm at peace.

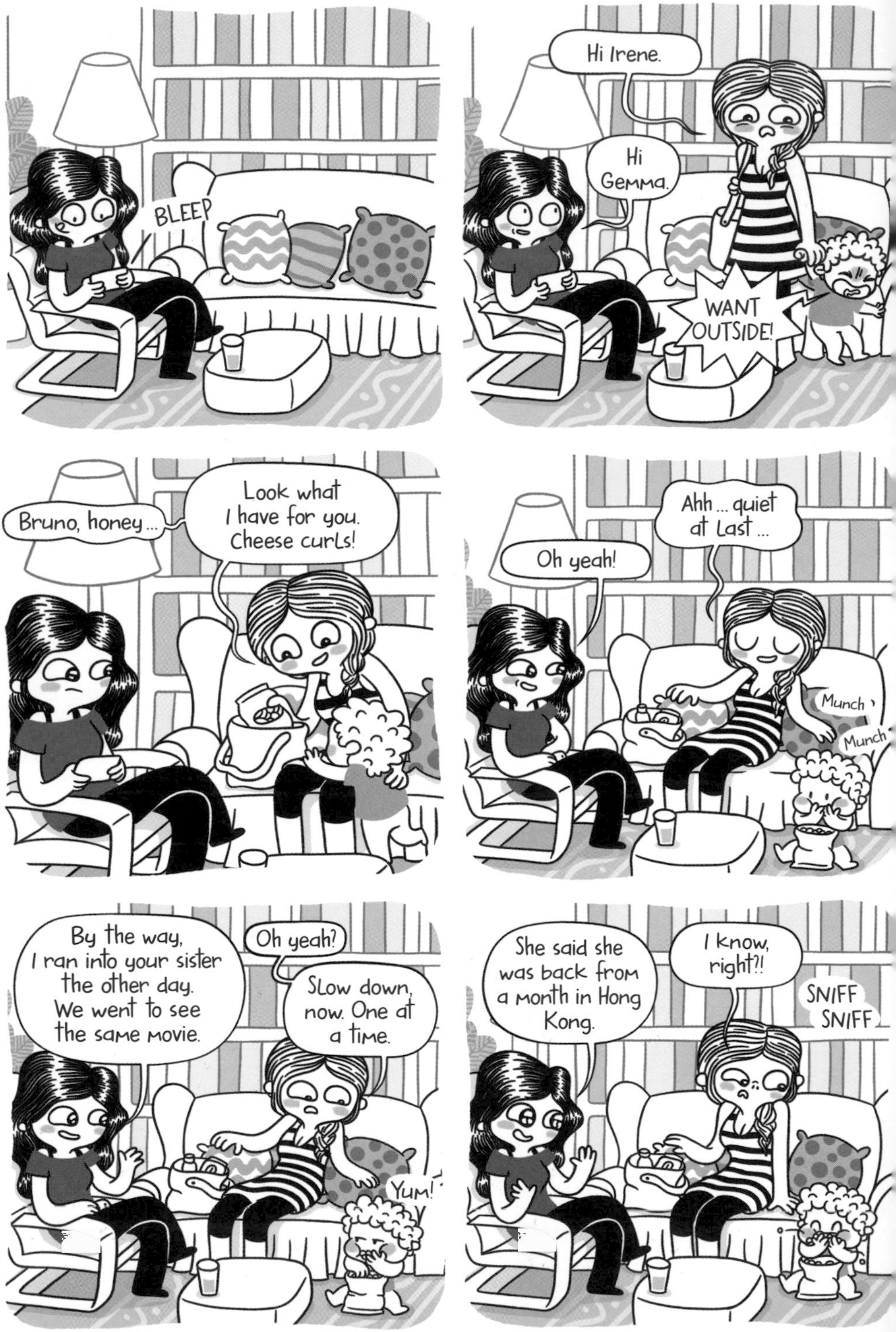
BLEEP
Hi Irene.
Hi Gemma.
WANT OUTSIDE!
Bruno, honey ...
Look what I have for you. Cheese curls!
Oh yeah!
Ahh ... quiet at last ...
Munch
Munch
By the way, I ran into your sister the other day. We went to see the same movie.
Oh yeah?
Slow down, now. One at a time.
YUM!
She said she was back from a month in Hong Kong.
I know, right?!
SNIFF SNIFF

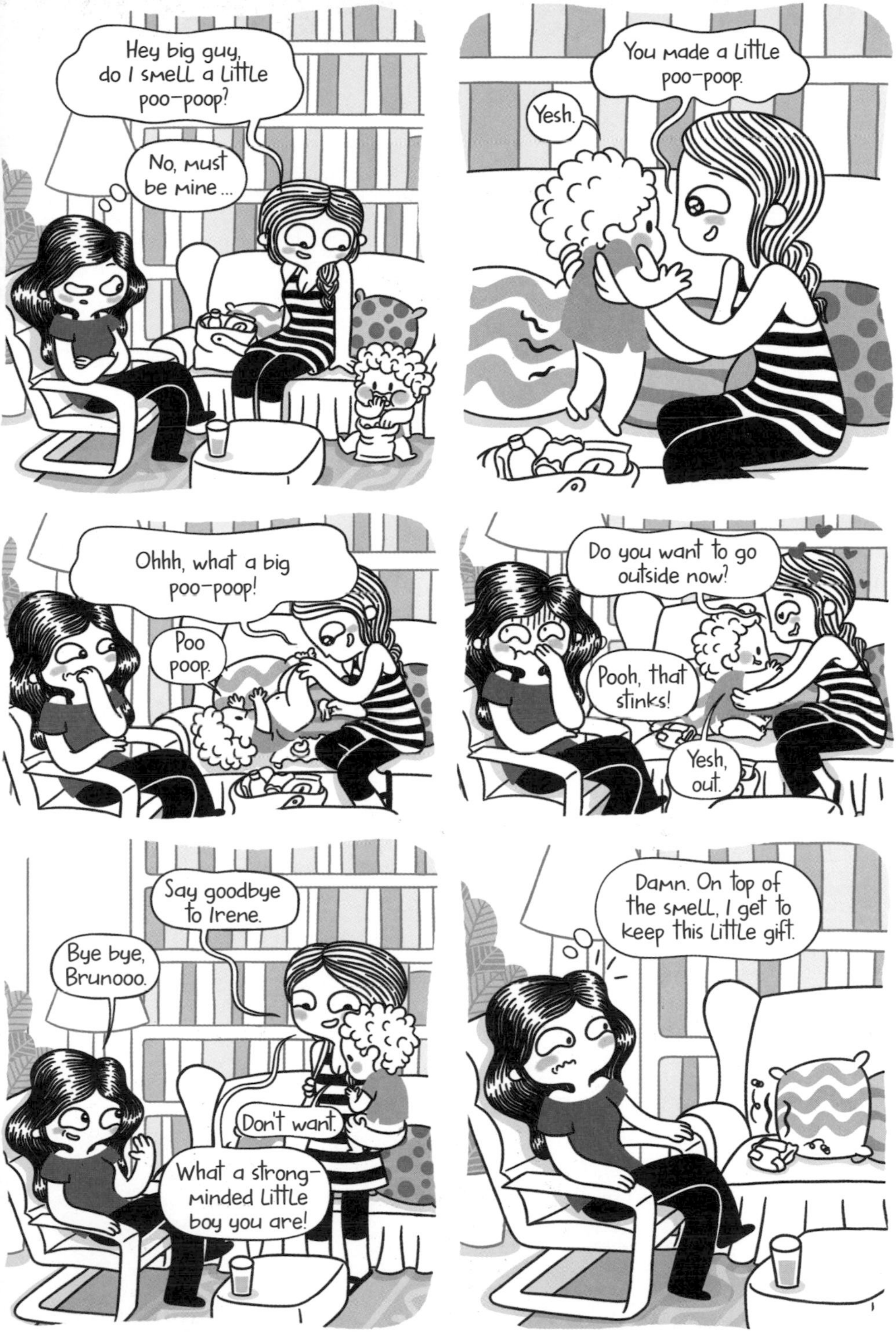

Hey big guy, do I smell a little poo-poop?
No, must be mine ...
You made a little poo-poop.
Yesh.
Ohhh, what a big poo-poop!
Poo poop.
Do you want to go outside now?
Pooh, that stinks!
Yesh, out.
Say goodbye to Irene.
Bye bye, Brunooo.
Don't want.
What a strong-minded little boy you are!
Damn. On top of the smell, I get to keep this little gift.

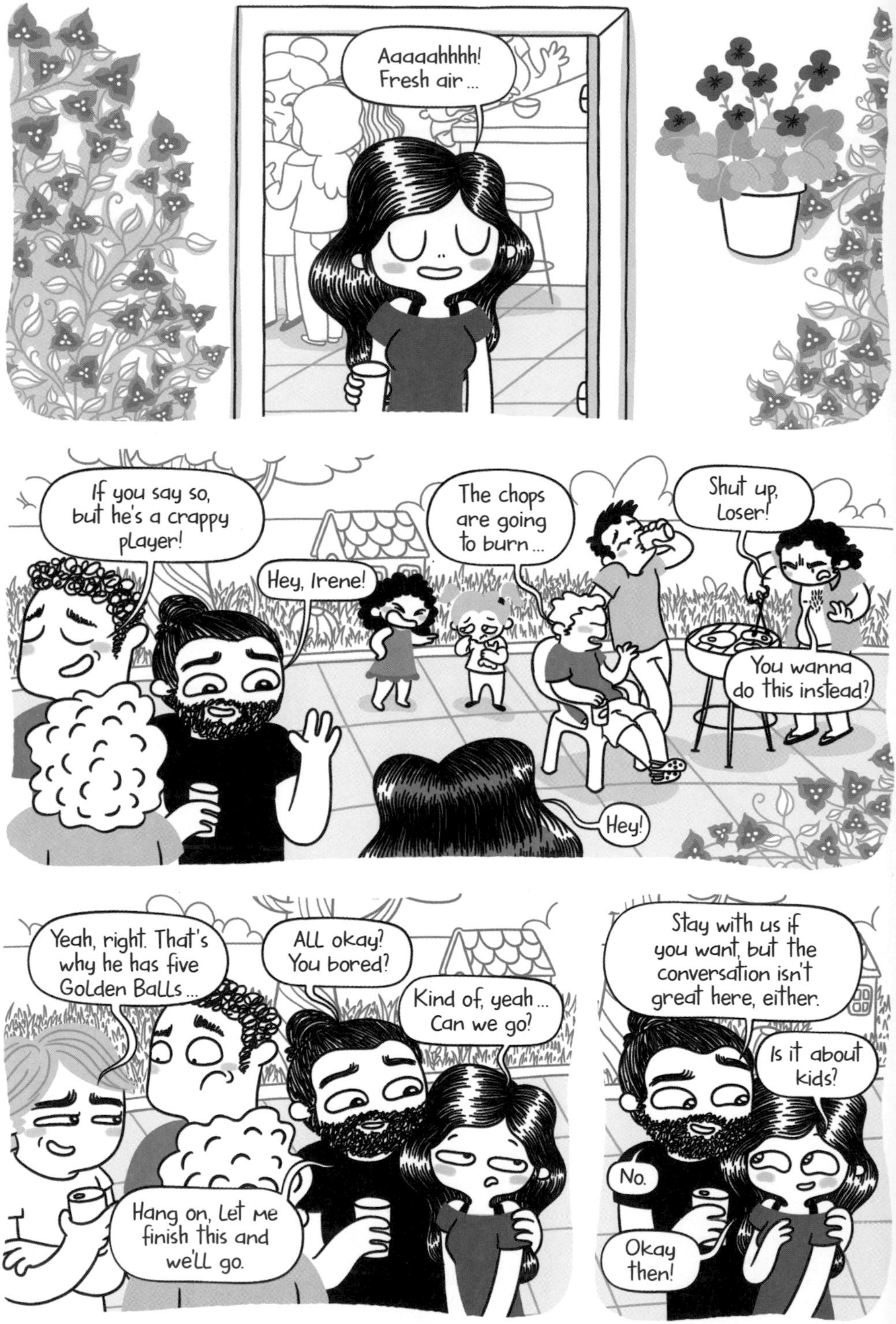

Aaaaahhhh! Fresh air...
If you say so, but he's a crappy player!
Hey, Irene!
The chops are going to burn...
Shut up, Loser!
You wanna do this instead?
Hey!
Yeah, right. That's why he has five Golden Balls...
ALL okay? You bored?
Kind of, yeah... Can we go?
Hang on, Let me finish this and we'LL go.
Stay with us if you want, but the conversation isn't great here, either.
Is it about kids?
No.
Okay then!

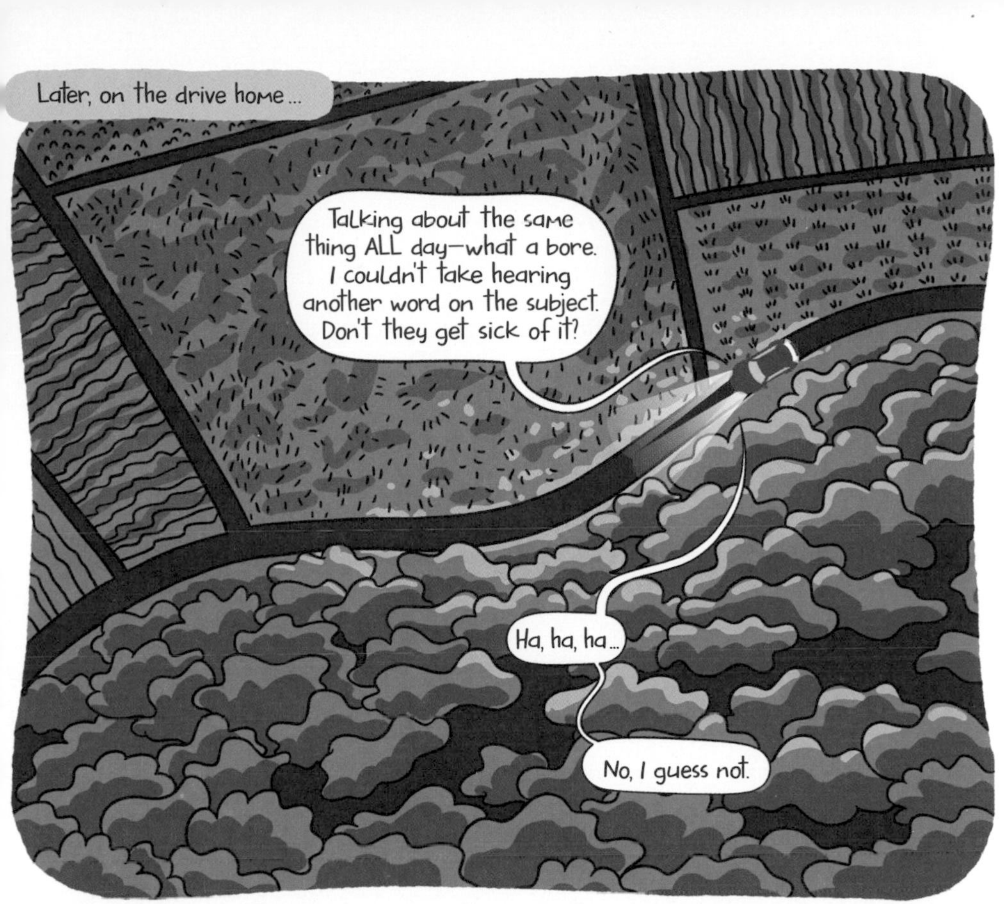
Later, on the drive home...
Talking about the same thing ALL day—what a bore. I couldn't take hearing another word on the subject. Don't they get sick of it?
Ha, ha, ha...
No, I guess not.

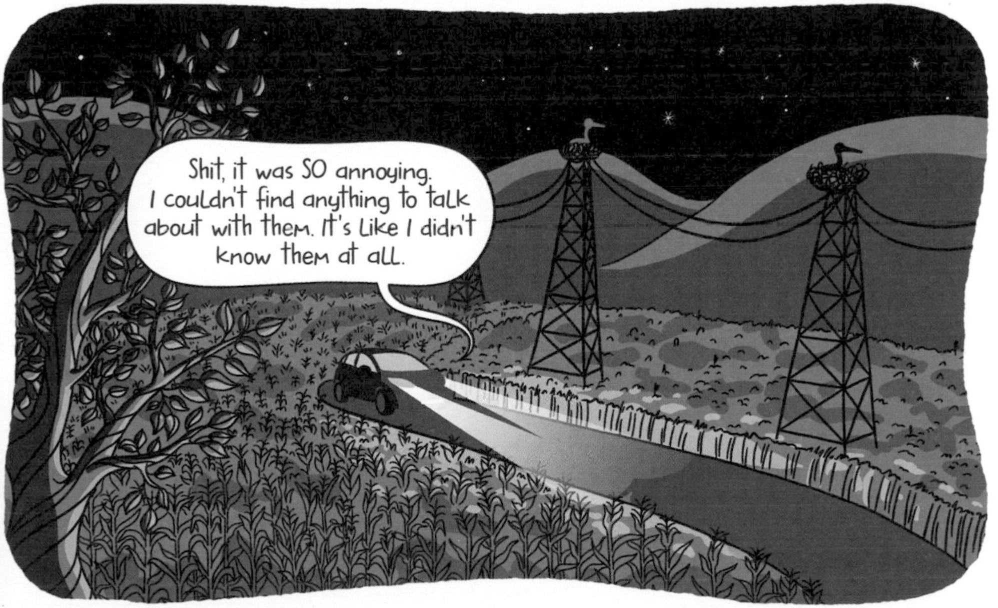
Shit, it was SO annoying. I couldn't find anything to talk about with them. It's like I didn't know them at all.

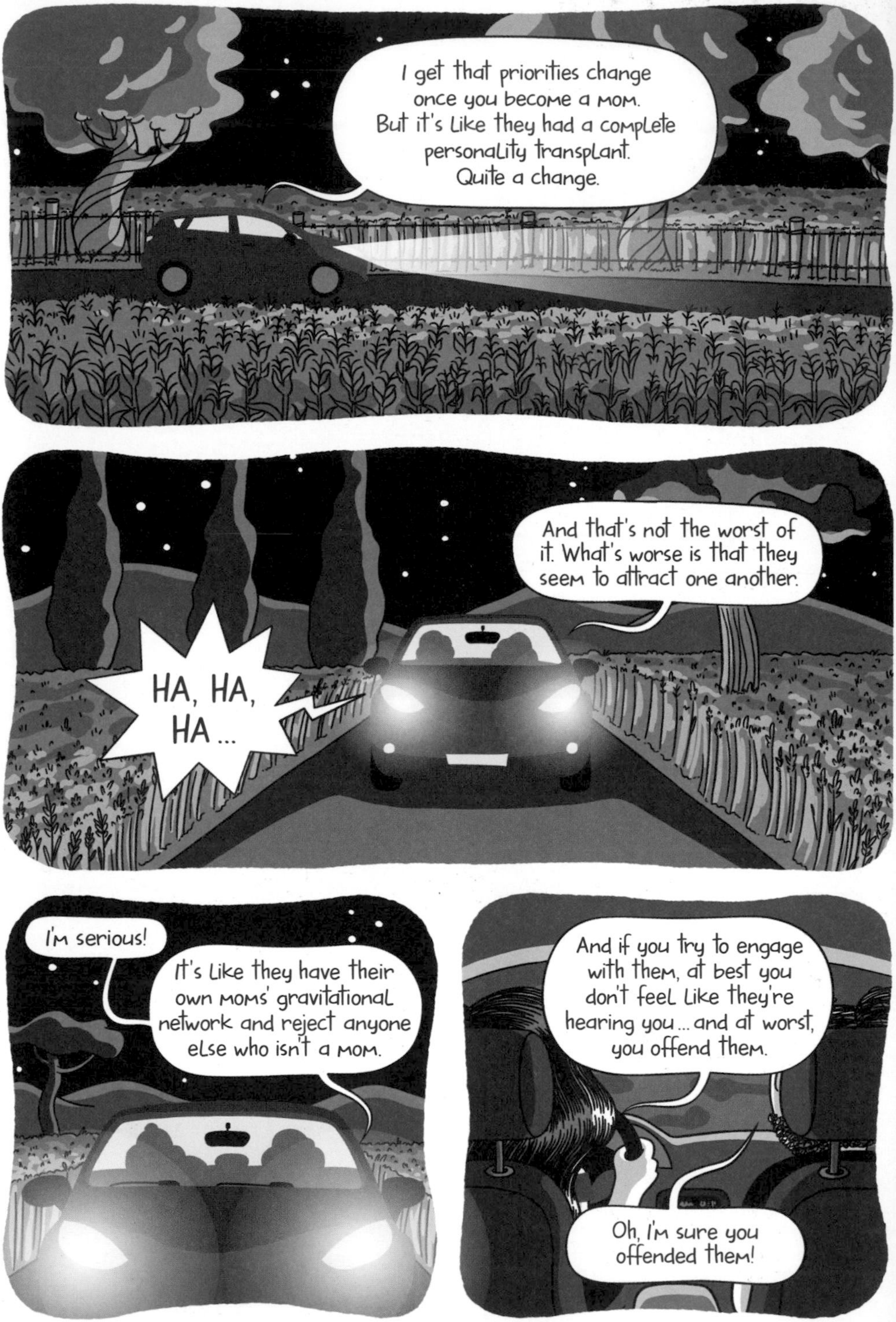
I get that priorities change once you become a MOM. But it's Like they had a complete personaLity transpLant. Quite a change.
And that's not the worst of it. What's worse is that they seem to attract one another.
HA, HA, HA ...
I'M serious!
It's Like they have their own MOMS' gravitational network and reject anyone eLse who isn't a MOM.
And if you try to engage with them, at best you don't feeL Like they're hearing you ... and at worst, you offend them.
Oh, I'M sure you offended them!

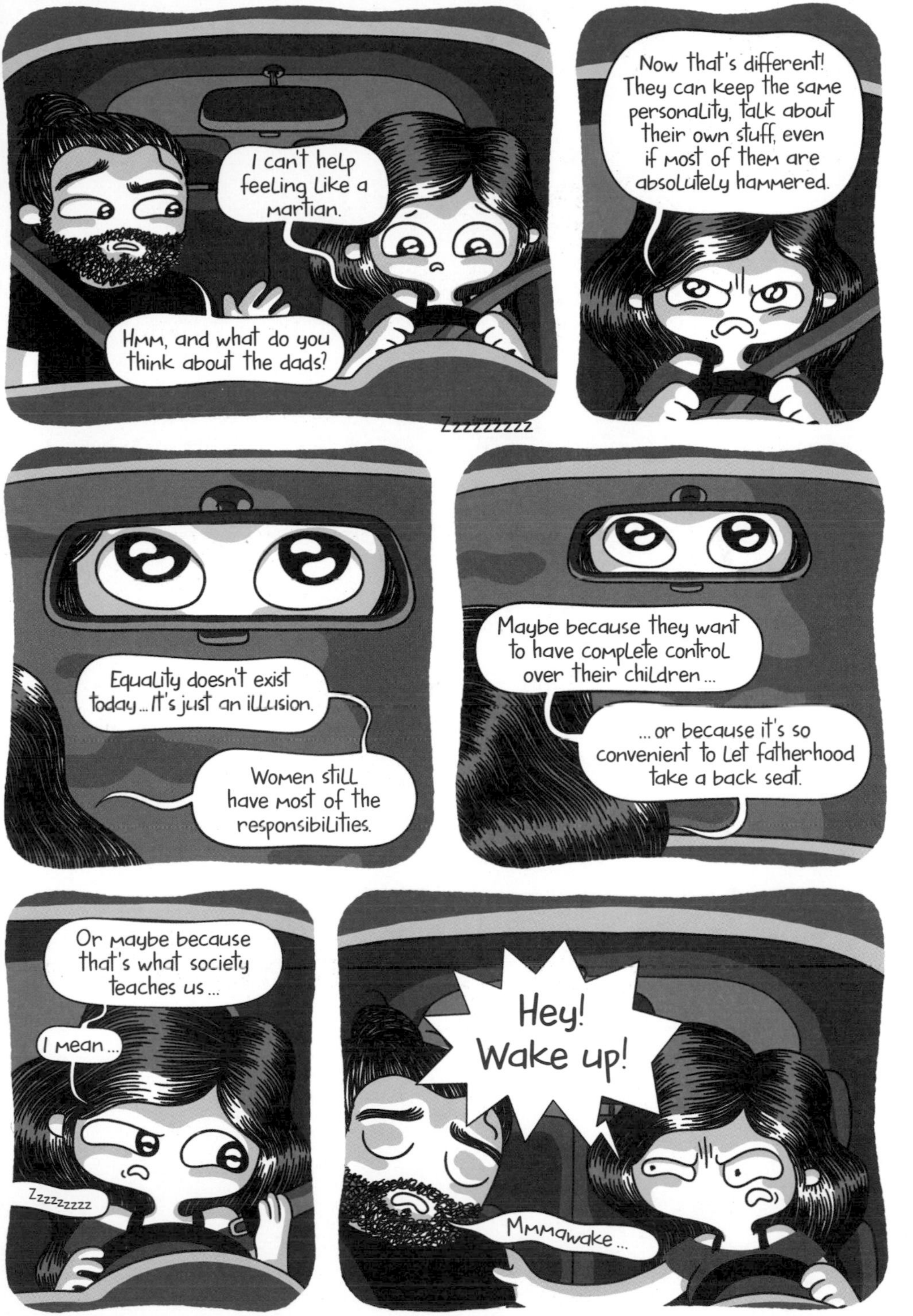
I can't help feeling like a martian.
Hmm, and what do you think about the dads?
Zzzzzzzzz
Now that's different! They can keep the same personality, talk about their own stuff, even if most of them are absolutely hammered.
Equality doesn't exist today... It's just an illusion.
Women still have most of the responsibilities.
Maybe because they want to have complete control over their children...
... or because it's so convenient to let fatherhood take a back seat.
Or maybe because that's what society teaches us...
I mean...
Zzzzzzzzz
Hey! Wake up!
Mmmawake...

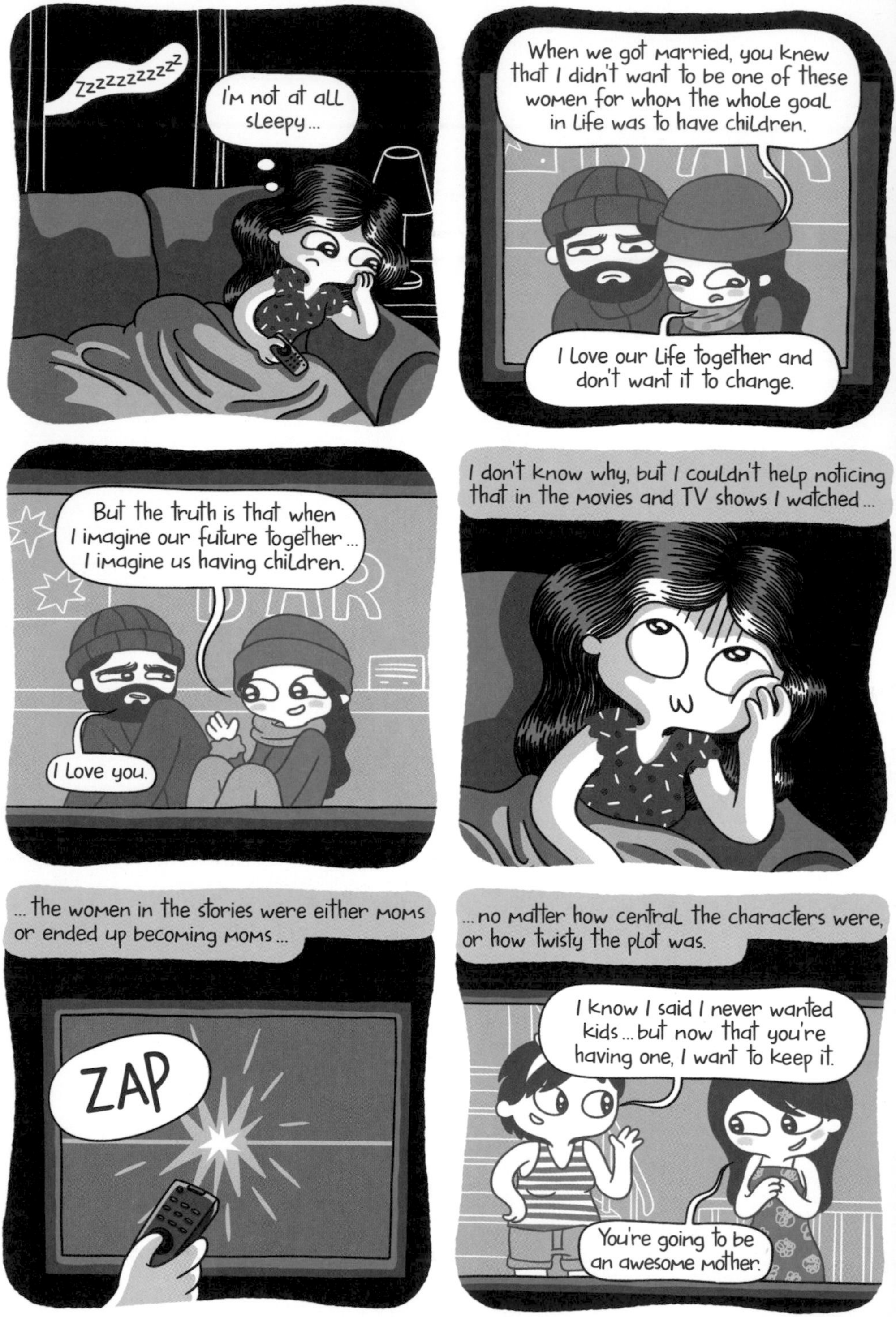
Zzzzzzzzzz
I'm not at all sleepy...
When we got married, you knew that I didn't want to be one of these women for whom the whole goal in life was to have children.
I love our life together and don't want it to change.
But the truth is that when I imagine our future together... I imagine us having children.
I love you.
I don't know why, but I couldn't help noticing that in the movies and TV shows I watched...
... the women in the stories were either moms or ended up becoming moms...
ZAP
... no matter how central the characters were, or how twisty the plot was.
I know I said I never wanted kids... but now that you're having one, I want to keep it.
You're going to be an awesome mother.

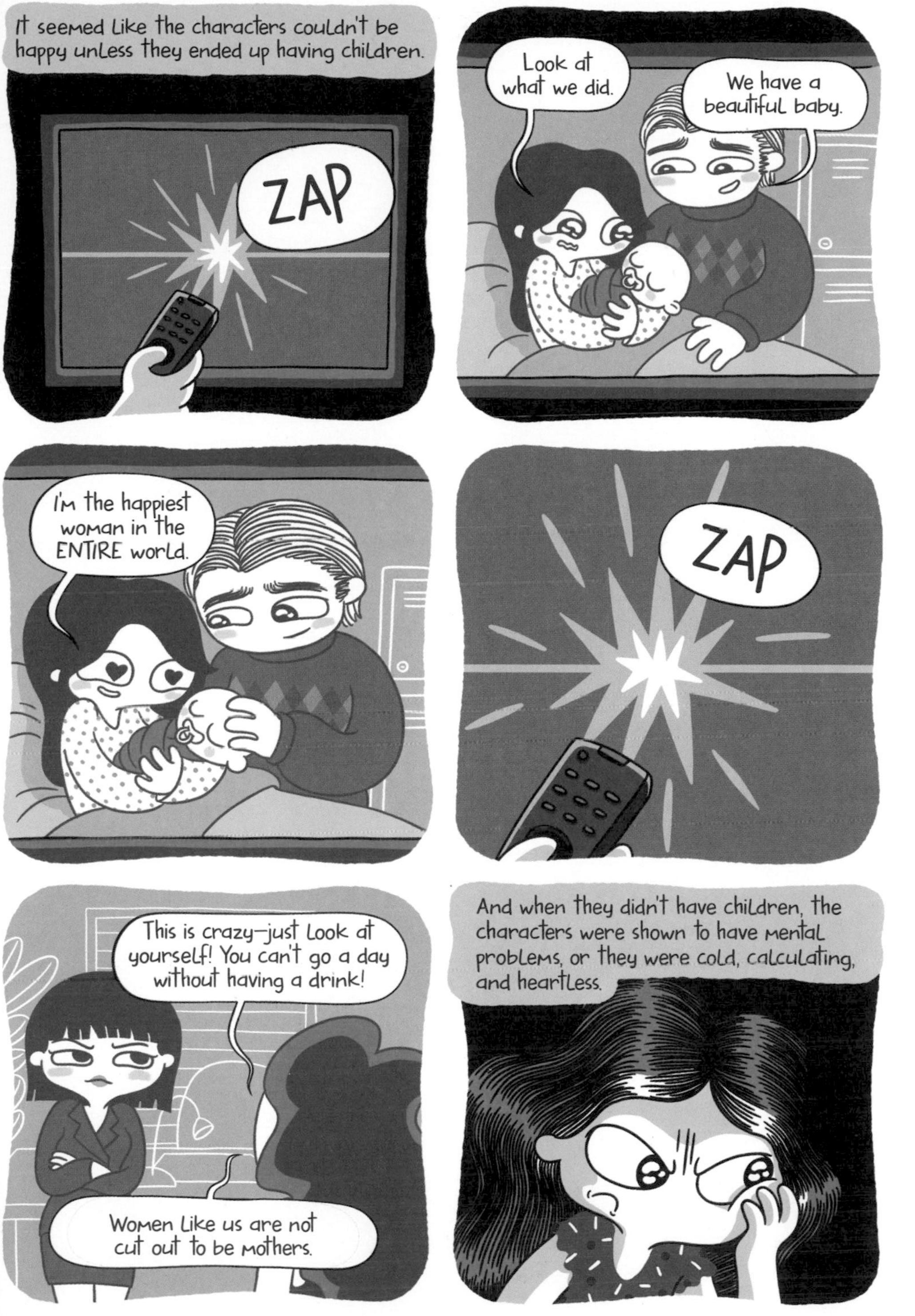
It seemed like the characters couldn't be happy unless they ended up having children.
ZAP
Look at what we did.
We have a beautiful baby.
I'm the happiest woman in the ENTIRE world.
ZAP
This is crazy—just look at yourself! You can't go a day without having a drink!
Women like us are not cut out to be mothers.
And when they didn't have children, the characters were shown to have mental problems, or they were cold, calculating, and heartless.

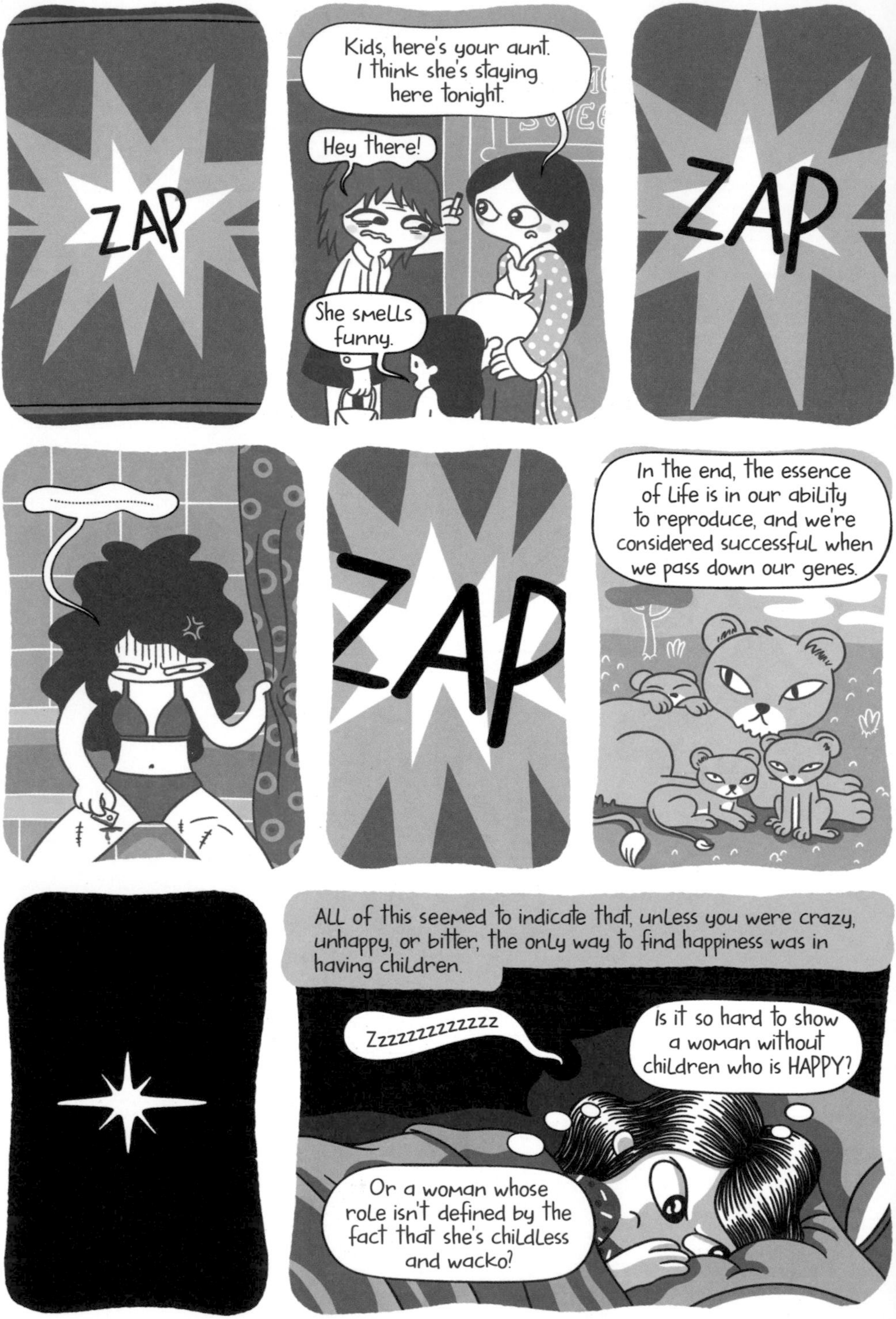
ZAP
Kids, here's your aunt. I think she's staying here tonight.
Hey there!
She smells funny.
ZAP
....
ZAP
In the end, the essence of life is in our ability to reproduce, and we're considered successful when we pass down our genes.
All of this seemed to indicate that, unless you were crazy, unhappy, or bitter, the only way to find happiness was in having children.
Zzzzzzzzzzzzz
Is it so hard to show a woman without children who is HAPPY?
Or a woman whose role isn't defined by the fact that she's childless and wacko?

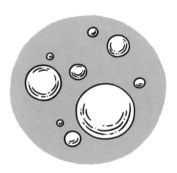

CHAPTER 6
Other Planets

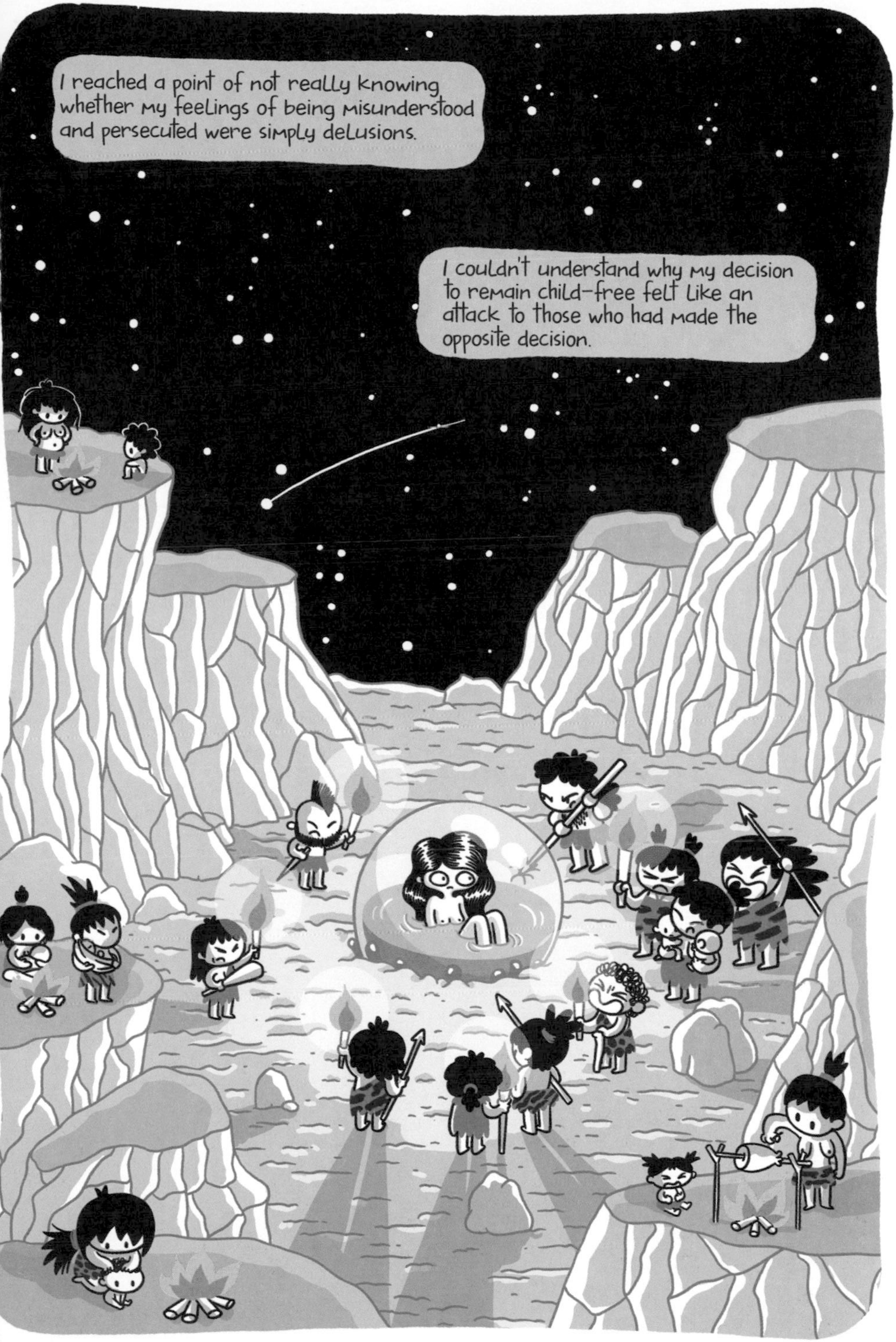
I reached a point of not really knowing whether my feelings of being misunderstood and persecuted were simply delusions.
I couldn't understand why my decision to remain child-free felt like an attack to those who had made the opposite decision.

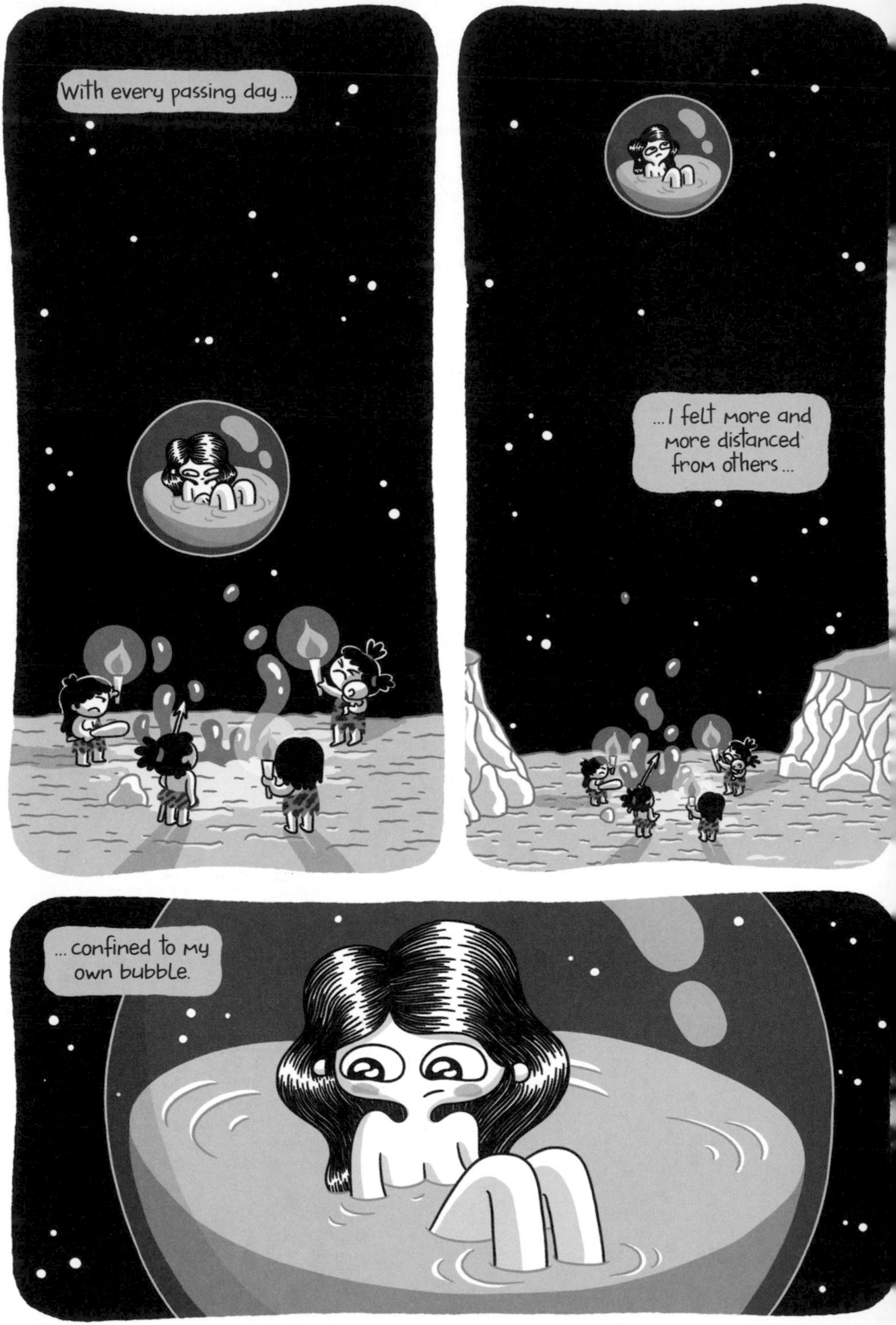
With every passing day...
...I felt more and more distanced from others...
...confined to my own bubble.

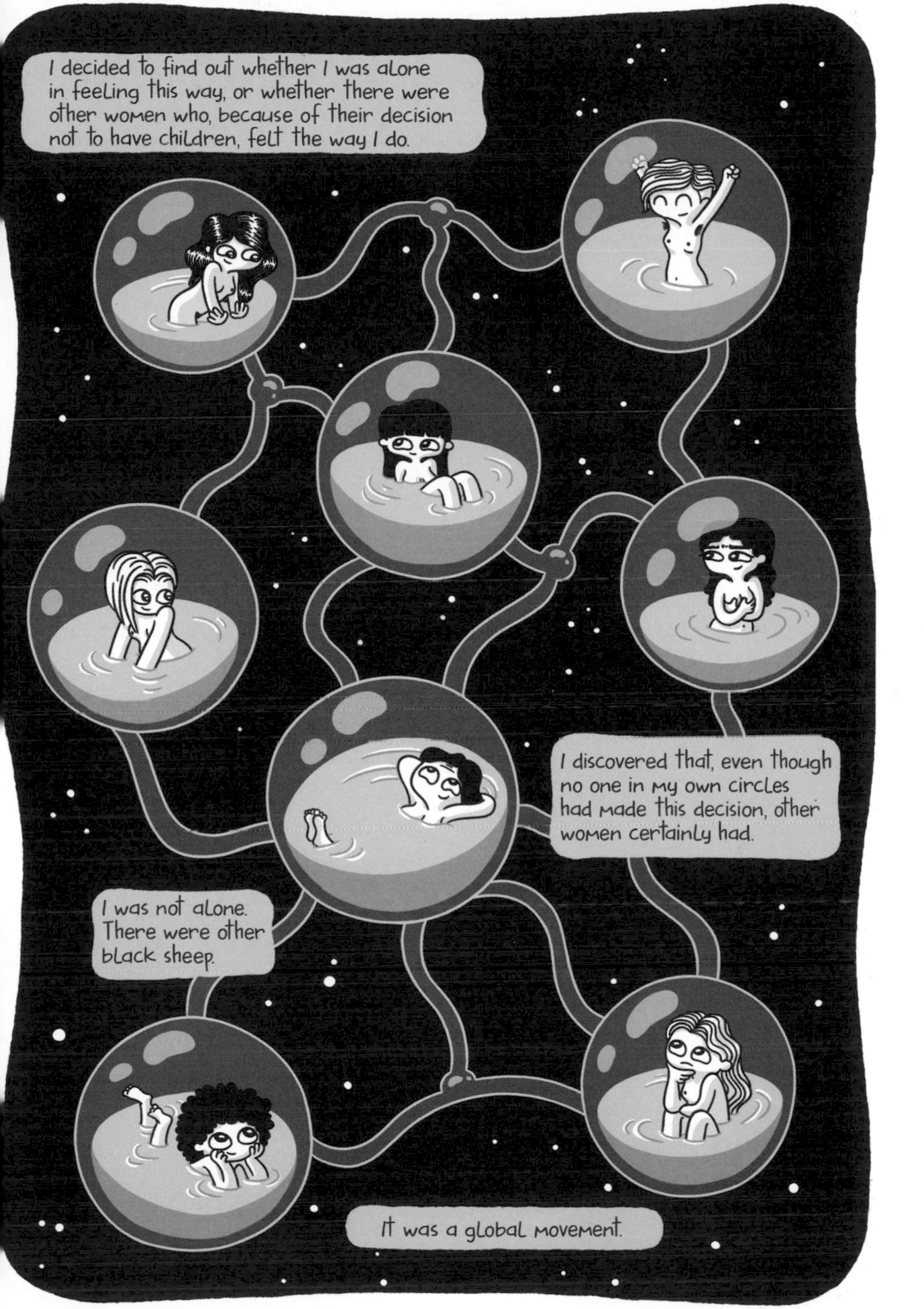
I decided to find out whether I was alone in feeling this way, or whether there were other women who, because of their decision not to have children, felt the way I do.
I discovered that, even though no one in my own circles had made this decision, other women certainly had.
I was not alone. There were other black sheep.
It was a global movement.

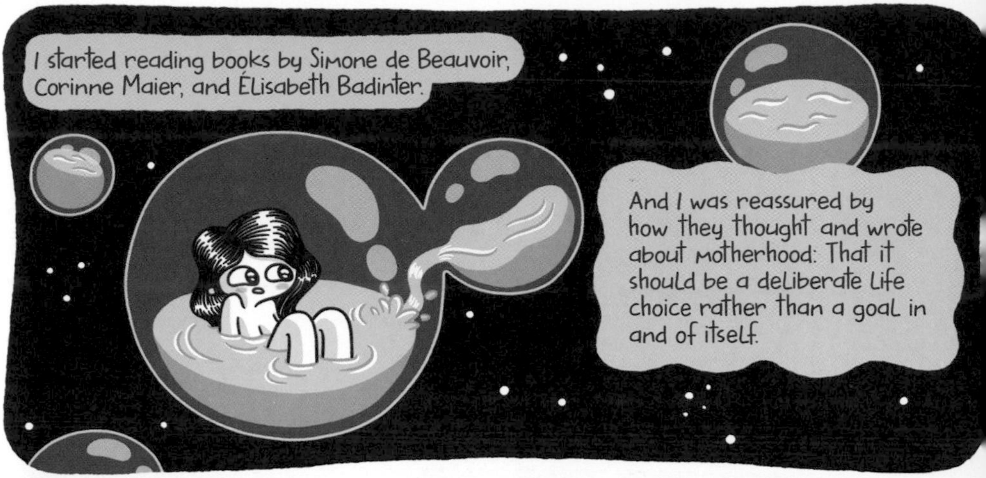
I started reading books by Simone de Beauvoir, Corinne Maier, and Élisabeth Badinter.
And I was reassured by how they thought and wrote about motherhood: That it should be a deliberate life choice rather than a goal in and of itself.

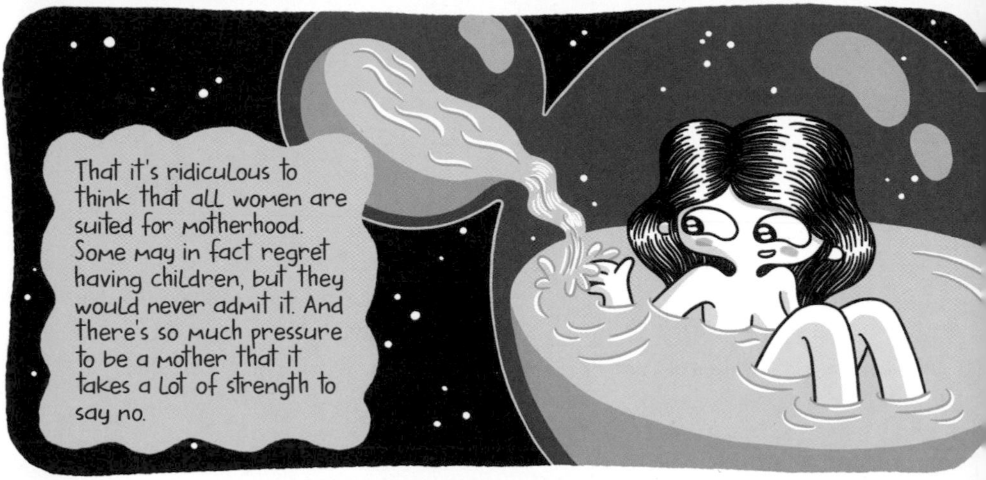
That it's ridiculous to think that all women are suited for motherhood. Some may in fact regret having children, but they would never admit it. And there's so much pressure to be a mother that it takes a lot of strength to say no.

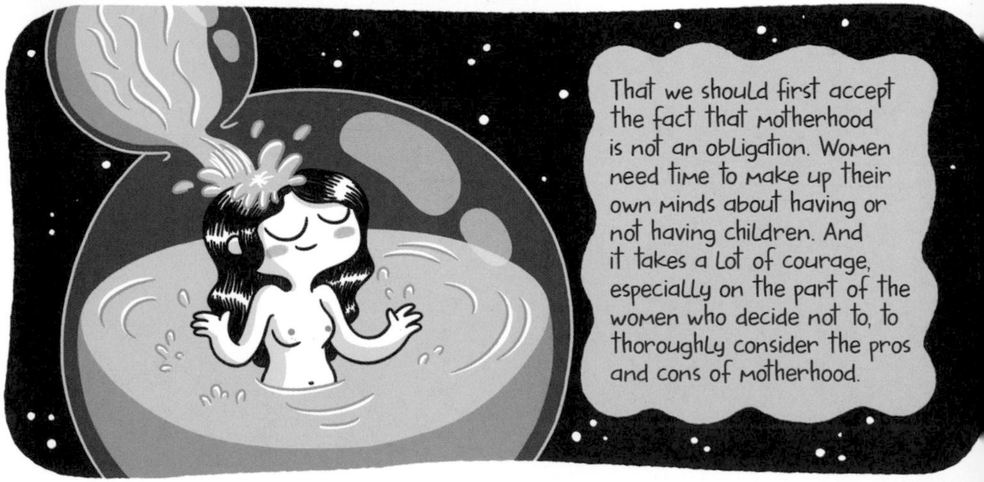
That we should first accept the fact that motherhood is not an obligation. Women need time to make up their own minds about having or not having children. And it takes a lot of courage, especially on the part of the women who decide not to, to thoroughly consider the pros and cons of motherhood.

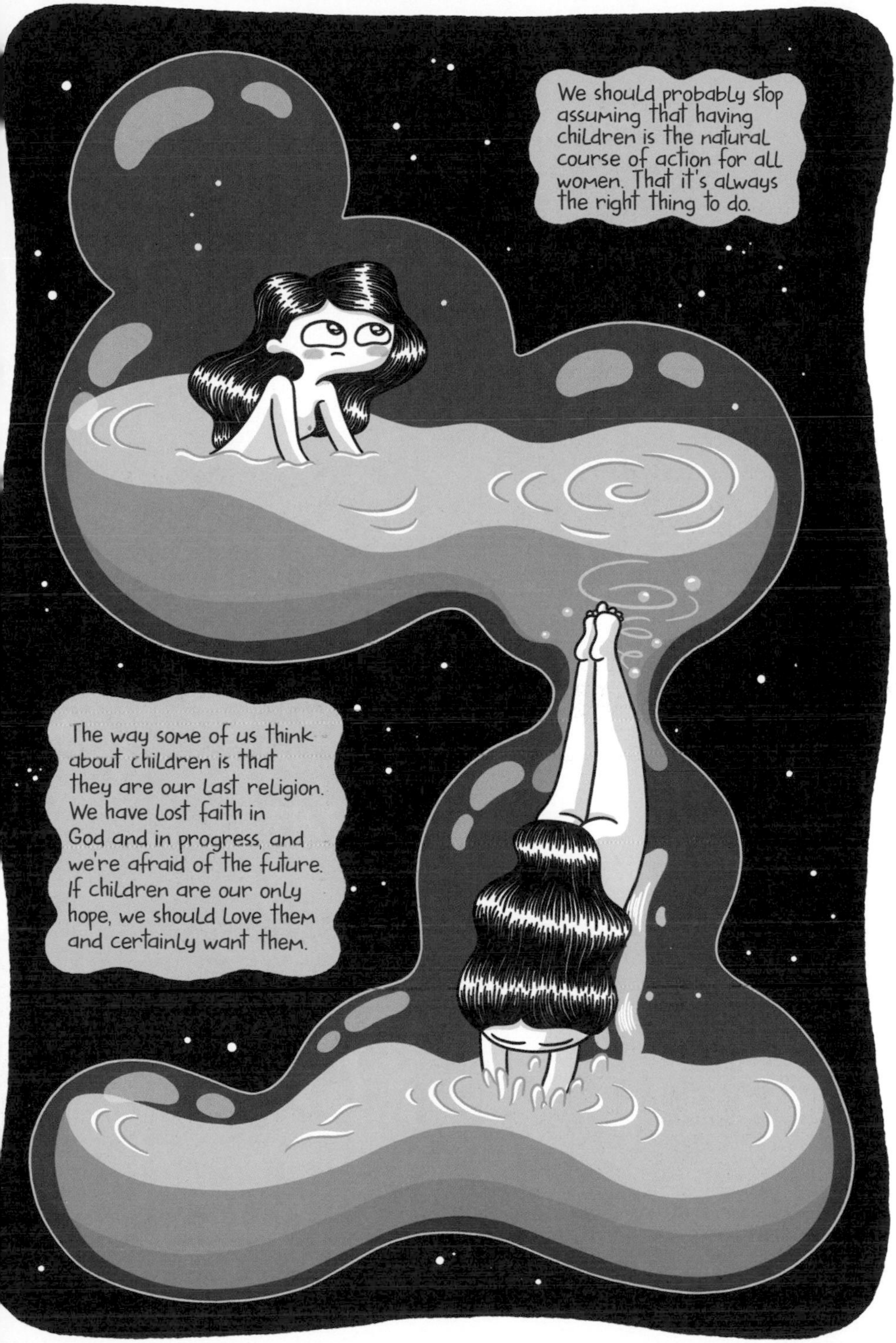
We should probably stop assuming that having children is the natural course of action for all women. That it's always the right thing to do.
The way some of us think about children is that they are our last religion. We have lost faith in God and in progress, and we're afraid of the future. If children are our only hope, we should love them and certainly want them.

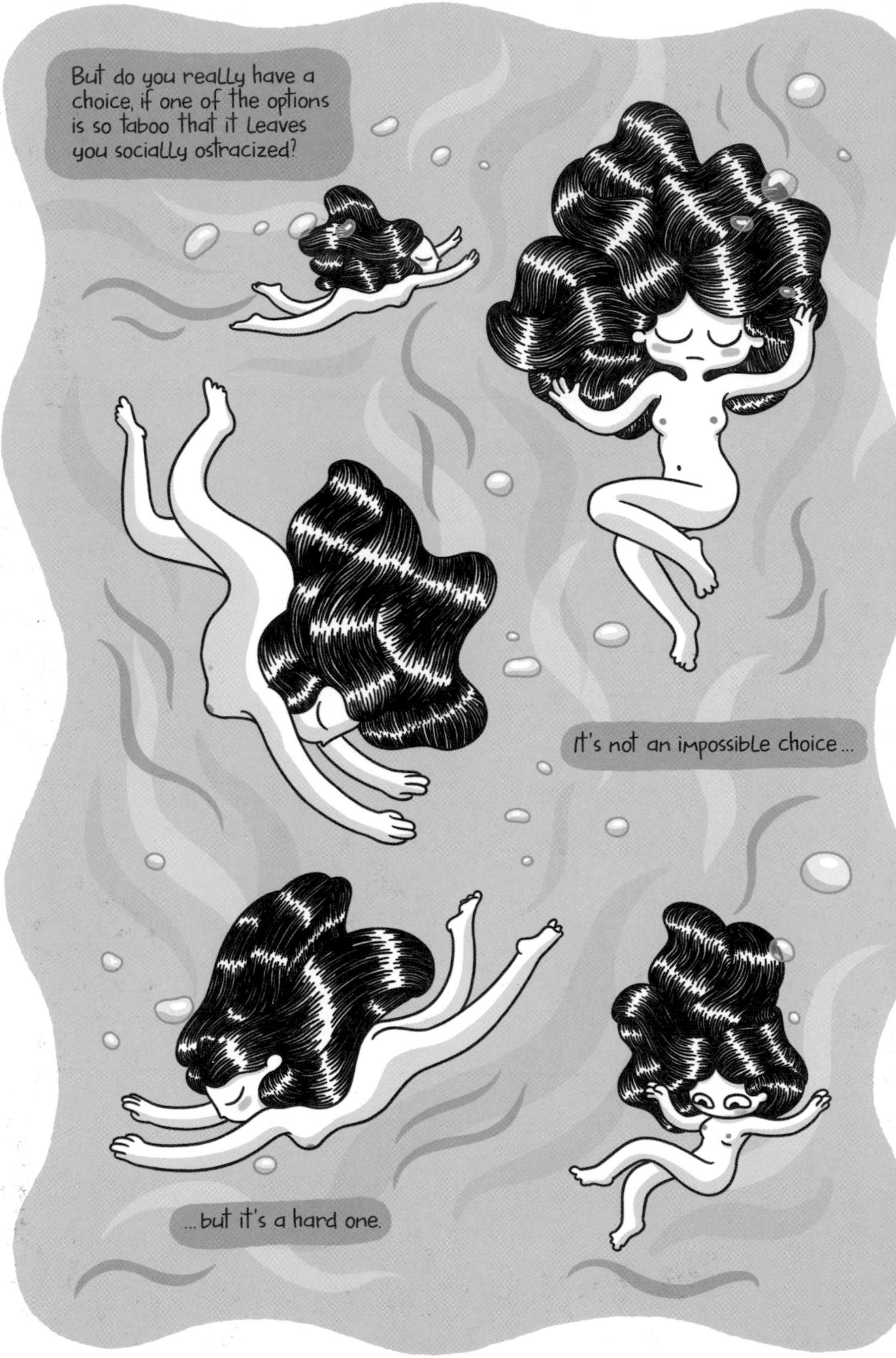
But do you really have a choice, if one of the options is so taboo that it leaves you socially ostracized?
It's not an impossible choice...
...but it's a hard one.

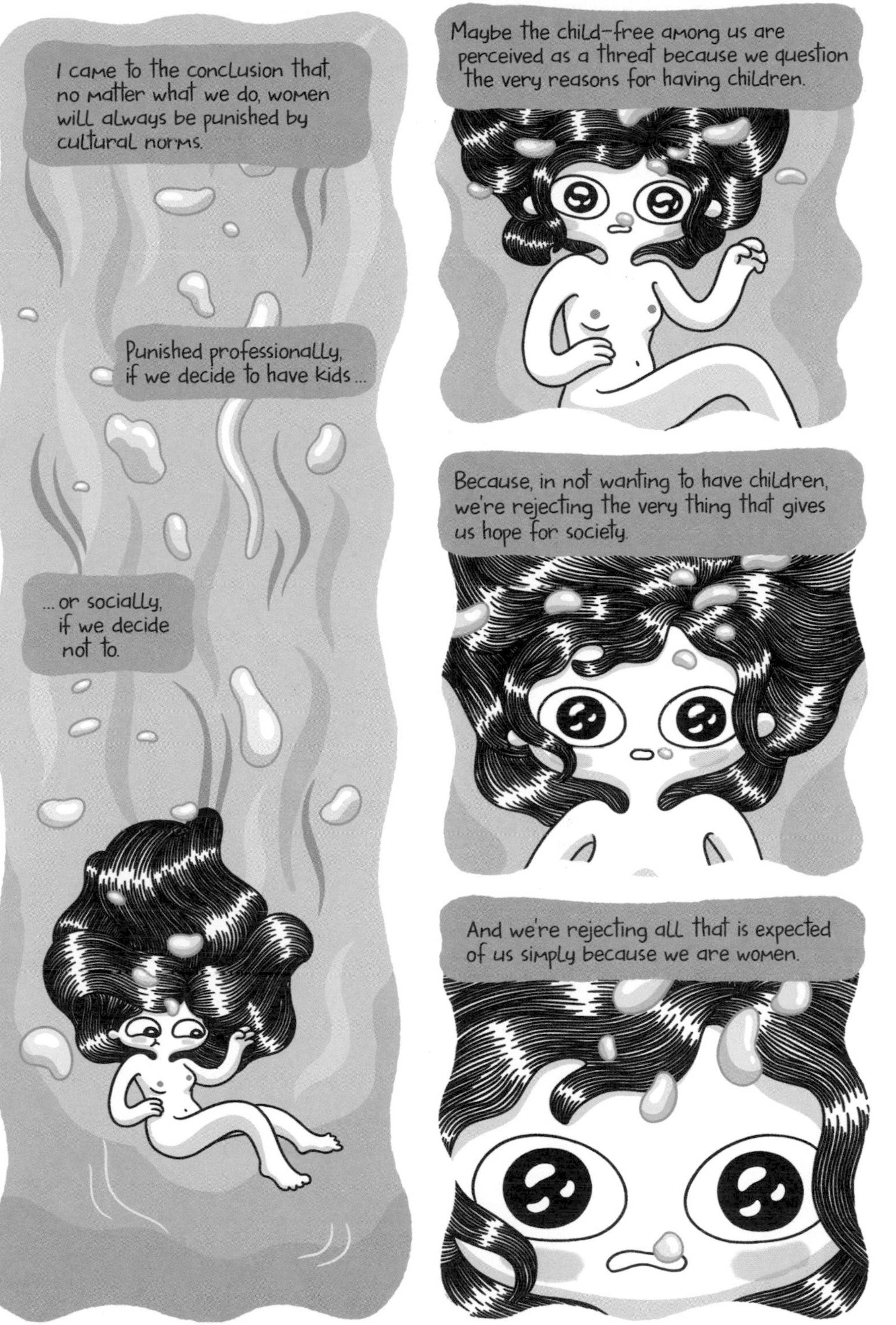
I came to the conclusion that, no matter what we do, women will always be punished by cultural norms.
Punished professionally, if we decide to have kids ...
... or socially, if we decide not to.
Maybe the child-free among us are perceived as a threat because we question the very reasons for having children.
Because, in not wanting to have children, we're rejecting the very thing that gives us hope for society.
And we're rejecting all that is expected of us simply because we are women.

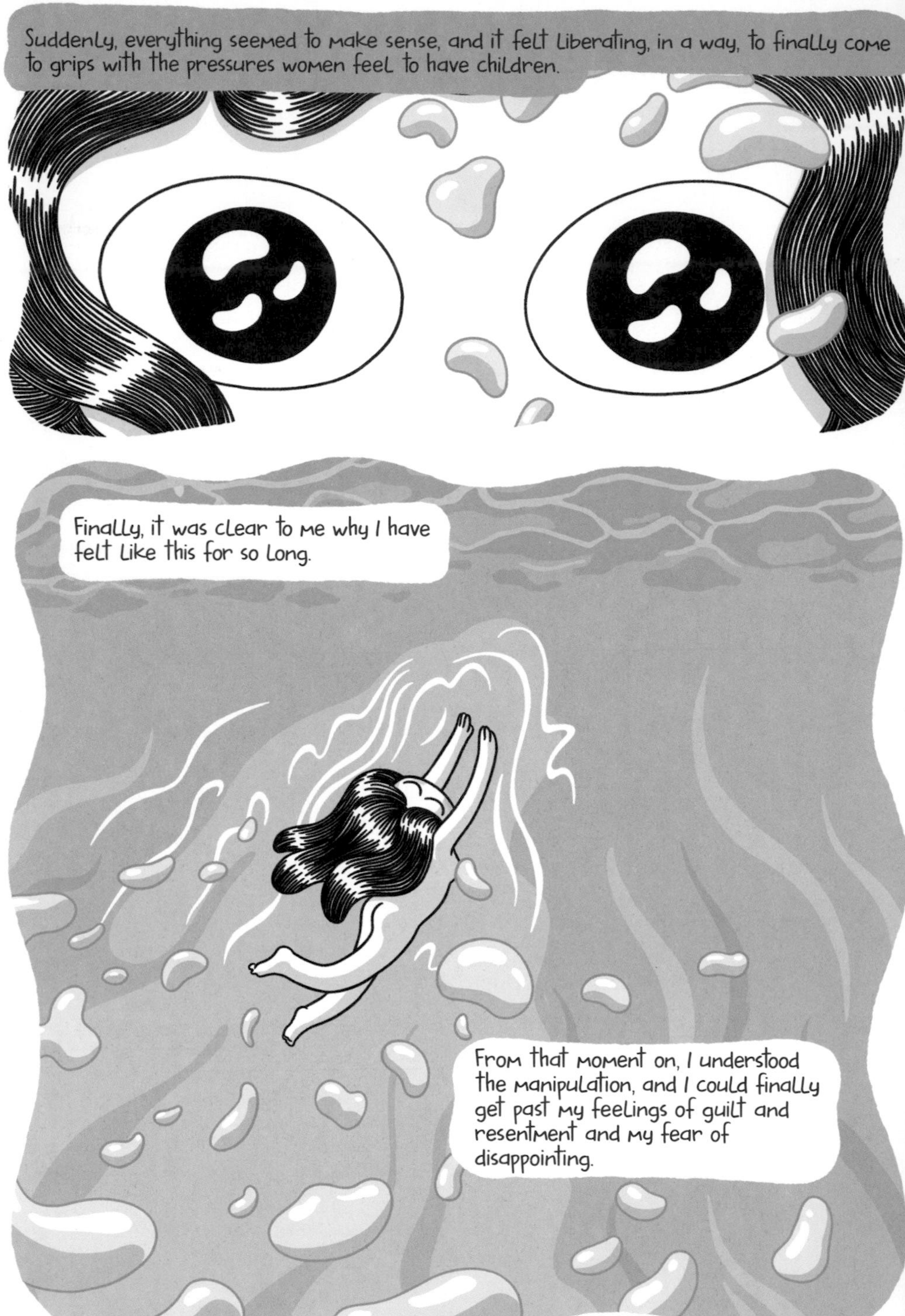
Suddenly, everything seemed to make sense, and it felt liberating, in a way, to finally come to grips with the pressures women feel to have children.
Finally, it was clear to me why I have felt like this for so long.
From that moment on, I understood the manipulation, and I could finally get past my feelings of guilt and resentment and my fear of disappointing.

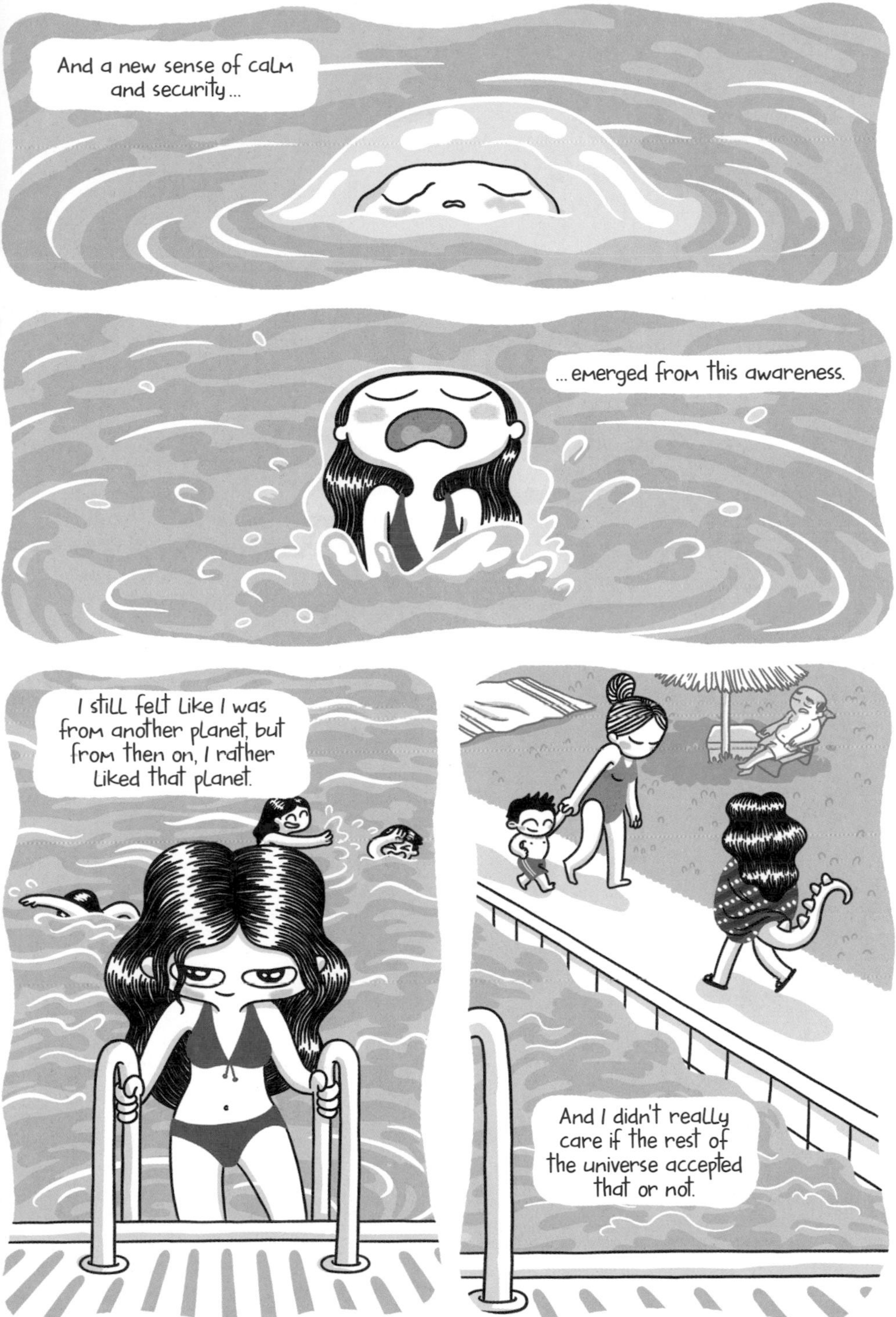
And a new sense of calm and security...
...emerged from this awareness.
I still felt like I was from another planet, but from then on, I rather liked that planet.
And I didn't really care if the rest of the universe accepted that or not.

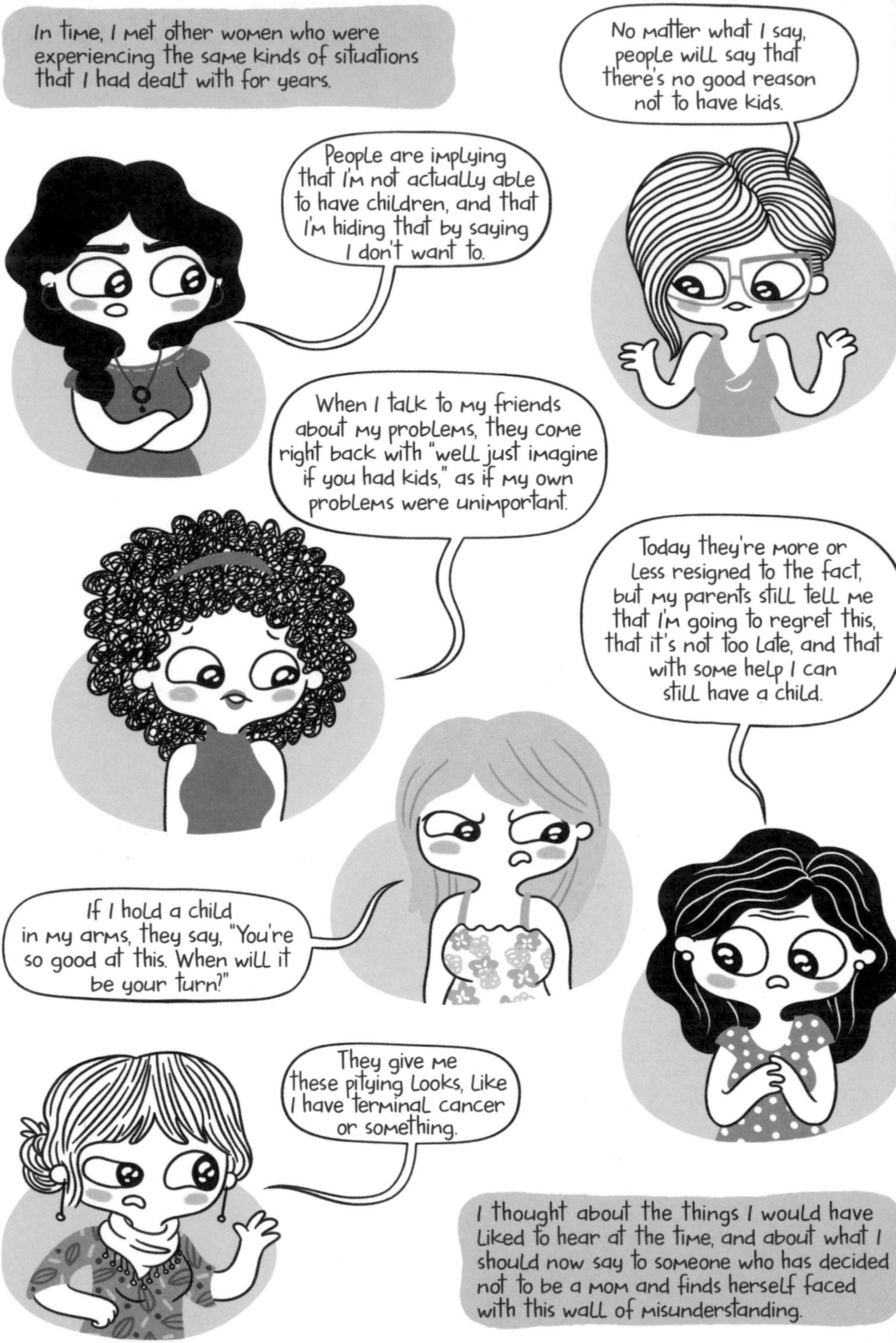
In time, I met other women who were experiencing the same kinds of situations that I had dealt with for years.
No matter what I say, people will say that there's no good reason not to have kids.
People are implying that I'm not actually able to have children, and that I'm hiding that by saying I don't want to.
When I talk to my friends about my problems, they come right back with "well just imagine if you had kids," as if my own problems were unimportant.
Today they're more or less resigned to the fact, but my parents still tell me that I'm going to regret this, that it's not too late, and that with some help I can still have a child.
If I hold a child in my arms, they say, "You're so good at this. When will it be your turn?"
They give me these pitying looks, like I have terminal cancer or something.
I thought about the things I would have liked to hear at the time, and about what I should now say to someone who has decided not to be a mom and finds herself faced with this wall of misunderstanding.

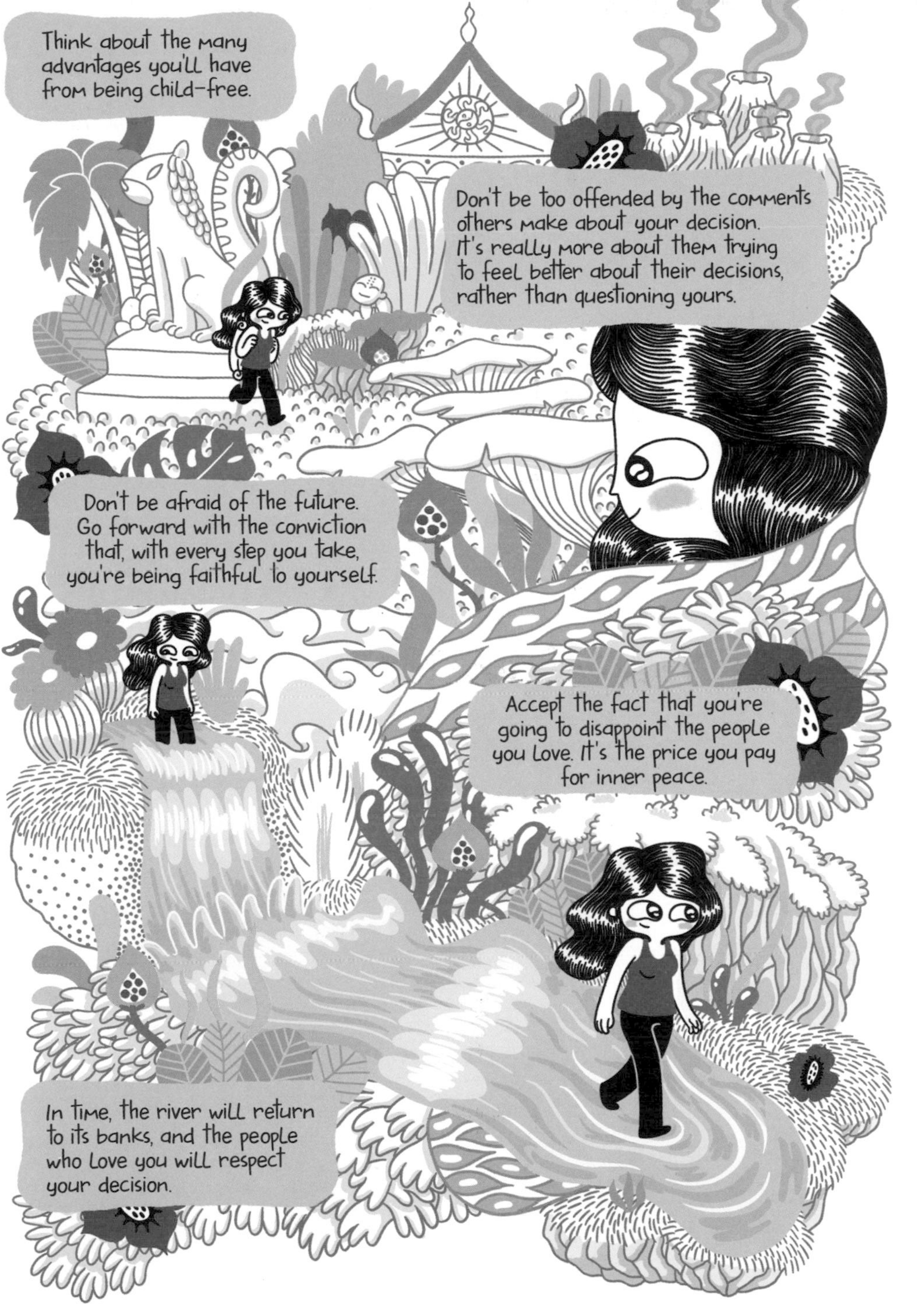
Think about the many advantages you'll have from being child-free.
Don't be too offended by the comments others make about your decision. It's really more about them trying to feel better about their decisions, rather than questioning yours.
Don't be afraid of the future. Go forward with the conviction that, with every step you take, you're being faithful to yourself.
Accept the fact that you're going to disappoint the people you love. It's the price you pay for inner peace.
In time, the river will return to its banks, and the people who love you will respect your decision.

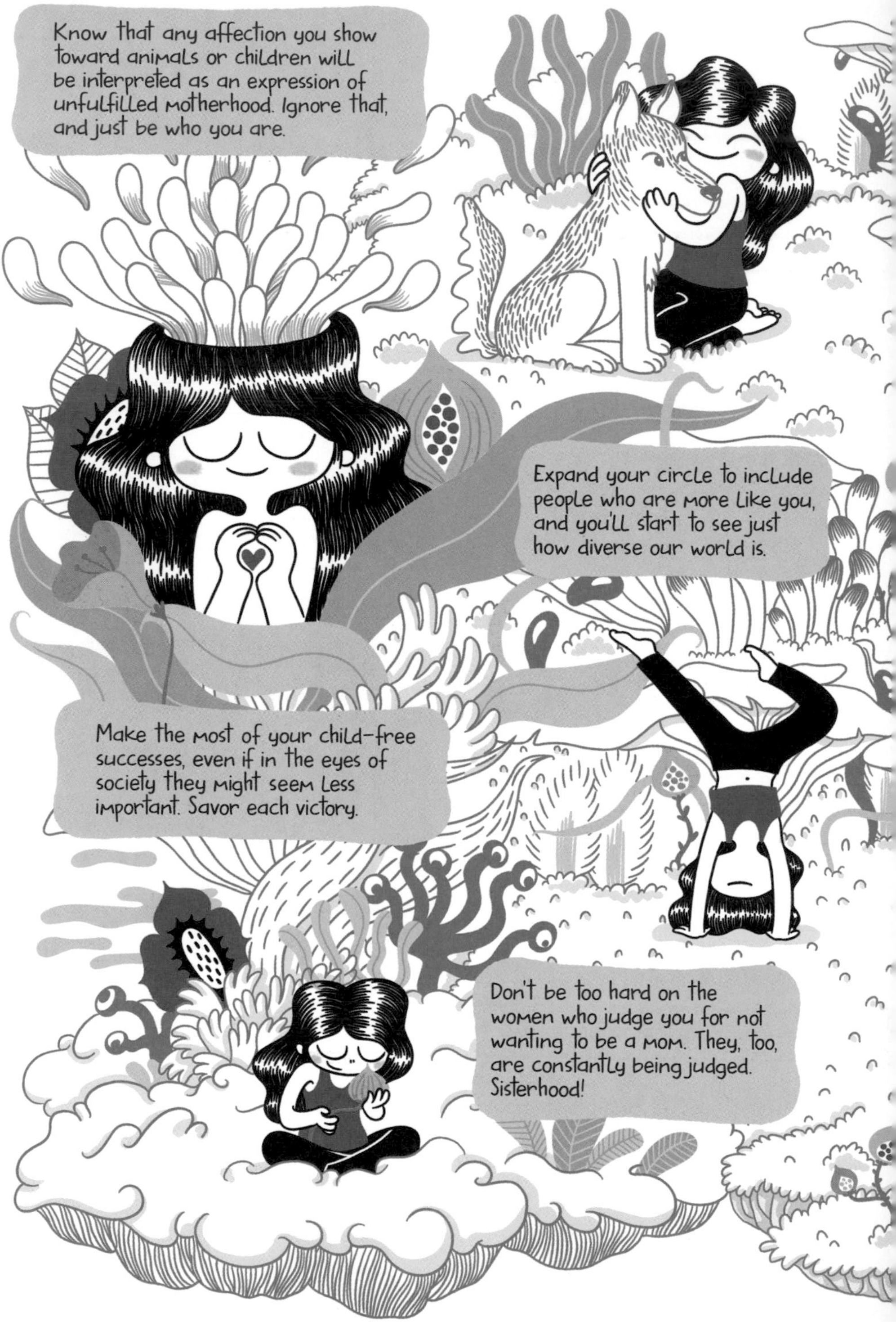
Know that any affection you show toward animals or children will be interpreted as an expression of unfulfilled motherhood. Ignore that, and just be who you are.
Expand your circle to include people who are more like you, and you'll start to see just how diverse our world is.
Make the most of your child-free successes, even if in the eyes of society they might seem less important. Savor each victory.
Don't be too hard on the women who judge you for not wanting to be a mom. They, too, are constantly being judged. Sisterhood!

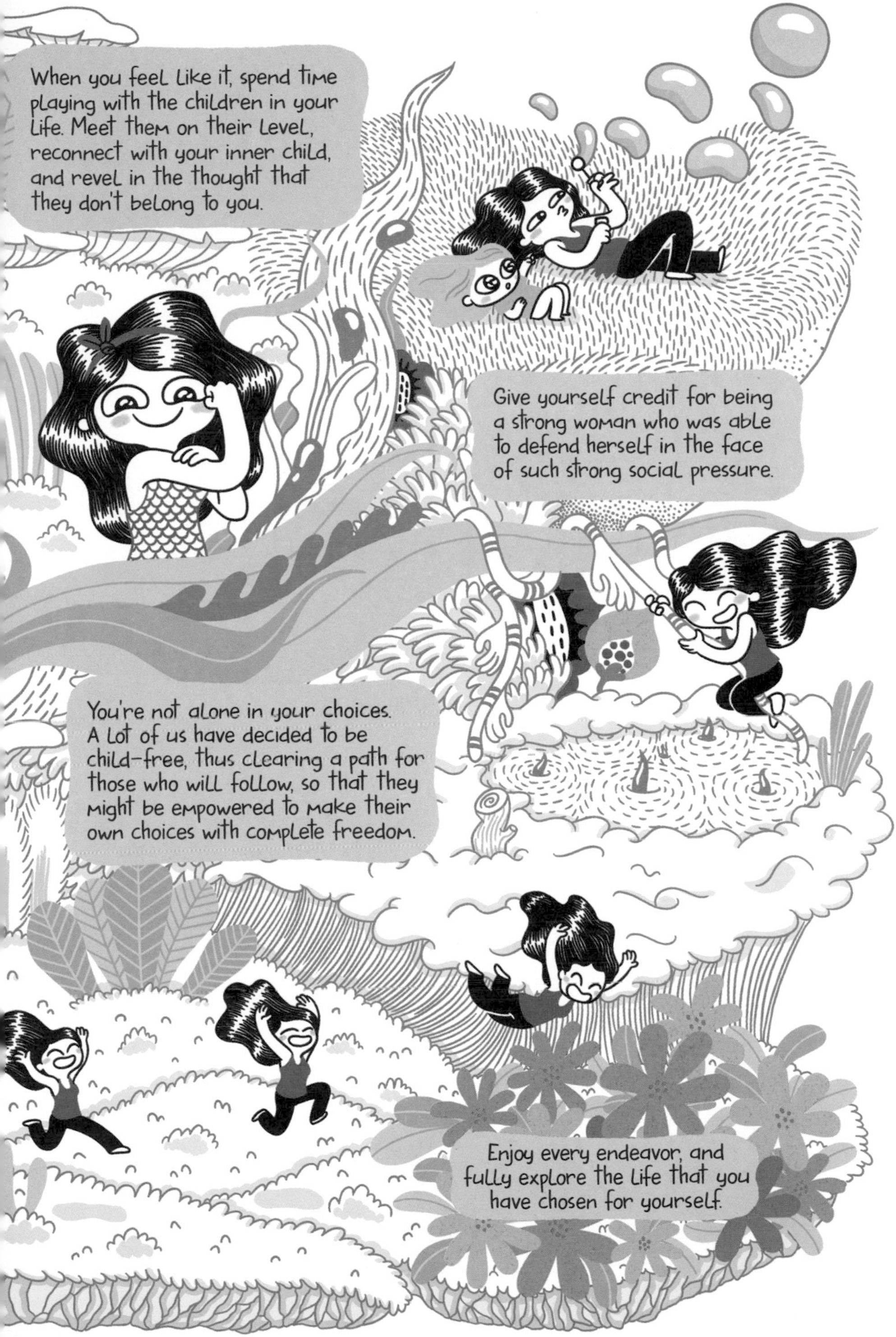
When you feel like it, spend time playing with the children in your life. Meet them on their level, reconnect with your inner child, and revel in the thought that they don't belong to you.
Give yourself credit for being a strong woman who was able to defend herself in the face of such strong social pressure.
You're not alone in your choices. A lot of us have decided to be child-free, thus clearing a path for those who will follow, so that they might be empowered to make their own choices with complete freedom.
Enjoy every endeavor, and fully explore the life that you have chosen for yourself.

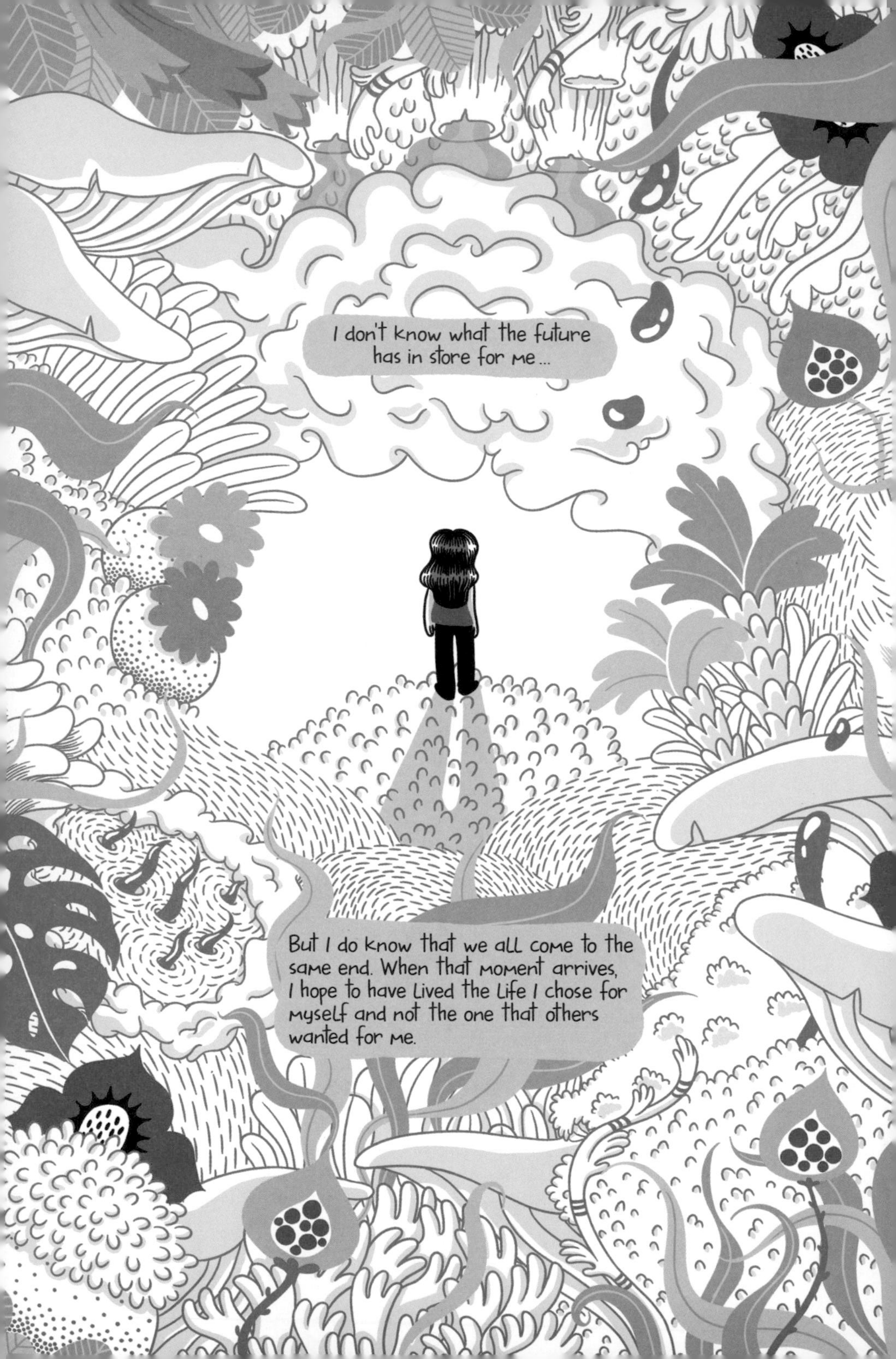
I don't know what the future has in store for me...
But I do know that we all come to the same end. When that moment arrives, I hope to have lived the life I chose for myself and not the one that others wanted for me.

Library of Congress Cataloging-in-Publication Data

Names: Olmo, Irene, 1978- author. | Boileau, Kendra, translator.
Title: I don't want to be a mom / Irene Olmo ; translated by Kendra Boileau.
Other titles: No quiero ser mamá. English
Description: University Park, Pennsylvania : Graphic Mundi, [2023] |
"Originally published as No quiero ser mamá / Je ne veux pas être maman."
Summary: "A recollection, in graphic novel format, of the author's
ambivalent feelings regarding motherhood while growing up, and an
exploration of the imposition of motherhood on women as both an expectation
and a path toward fulfillment"—Provided by publisher.
Identifiers: LCCN 2023022251 | ISBN 9781637790595 (paperback)
Subjects: LCSH: Olmo, Irene, 1978—Comic books, strips, etc. | Childfree choice—
Comic books, strips, etc. | Motherhood—Comic books, strips, etc. |
LCGFT: Graphic novels. | Autobiographical comics.
Classification: LCC HQ755.8 .O46 2023 |
DDC 306.874/3092—dc23/eng/20230513
LC record available at https://lccn.loc.gov/2023022251

Originally published as No quiero ser mamá /
Je ne veux pas être maman
® Text and illustrations, Irene Olmo, 2019
® Bang. ediciones, 2020
English translation rights arranged through S.B.Rights Agency –
Stephanie Barrouillet

Graphic Mundi is an imprint of
The Pennsylvania State University Press.

The Pennsylvania State University Press is a member
of the Association of University Presses.

It is the policy of The Pennsylvania State University Press
to use acid-free paper. Publications on uncoated stock satisfy
the minimum requirements of American National Standard
for Information Sciences—Permanence of Paper for Printed
Library Material, ANSI z39.48-1992.